ARCHAEOLOGICAL THEORY IN THE NEW MILLENNIUM

Archaeological Theory in the New Millennium provides an account of the changing world of archaeological theory and a challenge to more traditional narratives of archaeological thought. It charts the emergence of the new emphasis on relations as well as engaging with other current theoretical trends and the thinkers archaeologists regularly employ. Bringing together different strands of global archaeological theory and placing them in dialogue, the book explores the similarities and differences between different contemporary trends in theory while also highlighting potential strengths and weaknesses of different approaches.

Written in a way to maximise its accessibility, in direct contrast to many of the sources on which it draws, *Archaeological Theory in the New Millennium* is an essential guide to cutting-edge theory for students and for professionals wishing to reacquaint themselves with this field.

Oliver J. T. Harris is Associate Professor of Archaeology in the School of Archaeology and Ancient History, University of Leicester, UK.

Craig N. Cipolla is Associate Curator of North American Archaeology, Royal Ontario Museum, Canada.

ARCHAEOLOGICAL THEORY IN THE NEW MILLENNIUM

Introducing Current Perspectives

Oliver J. T. Harris
Craig N. Cipolla

Routledge
Taylor & Francis Group

LONDON AND NEW YORK

First published 2017
by Routledge
2 Park Square, Milton Park, Abingdon, Oxon OX14 4RN

and by Routledge
711 Third Avenue, New York, NY 10017

Routledge is an imprint of the Taylor & Francis Group, an informa business

© 2017 Oliver J. T. Harris and Craig N. Cipolla

The right of Oliver J. T. Harris and Craig N. Cipolla to be identified as
authors of this work has been asserted by them in accordance with sections
77 and 78 of the Copyright, Designs and Patents Act 1988.

British Library Cataloguing-in-Publication Data
A catalogue record for this book is available from the British Library

Library of Congress Cataloging-in-Publication Data
Names: Harris, Oliver J.T., author. | Cipolla, Craig N., 1978- co-author.
Title: Archaeological theory in the new millennium / Oliver J.T. Harris,
    Craig N. Cipolla.
Description: Milton Park, Abingdon, Oxon ; New York, NY : Routledge,
    2017. | Includes bibliographical references and index.
Identifiers: LCCN 2016056489 (print) | LCCN 2017017899 (ebook) |
    ISBN 9781315713250 (E-book) | ISBN 9781138888708 (hardback :
    alkaline paper) | ISBN 9781138888715 (paperback : alkaline paper)
Subjects: LCSH: Archaeology—Philosophy. | Archaeology—Social aspects.
    | Social change.
Classification: LCC CC72 (ebook) | LCC CC72 .H365 2017 (print) |
    DDC 930.1—dc23
LC record available at https://lccn.loc.gov/2016056489

ISBN: 978-1-138-88870-8 (hbk)
ISBN: 978-1-138-88871-5 (pbk)
ISBN: 978-1-315-71325-0 (ebk)

Typeset in Bembo Std
by Swales & Willis Ltd, Exeter, Devon, UK

For Sarah, my mother and teacher – OJTH
For Maya and Siany – CNC

CONTENTS

FIGURES

BOXES

TABLES

ACKNOWLEDGEMENTS

A conservative estimate might push the start of this collaborative writing effort back to the winter of 2014, when we had our first conversations about writing a book on contemporary archaeological theory. At the time, we worked together in the School of Archaeology and Ancient History at the University of Leicester. We were just beginning to discuss the possibility of teaching archaeological theory collaboratively. We also occasionally compared notes on the current state of theory and how it shaped our respective research directions. Perhaps it was in those conversations and comparisons that we began fleshing out this book. Upon further scrutiny, however, it is also possible to stretch this book's origins back in terms of a much deeper and more complicated history for each of us. Through the years we have both taken special interest in archaeological theory and pedagogy. As theory enthusiasts we have benefited from discussions with a number of our colleagues, including Ben Alberti, Anna Agbe-Davies, Asif Agha, Jo Appleby, Douglass Bailey, Alexander Bauer, John Barrett, Huw Barton, Penny Bickle, Lawrence Billington, Dušan Borić, Marcus Brittain, Bob Carter, Adrian Chadwick, Charlie Cobb, Hannah Cobb, Andrew Cochrane, Rachel Crellin, Zoe Crossland, Ben Davenport, Kristen Fellows, Kelly Ferguson, Chris Fowler, Severin Fowles, Jack Gary, Mark Gillings, Yannis Hamilakis, Kat Hayes, Terry Hopkinson, Matthew Johnson, Andy Jones, Jay Levy, Richard Leventhal, Diana Loren, Lesley McFadyen, Andy Merrills, Kevin McBride, Stephen Mrozowski, Paul Murtagh, Nick Overton, Tim Pauketat, Jordan Pickrell, Mark Pluciennik, Robert Preucel, John Robb, James Quinn, Phil Richardson, Uzma Rizvi, Peter Rowley-Conwy, Ian Russell, Bob Schuyler, Stephen Silliman, Marie Louise Sørensen, Tim Flohr Sørensen, Pwyll ap Stifin, Sarah Tarlow, Julian Thomas, Christopher Witmore and Alasdair Whittle. However, we would be remiss if we left out our students from this section. Our interactions and discussions with them – at Lafayette College, Cambridge University, the University of Leicester, the

University of Massachusetts, Boston and Newcastle University – also played crucial parts in motivating us and shaping the ideas that we present in this book.

We offer special thanks to Chris Fowler, Rachel Crellin and an anonymous reviewer for their detailed and helpful feedback on the first draft of the manuscript as well as Ben Alberti, John Robb and Gavin Lucas, who provided useful comments on versions of the original book proposal. Matt Gibbons and Lola Harre at Routledge also offered useful advice and feedback on the manuscript. K-Fai Steele created the fabulous cartoons you will find in each chapter. Adam Thuraisingam assisted nobly and with good humour in securing various image permissions. Ben Alberti, Beth Asbury, Emily Banfield, Alexander Bauer, Chantal Conneller and Zoe Crossland generously offered up photographs and image permissions. Kelly Ferguson indexed and copyedited the manuscript. A Marie Curie Research Fellowship from the European Commission (grant number 333909) provided financial support for commissioning K-Fai's cartoons, image permissions, indexing and copyediting.

Ollie would like to thank friends and colleagues at the University of Leicester for their support and the granting of research leave during the period when this book was completed. Thanks to Craig for being such a fun co-author to work with too. His family, both on the Harris and Rowley-Conwy sides, have provided ongoing help and love, and a special thanks must be offered to Sarah Harris, now sorely missed, who taught him so much and uttered these fateful words while looking over a copy of the Sheffield University prospectus in 1997: 'what about archaeology . . . ?'. Teddy and Maggie have offered structure to the days, cat hair to sweep up and distraction from the general stresses of life. Finally, the deepest thanks goes, as ever, to Ellie, a brilliant conservator who has a processualist for a father, a new materialist for a partner, has to put up with discussions of assemblage theory in the car, works for free in Ardnamurchan every year and yet maintains serenity throughout.

Craig thanks his friends, colleagues and students at the University of Leicester and the Royal Ontario Museum for the enthusiasm they showed for this project. He thanks all of his family, friends and colleagues who supported him as he worked on this book while in Leicester; New London, CT; Harwich Port, MA; and Toronto. He is grateful to Ollie for initiating this project and for putting up with the inconvenience of having a co-author decide to pack up and leave the country in the middle of it all. He offers special thanks to Jim and Laureen Cipolla for generously giving up their Harwich Port cottage to him and his family between November 2015 and February 2016. Large parts of this book were composed during that stay and a close reading might reveal the subtle traces of Cape Cod imprinted on a few pages. Kelly, Maya, Siany and Pete contributed love, support and motivation as this book took shape. Pete reminded him that there is always time to take a break and go for a stroll. Maya and Siany reminded him that there is so much more to life than work. Finally, Kelly reminded him that together they could accomplish anything, even another transatlantic move fraught with challenges.

1

AN INTRODUCTION TO CONTEMPORARY ARCHAEOLOGICAL THEORY

Confronting dualisms

Introduction

Why does the world need yet another book about archaeological theory? Hasn't everything already been said? On the shelves of university libraries you can find lots of texts that address different aspects of archaeological thought, and even books declaring that archaeological theory is dead.[1] Matthew Johnson has already published two excellent editions of his lucid book, *Archaeological Theory: An Introduction*, which covers the history of theory in the discipline from the mid-twentieth century.[2] So, what sets this book apart? Archaeological theory in the last 15 years has grown increasingly diverse and complicated. The last 'great revolution' in archaeological theory, which we sometimes refer to as a 'paradigm shift', took place 30 years ago or more, and increasingly the discipline's structures of thought appear to be fragmentary. From claims that human behaviour is driven purely by evolution, via an emphasis on human identity and agency, to arguments that we need to move away from talking about people at all, archaeological theory sometimes feels less like a toolbox and more like a random collection of unrelated approaches that talk past – rather than to – one another. Despite laudable attempts to bring some of these approaches into dialogue,[3] there remain major rifts across the discipline. These divisions lie behind the spurious claims that archaeological theory is stuck in a rut, in some way unhealthy or that it has perhaps perished altogether.

We take the opposite view. Contrary to such arguments, we see recent debates in theory as exciting, vibrant and absolutely essential to the discipline of archaeology. Behind the scenes there are a number of interrelated developments in a series of critical areas that are opening up radical new possibilities for archaeological thought. Hidden in diverse and difficult texts, these can sometimes seem to pass unnoticed, with the arguments between differing positions obscuring what they have in common. As two authors from different backgrounds, studying different periods of the past, with different sources to draw on, we have come together to set out what we think are the most important developments in archaeological thought in the current climate. In this sense, this book emerges from us teaching together and thinking about how to communicate these important ideas to our students and our colleagues.

Before we get into any of that, though, we need to address a vital question: what do we mean by theory anyway? Johnson[4] begins the second edition of his book by defining theory as 'the order we put facts in'. But as he goes on to show, even the notion of a 'fact' cannot be separated from the theoretical understandings we have of the world. We could even extend this notion beyond the facts we use to answer our questions, to critically reflect on *the very kinds of questions* we ask in the first place. Let us think this through in relation to a puzzle that compares our two different areas of research. We will often use puzzles in this book as a device to help us think through different archaeological dilemmas, and our first example starts with something archaeologists often encounter on excavations: a humble, unworked stone. How do we know if this stone is an artefact or not? Is this something you can demonstrate factually? If you were digging an Iron Age promontory site in western Scotland and you came across our stone in a pit, you might ask your supervisor whether the stone was an artefact. The supervisor would look at the stone and, recognising that it has not been modified, declare it simply to be natural and throw it on the spoil heap. Here the 'fact' is that this stone is not a 'cultural object' because it had not been modified in any recognisable way in the past. Take a similar feature encountered on an excavation on a Native American reservation in New England, where indigenous people are involved in the research. You find a similar stone and again ask your supervisors whether this is worth keeping. Perhaps the Anglo-archaeologist might have a similar response to the one you got in Scotland, but the indigenous archaeologist might tell you that the stone is an important spiritual element from Mother Earth, a prayer set in stone by her ancestors that requires respect and attention. Here the 'facts' have changed because of the different theories. Theory one says that physical modification defines human involvement; theory two says that no such modification is required. While your initial response might be to presume that one of these theories is correct – we might call it a science – whereas the other is merely belief, one of the things we will explore in this book is how such a position is deeply problematic. As suggested above, however, we can also go beyond this to think about the very question we posed: 'is this stone an artefact?' This question itself is based on a theoretical premise that we can divide the world into things that are artefacts and things that are not – *which is in itself a theoretical position*. Instead we might ask: 'is this stone alive?'[5] This might prompt a whole host of other responses. While you might think that asking if a stone is alive is a pretty strange – maybe even silly – question, we will see later on that this is not necessarily the case.

So, what is theory? Turning back to Johnson's initial definition, what we are left with is the notion of *order* – how we organise our interpretations; how we recognise and define data; the different preconceptions, ideas and beliefs we bring into dialogue with one another. This notion of ideas in dialogue is what makes theory so vibrant and so alive. It is always an ongoing debate and story that we are a part of. It is not something that 'happened' in archaeology for us to learn about, but rather a process that goes on in our discipline that we need to embrace. As we will see throughout this book, what theory does is grab the assumptions you hold dearest and shake them until they fall apart. It makes you look at yourself and the world around you in new ways, and it also challenges you to embrace what you would otherwise dismiss and reflect critically on your most fundamental truths. 'Common sense is not enough', as Johnson so rightly points out.[6] To this we can add that theory forces us to ask different kinds of questions of our material, and to define our material in new and interesting ways. Not only are the answers to our archaeological conundrums up for grabs, but we can generate whole new sets of questions to ponder.

Beyond paradigms

On occasion, we have both encountered senior colleagues who claim that 'nothing has happened in theory since the 1990s'. Here and throughout the book, we are going to show you how wrong that notion is. Most archaeologists think of the history of our discipline in terms of three big transformations. We are told of culture historic archaeology, processual archaeology (or the 'New Archaeology') and postprocessual archaeology. We will discuss each of these further in Chapter 2, but for now here is a one-sentence introduction to each. Culture history emphasises the when, where and what of different human 'cultures', placing great importance on description, typology and the transformation and spread of material culture through space and time. Processual archaeology, modelled after the natural sciences, asks why and how human culture changed through time, often looking to the environment for explanations. Postprocessual archaeology rejects the idea that archaeology is only a science, and instead embraces questions concerning multiple meanings, symbolism and identity. All histories of archaeological thought rely on this tripartite structure, including the gold standard in our discipline, Bruce Trigger's *A History of Archaeological Thought*.[7] The transformations just described are characterised as paradigm shifts,[8] a term that comes from the work of the philosopher of science, Thomas Kuhn.[9] Kuhn defined a paradigm shift as a moment when one set of ways of understanding the world is replaced by another in a revolutionary event. We want to challenge the idea that this captures the way in which archaeological thought has changed through time.[10] A true paradigm shift entails a complete rejection and replacement of what came before. When we look back at the history of the discipline, we find little evidence for such a change. For instance, Ian Hodder, who many archaeologists consider the founder of postprocessual archaeology, still uses typology (from culture history) and radiocarbon dating (a scientific technique) to understand chronology at the sites he excavates. We argue that you cannot be an archaeologist without referring to typologies, employing scientific techniques or concerning yourself with the complexity of meaning and identity in the past. These divisions may be useful as a device for telling the history of archaeological thought, but they have little intellectual value in the present and do not actually exist in practice.

Contrary to those claims that 'nothing new has happened in theory since the 1990s', we argue that change in archaeological thought is *continuous*. This means that change runs throughout the three 'archaeological paradigms' up to the present. The subject matter of this book is the development of archaeological thought in the new millennium – what many archaeologists might consider later postprocessual thought up to the present. As we just reasoned, however, these debates are built upon the bedrock of theory set in place by the history of earlier 'paradigms'. Of course, we do not see this bedrock as static and completely intractable either. We regularly go back and rework our understandings of 'older' concepts like typology even as we pursue new research agendas.[11] In short, we find that many aspects of our concerns predate the later postprocessual label that some will attach to this book.

Theory in the new millennium

What this book examines, then, is developments in archaeological thought since the year 2000. We won't be strict about this date, of course, with various chapters dipping a little further back in time, but it does represent our primary focus. What this book is not, however, is an encyclopaedia of archaeological thought during this period. We are not trying to cover every perspective, or indeed every single approach. There are several reasons for this. First, such a book would be enormously long, and still have too little space to do justice to each approach it would need to cover. Second, it would be hard to develop a coherent argument through a book whose aim was to be encyclopaedic. Third, and most importantly, archaeological theory and archaeological theorists are situated – that is, we come with our own interests and expertise, as we discuss below. We are not the best people to write about human behavioural ecology or Darwinian notions of evolution, or other approaches that we will not cover in these pages. These approaches, which play important roles in certain parts of the field, are not directly connected to the questions we are interested in asking, or that we want to engage our readers with (although we will touch upon evolution and ecology from different perspectives in Chapter 9). For similar reasons we focus primarily on archaeological theory from Britain, America and Scandinavia because these approaches form a coherent group, engaging with a particular set of questions.

Our book is about a specific set of interrelated developments that have garnered a range of labels. You can variously encounter these notions described as 'the material turn', 'the ontological turn', 'the turn to things', 'thing theory', 'the relational turn' and so on. They include approaches with names like 'symmetrical archaeology', 'new materialism', 'object agency', 'materiality' and 'Peircian semiotics'. Are these all the same? Perhaps according to those senior colleagues mentioned above, yes, but not to us. These debates are related, as we will see, but not identical, and they offer a dynamic and challenging new set of approaches to thinking about

TABLE 1.1 Some dualisms that impede archaeological thought

Nature/culture	Material/ideal	Object/subject
Fact/interpretation	Nonhuman/human	Agency/structure
Women/men	Body/mind	Past/present

archaeology that have not yet been brought together in an accessible manner – that is what we aim to do here. In this sense, then, this book is both an introduction to contemporary archaeological thought and an argument about where archaeological theory is going.

What unifies the different approaches we will discuss in the book is an attempt to deal with a central tendency not just in archaeological theory, but also in western traditions of thought more widely, to conceptualise the world in terms of *dualisms*.[12] What do we mean by this? Think of the example we discussed earlier about our stone, the one found in either Scotland or New England. The fundamental debate was about whether this stone was a cultural artefact. If it wasn't, the default position of the supervisor in Scotland was that it was natural, that it belonged to nature. Okay – what's the problem with this? The answer is twofold. First, as our Native American colleague showed us, not everyone divides the world up like this. To her the stone was alive; the division between nature and culture was not clear. This means when we are digging other sites, like our Iron Age promontory enclosure in Scotland, we cannot be certain that 'natural' objects were perceived as such by people in the past there either. So imposing our dualism onto the past gets in the way of understanding *their* point of view. See Table 1.1 for a list of problematic dualisms that often impede archaeological thinking.

Unfortunately, this is only one half of the problem. The other issue is that this system of categorisation itself impedes us from understanding *our* world as well. To think about this, let's move away from our stone for a moment, and think about an example we have all encountered – the human body. In the modern world we tend to think about the biological structures of the body as completely natural.[13] In fact, when it comes to the achievements of human bodies we police these boundaries rigorously. If you are an Olympic sprinter you have to work at improving your body 'naturally'. This means that you can exercise, you can work on your diet and you can make sure you sleep properly. What you absolutely cannot do is take an 'artificial' – or cultural – enhancement like human growth hormone. Using this chemical compound, synthesised in a lab, would mean that your body was no longer 'natural' and thus not a reasonable point of comparison with others involved in the sport. This is why drug testing exists, scandals occur and records are re-written. Yet at the same time, this distinction actually makes no sense. The same athlete will wear shoes made from the latest compounds that allow them to run faster. They will eat foods with genetically modified proteins that allow their muscles to regenerate quickly. If they suffer injury, their ligaments will be reattached by modern medical techniques employing all kinds of 'cultural' equipment. The distinction between what is natural and thus allowed, and what is cultural and thus cheating, is not obvious or clear, but rather constructed by the rules of the organisations involved, both explicitly and implicitly. Look at your own body and try and divide it up into the natural parts and the cultural parts. At first it might seem obvious – strip away all the things and nature is what is left behind. But inside your body, the antibodies that you were injected with as a child continue to work and keep you free of disease. The chemicals you inhale continue to attach themselves to your red blood cells; the fact that you worked all summer on an archaeological site has shaped your muscles and the muscle attachments on your bones. For example, both of us are right handed, so we use our trowels primarily in that hand, creating calluses on the skin and stronger muscles in the forearm. If you think about the process of digging a site, these dualisms become even more blurred. Where is the edge of your body as you start digging into the ground, the edge of your skin, your clothing or your trowel? As Figure 1.1 suggests, some of the approaches we will be exploring in this book will start to make us think about the material things of the world around us as more 'alive' than we might previously have done. The key point to emphasise here is that we cannot understand the human body in terms of dualisms like nature and culture; they simply get in the way of us grasping anything interesting about it at all. We will look at more of these examples when we talk about people and things in later chapters.

Archaeologically, these divisions are equally as arbitrary, and in fact the opposition between nature and culture is only one of many ways in which we have learned to divide the world up. We oppose mind and body, ideas and materials, women and men, individuals and collectives, and past and present, just to name a few. In our everyday lives we use these divisions when we divide 'mental' illness off from regular everyday bodily illness, or when we debate whether our love (or hatred) of baked beans came from 'nature or nurture'. Even the way in which the history of archaeological thought has been told relies on a dichotomy between change and continuity. Either you have one (and thus a period of paradigm shift) or the other (stasis). In fact, as we have argued so far, these two are part of the same process and are largely indivisible from one another. We return to this point in the next chapter, where we explore the long history of these dualisms.

The different approaches we will look at in this book have different tendencies, influences, histories, taken-for-granteds, and strengths and weaknesses. Each tries to wrestle with dualistic thinking that has come to us via a long and wandering path. This shared starting point, however, should not be used to obscure the differences between them that are real and at times profound, as we will see throughout the book.

Imagining theory

One of the ways in which we have tried to think through the problems we want to explore in this book is in the use of images of different kinds. Some of them are very familiar (for example, we might illustrate a particular archaeological example with a photo of the object under discussion). However, there are two other kinds of images

FIGURE 1.1 Where are the boundaries between the body and the world around it?
Drawing by K-Fai Steele

we use that are worth a little more explanation. The first is our cartoons, drawn by the fantastic San Francisco artist K-Fai Steele. These feature a skeleton archaeologist and a trowel that comes to life and begins to explore the world for itself. On the one hand, these cartoons are designed in each chapter to bring to life the kinds of questions we will be discussing and help us to think about them differently. On the other, they allow us to make the visual point that new archaeological theories question the boundary between living and non-living things in interesting ways. Putting things down as images always raises questions, though; for example, you might wonder why we have used a skeleton as one of our protagonists. The answer is that beyond the archaeological element to it, it gets us out of having to provide our character with gender or ethnicity – in that sense it is a much more accessible figure! The second issue worth flagging up is the trowel itself and its anthropomorphic qualities – that is, the way it has taken on elements of a human (with eyes and so on). Later in the book we will be very critical of anthropocentrism (making humans the centre of everything), so why have we opted for this act of anthropomorphism? The simple answer to this is that it makes our cartoons intelligible and understandable; it allows them to work in the way we want.[14] To think about the way in which objects help to bring our identities into being (Chapter 4), have agency (Chapter 5) and so on, we depict our trowel as a person to provoke our readers to think differently about the way in which people and things explore the world together.

The second set of images that are a little unusual begin in the next chapter and can be found in the form of the different boxes we have included about thinkers, both inside and outside archaeology, who have had an impact on the theories we discuss. We chose to illustrate these boxes not with photographs of the thinkers we are discussing, but instead with images of things connected to their ideas – often, but not always, objects of different kinds. One of the key ideas explored in this book is that objects and people bring each other into being in different ways, and so our use of objects to stand for people in these boxes helps us to explore how the theoretical ideas we are discussing are themselves often in part produced by encounters with the material world. The selection of who to include in boxes was a very difficult one – there are many archaeologists and theorists from other disciplines who we would have loved to incorporate, but could not find room for in the end. The other issue is that selecting boxes forces you to examine the people who have come to dominate theoretical debates in archaeology and other disciplines. More of our boxes contain men than women, and very few are of persons of colour. This is crucial to point out as it represents the way in which white men continue to dominate theoretical debates. We hope that it serves as a reminder of the profound challenges we face to broaden the scope of archaeology's inclusivity both in terms of gender and race.

Theory and us

Rather than present only a singular perspective on contemporary archaeological theory, we rely on co-authorship to help us integrate our distinctive approaches and opinions. Despite coming from two very different backgrounds and working in distinct archaeological contexts, we find a level of unity in our thinking that we hope will prove useful and interesting for our students and colleagues. This unity begins with our mutual passion for archaeological theory and for teaching in general. It continues through to our independent struggles with dualisms in archaeological theory prior to teaching together and writing this book. Of course, the ways in which each of us came to engage with archaeological theory, find fault in the dualisms mentioned above and endeavour to grapple with these issues are distinct and worth further elaboration.

Oliver is a British prehistorian focusing mainly on Neolithic Britain. He became fascinated by archaeological theory as an undergraduate because of the way in which it challenged his assumptions about how the world worked. His field research looks at long-term change in western Scotland, and how we cannot solely rely on writing an archaeology that is only about people to understand this. The theoretical topics he is particularly interested in are new materialism and assemblage theory, which we will encounter later in the book.

Meanwhile, Craig is an American historical archaeologist trained in anthropology. He is interested in the long-term indigenous prehistory and history of New England and the Great Lakes, particularly the complicated intersections of indigenous societies and European colonists that took place in those areas. In studying these topics, he strives to foster working relationships with indigenous descendant communities. This, he argues, makes the archaeological process more visible and relevant to those traditionally situated outside of academia while incorporating contemporary indigenous knowledge and sensibilities into the research. Some of the topics in archaeological theory that Craig feels most passionate about are practice theory, postcolonialism and semiotics.

These differences in nationality, disciplinary training, regions and period of study, and lines of evidence employed in our interpretations certainly set us apart, but not to the degree where we talk past one another. This is not a book about theory in Britain *or* America, in prehistory *or* historical archaeology, or in archaeology *or* anthropology. It is all of these things. As outlined above, most of the book is about how we, as a team, think about the history of the discipline and the problem of dualisms therein. In the following nine chapters, we present the different positions that we agree are most relevant to this set of debates without being too judgemental. In the final chapter, we step back and begin to explore how our own approaches diverge.

Structure of the book

The book follows a loose chronological sequence. We divide our discussion into three main sections. The first section covers the introduction and background for this project, outlining where our history of dualisms originates. The second section explores what we see as some of the key responses to these problems along with several more recent approaches. Here, we highlight a specific set of trajectories involving what we will refer to as the rise of 'relational approaches' in archaeological theory. By relational we mean that these approaches focus primarily not on bounded entities (things, people, agents or structures) but rather on the relations between them. The final section of the book delves into contemporary debates, which are currently in process as we write.

The first section is made up of this chapter and Chapter 2. There we present a brief history of archaeological thought, further exploring transformations in archaeological theory – often referred to as paradigm shifts – and their continuities with one another. These continuities relate to the core theme of the book: dualisms, to which we will also refer from time to time as dichotomies or binary oppositions to limit repetition (all three terms have the same meaning). We frame this background chapter as a history of dualisms, the opposition between nature and culture being the earliest and most fundamental of binaries that continues to influence the discipline. Just think back to our rock problem introduced earlier: natural or cultural? We find a deeper antiquity to this puzzle and its interpretive hazards than a standard 'three-paradigm' approach to archaeological theory allows.

The second section of the book consists of four chapters. Chapter 3 explores notions of practice and agency in archaeology. A key move of the 1980s and 1990s was the realisation that archaeologists needed to think both about people's actions and how they related to the world around them. These concerns led archaeologists to move away from thinking solely about what things meant to people, to emphasising critical questions about what people did with things and what things did to people. This ushered in what we will refer to as recursive models of social action. Chapter 4 considers issues of identity and personhood. The crucial questions about agency discussed in the previous chapter connected up with studies of gender that emerged in the 1980s. This led to new emphases on critical questions of identity and personhood over the last 20 years. Identity raises important issues about the historically contextual nature of who people were. Questions about personhood go a step further, asking what it means to be a person in a particular context, and whether personhood is limited to human beings. Chapter 5 builds upon this last point in its focus on object agency and biography. We start off by considering the ways in which objects relate to personhood and therefore come to have agency and biographies of their own. Here, we trace the moment that archaeologists began to look at objects as more than just the simple outcomes of people's actions, as things people understood as being meaningful or even as structuring elements of people's lives, but as agents in their own right with biographical qualities akin to those of humans. Chapter 6 closes this section of the book with a discussion of materiality, phenomenology and entanglement. These approaches, directly related to studies of object agency and biography discussed in Chapter 5, consider how the experience of the material world was crucial to further transcend dualisms such as nature/culture, mind/body and structure/agent that previous attempts failed to solve.

The third and final section of the book includes five chapters. Again, we see the debates discussed here as ongoing. Chapter 7 explores a more recent approach to the study of meaning and symbolism in archaeology that takes direct influence from the writings of philosopher Charles Sanders Peirce. This bourgeoning set of theories offer valuable critiques of the dualisms of earlier approaches to symbols and meaning based initially in structuralism. This chapter offers a logical transition between ideas of materiality, discussed in Chapter 6, and a newer set of theories often labelled as 'posthumanist'. Chapter 8 engages in posthuman approaches in its exploration of symmetrical archaeologies and new materialism. The chapter looks at the ways in which recent concerns with material things have prompted certain archaeologists to go beyond thinking about how things and people 'co-constitute' each other to thinking about how people can only act in the world with things. These thinkers even problematise the division between things and people. As we will show, this move towards symmetry raises a host of questions for how we think about the past, and these cutting-edge ideas are increasingly influential in archaeology. Chapter 9 follows along this line of reasoning to examine emergent ways in which archaeologists are now thinking about relationships between people, plants and animals. Inspired by developments in biology and evolutionary thinking on the one hand, and the new materialist approaches outlined in Chapter 8 on the other, archaeologists are rethinking the roles of plants and animals in past worlds, and moving towards a multi-species archaeology. Whereas they might once only have been of interest in their calorific or symbolic value, plants and animals are now starting to play their own roles in what we think of as a more-than-human approach to the past. This chapter allows us to demonstrate certain continuities between what some think of as wholly different approaches. We find common ground here with studies of evolution and ecology, for example.

In Chapter 10, we engage with postcolonial concerns, framing our discussions around *the Other*. Here we discuss four related uses of postcolonial theory in archaeology: 1) as a means of rethinking the agency of people normally excluded from our writing (who we can term, in postcolonial style, 'subaltern'); 2) as a means of decolonising archaeological practice by collaborating with indigenous communities; 3) as a means of treating nonwestern thought as a form of theory and how this can create new ways of understanding the past; and 4) as a means of fundamentally rethinking people/thing relations in general. The last set of approaches argue that material things – in addition to certain groups of people – are subaltern and colonised by humans, and therefore in need of liberation. This chapter also considers 'alterity' as a general category. This term typically means alternative, different and *Other*. We explore current anthropological approaches that frame this term as representing radical and absolute difference. These raise serious issues about taking the point of view of nonwestern people seriously and also evoke interesting questions about how we think about the past.

Chapter 11 concludes the book. We consider the wider ramifications of the arguments explored throughout. These encompass challenges to the traditional history of archaeological theory, as we alluded to earlier in this chapter, along with wide-ranging consequences for the discipline of archaeology (beyond just theory). We finish this chapter with a dialogue between us exploring some of our own perspectives on the different approaches covered in the later chapters of the book. This serves to highlight our individual views on these problems and debates.

We argue that archaeological theory remains an important toolbox. It gives you a choice of different approaches that are useful for answering differing kinds of questions, and indeed for posing different kinds of questions in the first place. In this book we are going to look at the tools that we think have proved especially useful to us, and to others like us, in thinking about the past in new and interesting ways since the turn of the new millennium. What is essential to recognise, however, is that whichever of the approaches in this book – or indeed of other approaches we do not address – you happen to choose, remember that *there is no archaeology without theory*.[15] If the simple act of excavating a pit and finding an unworked stone involves theoretical engagement, as we saw in the puzzle earlier, then there really is no area of our discipline that sits apart from theory. This book aims to provide a comprehensible narrative about the development of some of the central theoretical approaches of the last two decades. It is a story we cannot afford to ignore.

Notes

1 Bintliff 2011; cf. Thomas 2015a, 2015b.
2 Johnson 1999, 2010.
3 E.g. Cochrane and Gardner 2011.
4 Johnson 2010: 2; Wallace 2011: 8–10.
5 As the anthropologist Alfred Irving Hallowell (1960: 24) has shown, this is actually a very useful question to ask.

6 Johnson 2010: chapter 1.
7 Trigger 2006.
8 For a recent example see Zubrow 2015.
9 Kuhn 1962.
10 For interesting discussions touching on this see Jones 2002; Last 1995; Thomas 2015a, 2015b.
11 E.g. Fowler 2013.
12 Shanks 2012; Thomas 2004.
13 This is the dominant approach; of course in all contexts, modern, archaeological or otherwise, there are multiple understandings at play (cf. Harris and Robb 2012).
14 There is also a more complex argument about the difference between anthropomorphism and anthropocentrism, and the way in which the former can be used judiciously to challenge the latter, but it is a little early in our story to be getting into that! (See e.g. Bennett 2010; Harman 2016; Malafouris 2013: 130–1.)
15 Wallace 2011.

2

BEYOND PARADIGMS

A potted history of archaeological thought

Introduction: understanding a pit with different theories

To understand the development of archaeological theory over the last 15 years or so, we need to start by outlining the broader history of the subject so we can see in later chapters exactly what is 'new' about more recent developments. To help set the scene, let's start with a simple thought exercise. Imagine you are out on an archaeological site digging a very common kind of archaeological feature, a pit (Figure 2.1). Emptying out the soil, you recover a variety of artefacts. These include a number of pieces of pottery, a polished stone axe, an antler digging tool known as a 'pick' and the skull of a cow. How can we understand and interpret these artefacts in this context? What do they tell us about the past? How can we even begin to move from this seemingly random selection of artefacts to a coherent story? As you turn to ask for advice, you encounter three senior professors from different generations and of different theoretical persuasions who all declare that they know exactly how you should go about interpreting this pit.

FIGURE 2.1 Archaeological pits under excavation. Drawing by K-Fai Steele

The first professor (he looks like the oldest of the three) explains that what you need to do is to compare the finds from the pit with others known from the local area. This will reveal, he tells you confidently, that the pottery in your pit is the same as other kinds of pottery known as 'Carinated Bowl'. This 'typological' match can help tell you about the kinds of people who dug the pit as well as the broad period the pit belongs to, in this case the Early Neolithic. The other types of artefacts in the pit are often discovered in association with this kind of pottery at other archaeological sites. Carinated Bowls, the professor declares, are found in other nearby countries at a slightly earlier date, and this clearly shows that people had moved into the region where you are working from elsewhere; a classic example of 'diffusion', he announces proudly. From this perspective, these pots stand for people; their movement indicates the movement of people. Knowledgeable as he is (rumour has it that he has hand drawn every piece of Neolithic pottery in Britain), the professor informs you that ditches at a nearby monument have been excavated with Carinated Bowls on the bottom and other kinds of pottery, 'Peterborough Ware', closer to the top, showing that Peterborough Ware dates to a period after Carinated Bowls. This suggests that other pits nearby which contain this second kind of pottery are later than the one you have excavated, and show either the arrival of new people with new kinds of beliefs and new kinds of ideas about the world, or that local people adopted neighbouring ways of making artefacts. This professor is a profound advocate of culture history, the first of our alleged 'paradigms' of archaeological theory.

The second professor is somewhat younger, and she looks very scornful of the ideas the first professor has been expounding. All very nice descriptions, she mutters, but what about trying to actually explain the past? What we need, she says, is a much more scientific approach. The material in this pit, she informs you, will allow us to think about how these people adapted to the world in which they lived. The pottery, for example, allowed them to cook their food more efficiently and to store calories in the form of milk, enhancing the economic effectiveness of their cattle herds. To prove this was the case, the second professor challenges you to test her hypothesis by taking the pot back to the lab and using residue analysis to examine its former contents. Looking at the other artefacts, the second professor suggests that the presence of the polished stone axe, as a prestige tool, shows that this was a ranked society, and perhaps these things belonged to a chief. He would have been very powerful, she says with an air of scientific authority. She suggests that a battery of scientific analyses like radiocarbon dating can help test the order of events, and wonders if we might conduct some experiments to see if the pit filled in naturally or not. Having conducted some 'ethnoarchaeology' a few years ago (that is, she spent several freezing winters observing and recording how Inuit people organise their houses, including learning about what they do with their waste), she says that we can link up the static deposits you have excavated to the real processes that happened in the past. Ideally, she says, we might be able to gen- erate some laws about the kinds of societies that dig pits. These laws will apply to all human societies everywhere. Processual archaeology, she says, is a far superior paradigm to the first professor's outmoded ideas of culture history.

At this stage the third professor – the youngest of the three but still pretty old – cannot contain herself. Honestly, she announces, you processualists are the living end! When you're not making sexist assumptions – see how you referred to the chief as a man automatically – you are dismissing the importance of the wonderful work our first professor did. Of course, our third professor confesses, the work of culture historians is a little old-fashioned, but at least they tell specific stories about the past, and don't just generalise about laws that make no sense whatsoever. The third professor is very clear; if we want to understand your pit instead of trying to be scientific, we need to be creative. Have you read any Derrida, she asks? Without waiting for a reply (you see, her question was actually designed to show you that she had read Derrida . . .), she suggests that the critical thing here is the meaning behind these objects. Look, she declares, the presence of the cow skull and the antler pick show how people in the past had sought to combine the forces of the domestic world (in the form of the cow) as well as the spirits of the wild (in the form of the antler). The pottery and the axe show how the pit also combined the work of differing genders together, telling the archaeologist about the identities of those who had dug the pit and filled it. The axe isn't a symbol of a chief, but rather a meaningful object hinting at mythological connections to distant mountains. For professor number three, rather than thinking of these objects as rubbish, the whole deposit can be conceptualised as a deliberately structured statement about the beliefs, concerns and intentions of people in the past. Like an ancient text, these different deposits can be read to reveal the multiple meanings behind them, especially if we look at the relationships between them rather than at the objects individually. The only way forward, she tells you, is to align yourself firmly with the paradigm of postprocessual archaeology.

So here we have the same pit, with three different explanations: identifying cultures and diffusion versus studying adaptation to the environment versus teasing out past meanings. Each of our three fictionalised and (slightly) over-the-top professors is advocating one of the three main 'paradigms' of archaeological thought that have dominated the way archaeologists write about theory. The aim of this chapter is to explore each of these different approaches to establish some background against which we can compare more recent developments. We will work through these in broadly chronological order, though we should stress that this in no way will be a total history – if such a thing would ever be possible – and there are many excellent texts that provide far more detail than we can here.[1] In the next three sections, then, we consider culture history, processual archaeology and postprocessual approaches. This sequence represents a pretty standard narrative for the history of archaeological thought. There are two major issues with this, however. The first is that none of these 'paradigms' have ever gone away; they continue to play a role in the work that all archaeologists do. Second, as we will see, there are fundamental assumptions shared between these different approaches. In particular, they are all structured around the same set of dualisms. We argued in the last chapter that these dualisms are quite problematic; we focus on this issue again towards the end of the chapter.

BOX 2.1 VERE GORDON CHILDE

Vere Gordon Childe (1892–1957) was an Australian archaeologist and probably the most influential figure in the history of the discipline. He taught at the Institute of Archaeology in London, now part of University College London, and before that at the University of Edinburgh. He published numerous books on European prehistory including *Man Makes Himself*,[2] *The Dawn of European Civilisation*[3] and *What Happened in History*.[4] He defined many of the debates that we still wrestle with today. An active and committed Marxist, he drew on his political convictions to examine a number of different 'revolutions' in the past including the 'agricultural revolution' with the onset of farming and the 'urban revolution' with the emergence of large, densely occupied settlements. Here is one of Childe's famous diagrams of archaeological cultures, showing which cultural groups lived where and at what point in time.

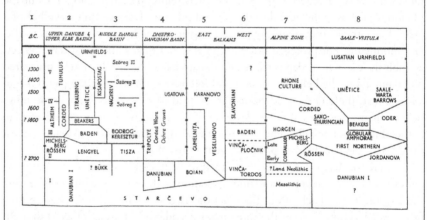

After Childe 1957 [1925]: 346, reprinted courtesy of Routledge

Culture history

The first major theoretical approach that emerged in the twentieth century is culture history. Although rarely concerned with 'theory' per se, in the manner that both processual and postprocessual archaeology would be, it nonetheless has a clear agenda and set of approaches.[5] Culture-historic approaches focus on the identification of past archaeological 'cultures' or groups. These are marked by particular ways of doing things like making pots, knapping stones and building monuments. When these occur together, archaeologists of this persuasion define them as a single culture. These then get named, and the names form the basis for how culture historians divide up the past (Box 2.1). European prehistory is full of these 'culture' names, many of which are still used in archaeology today. For example, there are the Linearbandkeramik in Central Europe who made timber long houses and pots decorated with linear bands (thus the name) and often buried their dead in cemeteries. Or there are the Beaker Folk, a Copper Age culture in much of Western Europe, who made – you guessed it – Beaker pottery (Figure 2.2), used copper tools and buried their dead with certain kinds of grave goods. These are just two out of countless examples. Although many culture historians, including Gordon Childe (see Box 2.1), were at pains to stress there was no direct link between archaeological culture – the particular set of material things – and an ethnic group of people, it was nonetheless pretty commonplace for people to assume that there was a direct relationship between the two. The slogan we tend to use about culture history is that for archaeologists of this persuasion, pots = people. Certain pottery types indicate the presence of – or at least, influence from – particular *kinds* of people.

Okay, but why *culture*? And why *culture history*? Archaeologists were particularly inspired by the work of the anthropologist Franz Boas who had identified how the differences between people in the present could be understood based on their culture; this means the particular ways they conducted themselves, and crucially, the unique beliefs and understandings they had of the world.[6] So this isn't culture in the sense we think of 'high culture' today (like going to the ballet), but culture as a mental representation of the world. In effect, this idea of culture is like a guidebook for how to participate in a particular group, the rules for how

FIGURE 2.2 Beaker pot

© *Trustees of the British Museum*

to behave. For culture historians, the material things uncovered became indicators of the kinds of thoughts people had. This was *material culture*, literally culture made into physical stuff. A central point that we will return to below is that this element of culture history is *idealist* – that is, it focuses on the *immaterial*. What this means is that what is important for culture historians are the ideas people held in their heads. The things people made were not driven by environmental or material concerns, but by the notion of what it was to belong to a certain group. So a Beaker person had an idea in their mind of what a pot should look like – known to us as a Beaker pot. This internal image from which they worked is what archaeologists sometimes call a mental template. They then took a pile of malleable clay, and imposed this template on to it, making their cultural idea – what a pot should look like – material. In so doing, of course, they also made something for archaeologists to find. Reread this paragraph, keeping an eye out for dualisms. We'll revisit this idea again below.

So if the notion of culture comes from the way in which individual artefacts expressed a person's ideas of identity, where does the importance of history come from? The heyday of culture history was prior to the invention of radiocarbon dating. This meant that to create a sequence through time, archaeologists had to rely primarily on comparative dating sequences. They did this in part by sorting out the relationships between different kinds of artefacts stratigraphically, which might show which ones come later in the sequence, as we saw with Carinated Bowls and Peterborough Ware in our example above. By combining this with detailed analysis of typologies, culture historians began piecing together a sequence of different cultures. In the end this meant that the past could be broken up into a timetable of different groups occupying different areas for different periods of time (see Box 2.1). Archaeology thus had a sense of sequence, a sense of history.

This ordering posed a very important question: how and why did these cultures change? Why were the Late Neolithic Rinyo-Clacton folk replaced by the Copper Age Beaker folk, and them in turn by the Bronze Age Food Vessel people? Was it the case that people dropped one idea of how to make a pot and replaced it with another? Or was this simply a new group of people arriving in an area each time and replacing the old ones? Culture historians argued about this, but they tended in any case to always explain change as a result of *diffusion*; that is, the movement of people, or at the least ideas, into a new area. Of course, this raised the issue of how these ideas started in the first place and culture historians usually traced this back to centres of innovation like the Near East or Egypt when explaining change in Europe. This was rarely satisfactory, however, despite its continued prevalence in many areas of archaeology today. If people's movement caused change, then what caused them to move? How did innovation *actually* come about? What about local sequences of change and development? What about people within cultural groups that rejected the 'norms' everyone else followed? So while culture history is good at the what, where and when questions, it didn't really have any answer as to the *why* or even the *how*. As we will see in a moment, this was one of the crucial criticisms that processual archaeology made of culture history as it burst onto the scene in the 1960s.

Before we discuss processual archaeology, however, we need to reiterate a point made above. Remember that culture history is *not* something that exists in the past; it was not a mode of thinking that archaeologists went through between 1920 and 1960. Not only is culture history the dominant archaeological approach across the world today, it remains an essential part of what all archaeologists do. When an archaeologist recognises a particular kind of pot, or metalwork, or stone tool, and assigns a name to it and thus a date, they are drawing on ideas from culture history. Typology remains an essential part of the archaeological tool kit. Some archaeologists might now prefer to think of these things as particular forms of adaptation to the world, or as meaningful statements about identity, or as active agents, rather than culture-made material or the actions of a specific ethnic group, but the work culture history did continues to underlie much of what we are able to say about the past today.

Processual archaeology

New Archaeology and processual archaeology are one and the same (we suppose nothing stays 'new' for very long). This way of thinking exploded in the discipline in the middle of the twentieth century.[7] Inspired by Leslie White and led by his student Lewis Binford (Box 2.2) in America and by Colin Renfrew and David Clarke in the UK, processual archaeology seemed to shake the foundations of how we study the past. As already noted, what mattered to these archaeologists was that archaeology should seek to *explain* and not merely to describe the past. It wasn't just about telling the story but rather about explaining why the people of the past acted in certain ways and not others. To do this, they sought to make archaeology much more like the natural sciences than history. This meant two things. On the one hand, it led to a huge increase in the range of scientific techniques that could be applied in archaeology and the emergence of whole sub-disciplines focused on the study of everything from animal bones to pollen grains. This also meant that processual archaeologists paid a lot more attention to site formation processes[8] – how things end up in the ground and what happens to them once they are there – than culture historians had done. On the other hand, though, it meant something much more substantial than this; archaeology needed to be a science not just in terms of its techniques but also in terms of its outlook on the world. Archaeology needed to be *positivist*. That is, it needed to take ideas and test them, to put the past on a laboratory table and prove that the interpretations made about it were true or false. Ideally this might even lead to the generation of law-like principles that archaeology could hold up as the real success stories of the discipline. This also meant that processual archaeology was the first set of approaches to really take archaeological theory seriously and to think about what archaeology is philosophically. As David Clarke put it, this move marked archaeology's 'loss of innocence'.[9]

BOX 2.2   LEWIS BINFORD

Lewis Binford (1931–2011) was perhaps the most influential archaeologist of his generation. His major publications include *An Archaeological Perspective*[10] and *In Pursuit of the Past*.[11] He led the New Archaeology movement, developed the notion of middle-range theory (in archaeology), and pioneered ideas of ethnoarchaeology to develop analogies with processes in the past. The illustration here comes from Binford's ethnoarchaeological work. It shows his drawing of Nunamiut men sitting around a campfire and the kind of artefact patterning they regularly produced. By studying this process in the present, Binford felt he could explain the static archaeological record from excavated sites.

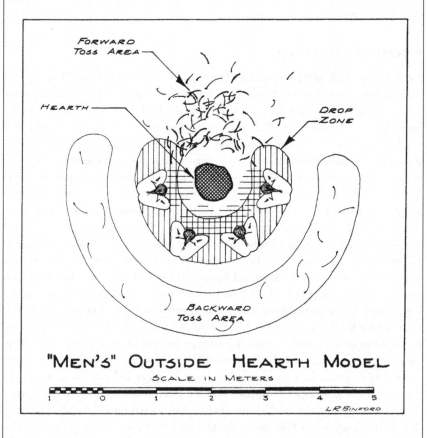

Image from Binford 1983: 153, reproduced with kind permission of the University of California Press

What did this newly scientific focus mean for how archaeology dealt with the materials it encountered? Rather than seeing them as historical expressions of particular ideas – particular mental templates – as culture historians did, processual archaeologists tended to focus on how material things were adaptive. In other words, artefacts were the means by which people adapted to the environmental conditions in which they found themselves. Material culture, they famously declared, was 'man's extrasomatic means of adaptation'.[12] Thus rather than being dictated by the immaterial ideas people had in their minds, it was the material conditions of the world that would have been the central driving factors in producing new kinds of artefacts, economies and societies.[13] This is one of two ways in which processual archaeology can be said to be *functionalist*. Adopting a functionalist argument in this context means that you believe that the reasons behind something being made were primarily driven by their adaptive function (see also our discussion of structural functionalism in the next chapter). So the reason someone made a pot is because there was a need to contain liquid or food. If someone made a sword, it was because they needed to fight and defend themselves to survive. Because material things were adaptations to the environment, they were determined by those functions. Yet functionalism has a second and related meaning. Functionalist approaches tend to compare societies to biological organisms, with different elements of a society (the economy, religion, politics) acting as different 'organs' keeping the 'body' in balance. Each part of the society, or system, has a role to play or a function in keeping things going just as the heart, liver and lungs all have different roles, relative to one another, within actual biological bodies. The importance of how these different elements of the system relate to each other, the structure of the system in other words, is why this is often referred to as *structural functionalism* (Chapter 3). It is also why processual archaeologists became very interested in so-called systems theory.[14]

Given the complex interactions between different parts of society and the critical role of the environment, it was clear to processual archaeologists from the start that it was no simple thing to test hypotheses against the material remains archaeologists excavated. What they required was a means of linking the static record archaeologists encounter in the present (the pot sherds, the flints, the animal bones) with the active processes that took place in the past (the people knapping flints, raising and butchering animals, shaping and using pots). To link these things up, Binford developed 'middle-range theory'.[15] This theory acted as the link between past and present – it literally filled in the 'middle range'. It often worked by drawing analogies between practices archaeologists could observe among living people and the archaeological patterns recovered from excavations. So Binford, for example, went and looked at how hunter gatherers sat around campfires and noted how different patterns of waste were generated (Box 2.2). He used this information to interpret finds from Upper Palaeolithic sites in France.[16] This is an example of analogy, where you make links between different kinds of society. Analogies remain very important to processual archaeologists both in specific cases like this, and also in how they generate comparisons between different kinds of society.[17] Just as adaptive thinking was important to understanding how people survived in different environments, so notions of social evolution were important to broader models of society. Many processual archaeologists continue to draw on anthropological models that divide societies into different evolutionary 'stages' such as bands, tribes, chiefdoms and states.[18] These different kinds of society share things in common, processual archaeologists argue, and produce particular patterns that can be examined and tested. So chiefdoms in the European Bronze Age could be understood through comparison with 'equivalent' chiefdoms in places like Hawaii that were known about in the much more recent past.[19]

This vision of social evolution, which implies an equivalence between western European pasts and the present of nonwestern groups and thus suggests that the latter are somehow stuck in 'our' past, is one of the many things that postprocessual archaeologists began to critique about processual archaeology in the late 1970s and 1980s. The others were the failure to recognise the role of women (see Chapter 4), the absence of human agency (see Chapter 3) and the idea that archaeology was a science that could prove things about the past. For postprocessual archaeologists, their field was not a science aimed at creating generalising laws about the past – it could never be positivist – but was instead better seen as a creative way of exploring the different identities, beliefs and power structures that made up the past. It was also an important political challenge to the present.

Postprocessual archaeology

If processual archaeology is a science generalising about the past, postprocessual archaeology is much more about specificity, about difference and about the unique ways of being human. Where functionalism dominated the concerns of processual archaeology – asking questions about an object's *function* – it was structuralism, which we define below, that dominated the early years of postprocessual archaeology.[20] Here the critical issue was the past meaning of objects. As one of the founding figures of postprocessual archaeology, Ian Hodder (Box 2.3), put it, 'material culture is meaningfully constituted'.[21]

Compared with culture history and processual archaeology, postprocessual archaeology is incredibly diverse.[22] The initial inspiration to challenge processual archaeology emerged from three main areas. First, archaeologists inspired by Marxism, the philosophy of Karl Marx, wanted to challenge the way in which processual archaeologists constructed very particular visions of power relationships in the past. These did not do enough, postprocessual archaeologists thought, to develop a critical analysis of how power worked and how certain kinds of authority were legitimised (we will discuss this further in Chapter 3). In particular these archaeologists, like Mark Leone, were interested in the notion of ideology, which

BOX 2.3 IAN HODDER

Ian Hodder is Dunlevie Family Professor of Anthropology at Stanford University, a post he has held since 1999. Prior to this he worked at Cambridge University where, in the 1980s, he played a leading role in developing postprocessual archaeology. He is author of numerous highly influential books including *Reading the Past*,[23] *The Domestication of Europe*[24] and *Entangled*,[25] and remains a central figure in archaeological theory. The photograph shows the famous Neolithic site of Çatalhöyük, where Hodder has directed excavations since 1993.

Image credit: https://commons.wikimedia.org/wiki/File:CatalHoyukSouthArea.JPG

is how power structures are naturalised and made to seem eternal and unchanging. Leone argued, for example, that the way in which gardens were designed in eighteenth-century America was not simply a product of fashion, but actively worked to make rich landowners feel comfortable in their positions of power and in their role as slave owners.[26] Similarly, Michael Shanks and Christopher Tilley argued that the way in which bodies were broken up inside Neolithic tombs in Britain and Sweden created an ideology of equality that cunningly disguised the real differences in power that existed in those societies.[27] In other words, people at the time saw that everyone was equal in death so were convinced that any inequalities in life were not really important.

The new commitment to Marxist interpretation related to the political climate in Britain and America in the 1980s and translated into political criticism within archaeology more generally. Feminism, the second critical stimulus behind postprocessual thought,[28] also drove this political critique. For anyone who is uncertain, feminism covers a range of different approaches, all of which are united by the aim of achieving equality for women. Inspired by this broader feminist work in the 1970s, archaeologists critiqued the way in which processualists assumed that modern patterns of gender inequalities were present in the past. This was not only inaccurate, they pointed out, it also helped to make it seem like modern issues were timeless, natural and therefore fixed and unchanging. Feminist archaeologists like Janet Spector (Box 2.4) not only challenged the androcentric (male-dominated) nature of the discipline, they also showed how archaeologists could employ creative ways of writing about the past to develop new understandings. These contributions were immensely important, so we return to them in detail in Chapter 4. Both Marxist and feminist postprocessual archaeologists[29] thus saw processual archaeology not only as wrong intellectually but as politically problematic. One of the great contributions of postprocessual theory has been this recognition that political ideas and archaeology are inevitably caught up with one another. The choice is not about whether to be political with the archaeology we do, but what kinds of politics we want to achieve, something we return to in Chapters 4, 10 and 11.

The third great influence on early postprocessual archaeology was the philosophies of structuralism and post-structuralism.[30] Structuralism was created by linguists such as Ferdinand de Saussure (who we discuss in more depth in Chapter 7), but principally came into archaeology through the work of the anthropologist Claude Lévi-Strauss. Lévi-Strauss was interested in the way in which different societies structured their myths and rituals around a set of binary oppositions, or dualisms, that he saw as underlying all human thought. These included nature versus culture, male versus female, raw versus cooked and so on; these are the very dualisms we encountered in Chapter 1! These binary oppositions quickly became influential in postprocessual approaches.[31] The second element of structuralism that archaeology embraced was its emphasis on the way in which language revealed these deeper meanings, or underlying dualisms. What if, postprocessualists like Hodder asked, material culture was used to communicate in similar ways to language? What if it had meanings coded within it that we could detect? Could the dualisms that underlay practices be revealed through this sort of analysis? Hodder, for example, looked at the material culture of Neolithic Europe and the Near East.[32] He argued that a close analysis of this material revealed that Neolithic Europe was structured around a set of binary oppositions, particularly ones he termed *the domus* and *the agrios*. The domus captured ideas of the home, of domestication and of life, while the agrios dealt with death, the wild and the outside. In the end, the critical thing for understanding the past through archaeology was to appreciate the meanings that material culture generated.[33]

BOX 2.4   JANET D. SPECTOR

Janet D. Spector (1944–2011) was a very important feminist archaeologist, best known for her work on gender archaeology in Native American contexts. Her 1991 article, 'What this awl means',[34] which was expanded into a book in 1993[35] of the same title, remains an astonishingly innovative account not only for its explicit engagement with gender but for the way it employed fictionalised narratives to highlight new ways that archaeologists could know and represent the past. Pictured here is the Dakota awl which was the focus of her inspiring narrative.

Image reproduced courtesy of the Minnesota Historical Society

Almost as soon as archaeologists became interested in structuralism, however, they also began exploring post-structuralism. This is an *enormously* diverse set of philosophical approaches, which would take several books to characterise. It includes figures like Michel Foucault, Roland Barthes, Jacques Derrida and many other famous – and often French – thinkers. Rather than try and detail all these philosophers here, let's instead emphasise the key elements that archaeologists took away from these approaches in the 1980s. The first was the idea that rather than language, a much better metaphor for material culture was *text*. This meant two things. First, it could be read just like a text; if you examined how objects related to each other, if you looked at the contextual associations between them, you could piece together the meanings behind them. This shows how important the notion of context was to postprocessual archaeologists trying to get at meaning. This relationship between text and context is the reason that Hodder's main approach in the 1980s and 1990s was known as con*text*ual archaeology[36] (our emphasis), and his first main book on archaeological theory was called *Reading the Past*.[37]

The second key point that emerged from this new metaphor for archaeology was that if material culture was like a text, then differing readings were possible. As we have seen, one of the key things about processual archaeology was that it was positivist – that is, processual archaeologists thought archaeology should be like a hard science and test hypotheses against the evidence in an attempt to prove things about the past.[38] In contrast, postprocessual archaeology asked: if you could have multiple readings of the same evidence, how could one *prove* anything? Think back to your last lecture. If you went and polled the class and the teacher the next day, you would find lots of different notions of what had taken place, whether it was interesting or boring, a success or a failure, whether the jokes were funny or not and so on. Which of these understandings of that experience were 'true'? Could you prove that one set of memories of the lecture the next day were more accurate than another? Rather than testing a hypothesis, postprocessual archaeologists argued that we needed to interpret the evidence, and more than one interpretation might be possible.

Let's take a second, more literary example. Think of any book you like and you can easily find lots of different possible interpretations. Is *The Lord of the Rings* a story of good and its triumph over evil? Or is it a parable about the dangers of industrialisation? Or is it a barely suppressed homoerotic love story? Or is it a racist narrative where dark figures 'in the east' threaten our white heroes 'in the west'? All of these readings are certainly possible, and so postprocessual archaeology embraced the potential for multiple meanings and multiple different possible interpretations. The notion that there might be more than one truth meant that postprocessual archaeology was often accused of *relativism* – the idea that anything goes.[39] If you can't prove anything after all, what is stopping you from simply making something up, from producing a story that is ridiculous, or even racist or sexist? The answer to this is that 'multiple' does not mean 'infinite', and just because more than one truth exists, this does not mean that 'anything goes'. If in doubt, think back to our example with *The Lord of the Rings*. You might agree or disagree with the readings above, but they are all more or less plausible. This 'more or less' is critical, in that it means the different views are available to be evaluated and critiqued. You might not be able to *prove* that one of them is true, but it does not mean that they are all necessarily equal. This also shows that the denial of positivism (that we can prove things about the past) does not mean that anything is plausible, what some refer to as 'hyper-relativism'. *The Lord of the Rings* is not a book about a supercomputer sending back a killing machine into the past to murder the mother of the resistance leader about to destroy it – that's the plot of the film *The Terminator*. Postprocessual archaeologists always knew that multiple readings did not mean that anything goes.

One final point is worth emphasising again. You guessed it – just as processual archaeology did not, in fact, replace culture history, postprocessual archaeology in no way replaced processualism. Scientific techniques remain important and are continually developed in archaeology. Even the most extreme postprocessual archaeologist never stopped using radiocarbon dates.[40] Our postprocessual interpretation of the Neolithic pit still refers to the pottery as 'Carinated Bowl' and would still happily test the pottery to see what residues it contained. Although the arguments between processual and postprocessual archaeologists became extremely heated, and at times personal, they were always as much about style as they were about substance. In part, that is because postprocessual archaeologists became the first archaeologists to embrace 'hardcore' continental theory in a serious way. Suddenly texts became full of references to numerous 'isms' never previously encountered, or to a philosopher whose work had never before seemed to connect to the concerns of archaeology. This acceptance of hardcore theory represented another step in the discipline's loss of innocence, and had much in common in reality with the progress that had been made throughout the 1960s and 1970s.

Tracing a history of dualisms

The sections above offered a brief, inevitably superficial and in the end fairly traditional narrative of the development of archaeological theory during the middle to late decades of the twentieth century. As we mentioned earlier, much more indepth and detailed accounts are available elsewhere. It is our contention, however, as we have stressed above, that a different reading of this history is possible. As we have seen, the three approaches do not really replace each other, so they cannot really be described as different paradigms.[41] Instead we suggest that they are actually arguments *within* a single paradigm, or a single way of understanding the world, that we might refer to as an 'ontology'. For the moment, we will define ontology as a technical word for how the world works. In this sense, the term ontology is usually opposed to epistemology, which means *how we come to know* how the world works. Although disciplines such as philosophy and anthropology define and use the term 'ontology' in different ways[42] that will become important in later chapters of this book, for now think of ontology as *what actually is*, or *what actually exists*. The different approaches to archaeology discussed up until this point all shared a single ontology, we suggest, and it is an ontology based around dualisms.[43]

Did you spot some of the dualisms in the 'paradigms' above as we went along? They were pretty explicit in the section on postprocessual thought a moment ago, but what about the others? Before we go any further, let's remind ourselves of what dualisms are again. As we saw in the last chapter, dualisms are a way of dividing the world into diametrically opposed categories. So we might divide the world into 'mental' illness and other kinds of illness, which maps neatly onto a distinction between 'mind' and 'body'. There are lots of these dualisms that seem to characterise western thought: they include mind and body, but also male and female, subject and object, immaterial ideas and material things, ritual and daily life and, most importantly, culture and nature. This last divide is the one that means we argue about whether or not sexuality is genetic (and therefore natural and fixed) or not (and therefore cultural and about choice), about whether you behave just like your mother because of nature (you share 50 per cent of her DNA) or culture (she helped bring you up). We saw in the last chapter how this way of thinking about the world gets us into lots of trouble, whether we are trying to decide what counts as 'cheating' when it comes to high-performance athletes, or when trying to decide if a particular stone counts as an archaeological artefact or not.

The arguments that have dominated archaeology, we suggest, are not really about different paradigms or ontologies – about what archaeology really is – but instead about which side of these dualisms is more important.[44] Imagine you are having an argument with a friend about nature versus nurture. Is it genetics that makes us who we are or culture? Whichever side of that argument you are on, what you and your friend are implicitly accepting is that there is a divide between those two things, that this way of splitting up the world makes sense. It is the same with the great debates of archaeological theory. Should archaeologists concentrate on the specific worlds of beliefs, ideas and culture or on more general notions of adaptation, materials and nature? To explore this point further, let's briefly retell the history above but backwards rather than forwards.

The role of dualisms in postprocessual archaeology was certainly explicit in structuralist accounts like Hodder's interpretation of Neolithic Europe. Yet underneath this, we can detect how postprocessual archaeologists placed their emphasis firmly on one side of our dualisms.[45] Postprocessual archaeologists emphasised meaning, language, belief, symbols and identity. All of these privilege immaterial, cultural concerns. What was important about nature and the material world was what people thought of them, how people engaged with them and what people believed about them. It is subjects not objects that matter here. Thus what mattered about an animal was what it represented, rather than the number of calories it provided; what mattered about a pot was what it symbolised, not what it could do. Even the discipline itself should be seen primarily as a humanities subject concerned with people and their cultures and our own *subjective* interpretations. Here culture is king.

In contrast, processual archaeology was the opposite. Nature is top dog and the question is: how will people adapt to it? How will the demands of particular environments shape and form the kinds of cultures that exist there? How did objects function in particular ways to allow people to meet their needs? The discipline here is an *objective* science, concerned with nature, the environment and certain kinds of laws. Follow the story back to the previous stage and the pendulum swings back the other way. In culture history what matters explicitly are the cultures people had, the way they express their ideas about those immaterial identities in material form and the history of those changing cultures. Matter is fundamentally shaped here by culture, object by subject, and the discipline is orientated towards history. So the criticisms made by processual archaeologists towards culture historians were about their failure to attend to the *nature of the material world*. Similarly, the huge arguments that took place between processual and postprocessual archaeologists in the 1980s were about whether nature or culture really mattered. What they were not about was whether it made sense to divide the world up like this.

So while it might seem that archaeologists have occupied a wide range of differing positions, what they have really done is flip-flopped back and forth between two opposed poles, one privileging subjects, ideas, beliefs, identities and cultures and the other looking at objects, nature, materials and science.[46] Of course, many archaeologists have also steered between those two extremes, or tacked from one to the other. Until the 1990s, however, what was rarely considered was *that the poles themselves were problematic*, that the very terms of the debate were artificial inventions that archaeologists were imposing on themselves. So where do these dualisms come from and why did archaeologists start relying on them? As you may have guessed from the fact that these dualisms crop up in our everyday arguments, they are much more widespread than just our discipline; in fact, we can trace them back into ancient history.

The central figure in the history of dualisms is often declared to be the French philosopher René Descartes, who lived and worked in the seventeenth century (Box 2.5).[47] He is such a critical figure that these dualisms are often referred to as Cartesian in his honour. Descartes, a radical sceptic, argued that we could not be certain of anything other than our own consciousness. His famous philosophical slogan – I think therefore I am – captures this sentiment precisely. What we could be certain of was our minds, but not our bodies, and thus the mental was separate from, and opposed to, the physical. Descartes divided the world between mind and body, but also between nature and culture, between animals (who were natural) and people (who were cultural). Blaming Descartes for dualisms is a little unfair, however. In many ways, he was drawing on much older histories of thought. The division between body and soul, for example, underlay his separation of body and mind, and this went back via Christian theology and the bible to Ancient Greek philosophers. Similarly Descartes was far from the only seventeenth-century thinker that divided the world up into two opposed camps. The critical realisation we need to make is that Descartes and others had not discovered some astonishing scientific fact that the world was divided up into two opposed categories of

BOX 2.5   RENÉ DESCARTES

René Descartes (1596–1650) was a French philosopher, and a key figure within the growth of philosophy and mathematics in the seventeenth century. Famous for his philosophical maxim, 'I think therefore I am', Descartes has become a symbol for the way in which western thought has sought to break the world up into opposed dichotomies. Included among his many publications is *Discourse on the Method* (1637). Many of the approaches we will examine in this book are an attempt to react against this kind of 'Cartesian' thought. As a radical sceptic, Descartes wasn't certain that anything – other than his own mind – was real, so we represent his work here with a photograph of Auguste Rodin's famous sculpture, *The Thinker*.

Andrew Horne via https://commons.wikimedia.org/wiki/File:The_Thinker,_Rodin.jpg

things; this was not the metaphysical equivalent of realising the world was round. Instead, what he did was begin to formalise a way of thinking that acted to *actively separate* things into these different camps, that imposed these ideas onto the world in ways that actually obscure its complex reality.[48] So, by embracing dualisms we are uncritically accepting one way of looking at the world, rather than thinking explicitly about how best to approach the past.

The problem with dualisms

It is these historical dualisms that lie at the heart of most archaeological debates of the last century.[49] Rather than differing understandings of the world being pitched against one another – differing paradigms – we instead have an argument about which aspect of a *particular* worldview works better. These dualisms are not just problematic because they are unconsidered assumptions, or simply because they are inherited historical traditions. Rather they are deeply problematic because of the way in which they prevent us from really getting to grips with the past. They do so for several reasons. First of all, people in the past almost certainly did not think exactly the same way that we do in the present. If we look around the world today at nonwestern groups, whether in Amazonia, Melanesia or elsewhere, we find countless examples of groups who have different perspectives about what the world is and how it works, differing *ontologies*. Do you remember our stone from Chapter 1? With one ontology, the stone can be dismissed as an unworked, unaltered piece of nature. In another ontology it had a very different set of relationships with the world in which it was found. This means that the past is certain to have been replete with all sorts of other ways of thinking too. So when Hodder argues that dualisms structure the world of Neolithic Europe, he is in effect colonising the past with present-day assumptions. He is not allowing the past to speak for itself, or for us to really start to think about how those people and times might be different from us and ours. Dualisms are *essentialist*, in other words – they take part of our world and make them eternal, or essential to all times and places. Now it is certainly the case that western thinking is not alone in employing oppositions, or dualisms, to structure the world. However, there is a significant difference between starting from the position that the world *is* structured by a specific set of dualisms (Cartesian ones) in reality, and the idea that in certain historical contexts we might reveal that some dualisms played an important role in how that world worked.

The second issue is that dualistic ways of thinking tend to impose categories onto people in the past that obscure the complexities of who they were and what they did. So, for example, if you want to explore the worlds of colonial America, like the archaeologist Barbara Voss, it is unhelpful to divide people up into opposed camps based on gender, ethnicity or sexuality because, as she argues, this forces you to miss all the complicated messiness that actually characterised people's lives.[50] Similarly, dualistic thinking assumes that 'men' and 'women' are opposed, timeless categories. Yet the evidence from both past and present suggests that other kinds of gender can and do exist (Chapter 4).

Third, dualisms make it difficult to explain change. A common archaeological dualism is between hunter gatherers on the one hand and farmers on the other. These two apparently opposed groups are seen as having completely differing ways of life and – especially on the hunter-gatherer side – as timeless and unchanging. Yet as soon as these groups are opposed to one another, explaining change from one to the other (what we often call in Europe the Mesolithic/Neolithic transition) becomes a major challenge.[51] We have to invoke seismic population replacement or a complete rejection of a former way of life, rather than looking at the changes that took place in detail. This ties to the opposition between continuity and change that we discuss in Chapter 3.

Finally, and fundamentally, these dualisms are deeply misleading. In all places and at all times, the world was *not* divided into nature and culture, body and mind, material and immaterial, or female and male. In reality that isn't even how we work in the modern west, where underneath our imposed dualisms, we can see all sorts of strange hybrid things that blur the two.[52] Just think back to our sprinter in the previous chapter with his genetically modified foods and artificially enhanced trainers. His achievements on the track are hardly 'natural' despite the fact that he is banned from ingesting certain chemicals. If dualisms and binary oppositions don't help us understand the present – the very heart of the dualist world – then there is no chance at all that they will help us understand the past.

Conclusions: the three professors

So where does this discussion leave the advice our three professors offered on your pit? Hopefully you can see that they all have something to offer. After all, assigning the pottery to a particular typology helps you date the pit; sending it off to be tested for residues will definitely help you understand what it was used for; and thinking about the meanings of these objects within this particular context also seems to be an interesting way forward. Yet with each case the professors' arguments seem to be caught in dualisms. Is it culture that matters or nature? Is it function or meaning? These things probably didn't matter in the past and they may not mean much in the present either. In contrast, next time you pick up your trowel, it might be better to build on some of the suggestions the postprocessual professor made and think about these issues in terms of relationships. How do the objects relate to one another? How did they relate to people? How did they emerge out of relationships? If you emerge as an archaeologist through the relationship you have with your trowel, these pits, your professors and so on, maybe we can think about the past like this too.

In this chapter we did two things. On one hand, we traced out a general history of archaeological thought, but we also attempted to show how much in common these different schools of thought actually have. They rely on dualisms, but simply tend to argue that one side of those dualisms is more important than the other. Archaeologists have known for some time that our thought is shaped by the political worlds in which we live and interpret the past. Trigger,[53] for example, famously traced how different priorities could shape archaeology into a nationalist, colonialist or imperialist project. What we have argued here is an extension of that. It is not just our politics that shapes our archaeology but our very assumptions about how the world works, our ontology – our theory of being. If we want to say something really challenging about the past, if we want to say something really *accurate* about the past, then it is these underlying assumptions we need to dismantle. This is what archaeological theorists have been trying to do for the last 20 years and it is on these efforts that we focus for the remainder of the book.

Notes

1 E.g. Johnson 2010; Trigger 2006.
2 Childe 1936.
3 Childe 1957 [1925].
4 Childe 1942.
5 Key culture-historic texts include those by Childe (e.g. 1936, 1942) and Piggott (e.g. 1954). During the 1950s culture history was already moving to think about the past in more scientific ways, something not always acknowledged by their processual critics. See, for example, the work of Graham Clark (e.g. 1952).
6 E.g. Boas 1911.
7 For key readings on processual archaeology see Clarke 1968; Binford 1962, 1968, 1983; Flannery 1967; Renfrew 1973, among many others.
8 See, for example, Schiffer 1983.
9 Clarke 1973.
10 Binford 1972.
11 Binford 1983.
12 White 1959: 8.
13 Dualism alert!
14 Clarke 1968.
15 Binford 1983.
16 Binford 1983: 157.
17 They also remain important in particular elements of postprocessual thought, including the study of personhood, as we will see in Chapter 4.
18 Service 1962.
19 Earle 1997.
20 Although it is important to note that structuralism actually has a long use in archaeology predating postprocessual thinking. It was used by the American historical archaeologist James Deetz (e.g. 1977), for example, and by André Leroi-Gourhan (1993 – first published in French in 1963) in his interpretation of Palaeolithic cave art.
21 Hodder 1982a: 13.
22 Hodder 1986.
23 Hodder 1990.
24 Hodder 2012.
25 Key references for reading on postprocessual thinking include: Hodder 1982b, 1986; Miller and Tilley 1984; Shanks and Tilley 1987a, 1987b, among many others.
26 Leone 1984.
27 Shanks and Tilley 1982.
28 E.g. Gero and Conkey 1991.
29 And of course these groups overlapped.
30 Spector 1991.
31 Spector 1993.
32 Hodder 1990.
33 Hodder 1982a: 13.

34 From the beginning postprocessual archaeology was also concerned with agency and practice – but we will deal with that in the next chapter.

35 Although from the very start they had something of an ambivalent relationship with them. So in one of the opening salvos of postprocessual archaeology, Hodder (1982a) is very critical of both dichotomies and of creating oppositions between things. Yet only a few years later he was publishing whole interpretations based on them (Hodder 1990). Many postprocessual accounts have wrestled with this. The first forays into phenomenology, for example (see Chapter 6), combined both a philosophy that tries directly to counter dualisms, and whole lists that specifically embrace them (e.g. Tilley 1994: 8).

36 Our emphasis.

37 Hodder 1986.

38 Whether this is an accurate representation of what the hard sciences actually do, of course, is very debatable.

39 E.g. Bintliff 1991: 276.

40 As neatly pointed out by Robb and Pauketat 2013: 17.

41 Cf. Thomas 2015b: 20.

42 In different subjects, and even in different areas of the same subject, ontology can have different meanings. So the use of ontology in computer science, for example, is very different from how it is used in anthropology and philosophy. Its use in the latter two subjects is of more interest to us as archaeologists. Even in that case, however, there is variation in how practitioners use and apply the term. In anthropology it can either mean the fundamental understandings people have of the kinds of things that exist and how they operate, or it can go further than this and refer to what *actually exists in reality, and how this can vary around the world*. The former is effectively a stronger version of the term 'worldview', while the latter means something more than that and might be seen as a kind of relativism (though its supporters would disagree). These positions capture the two sides of a debate between anthropologists on the subject (see Carrithers et al. 2010). In philosophy the word doesn't tend to reflect local understandings, but rather the attempt to generate a single model for how the world works (Graeber 2015; Heywood 2012; Jensen 2016). In this case we might discuss a dualist ontology on the one hand, for example, and contrast this with the kinds of 'flat' ontology we will discuss in Chapter 8. These distinctions may well be unfamiliar and difficult to grasp – don't worry, we will return to them in detail later in the book.

43 Later in the book we will examine how people tend to operate within multiple rather than singular ontologies; that is, rather than having one ontology, they switch between several (Harris and Robb 2012). So although we might discuss whether we are the product of nature or nurture (a dualist perspective), most of the time we get on with the world without worrying about these divisions. The same is true for archaeologists, of course. However, the way in which archaeology has traditionally been written about does not really engage with these other ontologies and so remains primarily dualist. We will return to the relationship between ontologies in Chapters 10 and 11.

44 Jones 2002.

45 Jones 2012: 6.

46 Jones 2002.

47 Thomas 2004.

48 Latour 1993.

49 Thomas 2004.

50 Voss 2008a.

51 Borić 2005; Jones and Sibbesson 2013.

52 Latour 1993.

53 Trigger 1984.

3

BETWEEN THOUGHTS AND THINGS

Theorising practice and agency

Introduction: encountering the mystery object

Already tired of theory? Let's take a quick break to consider some old-fashioned 'dirt' archaeology and a moment that many archaeologists are lucky enough to experience regularly, the instance of discovery in the field (Figure 3.1). Since most archaeologists and archaeology students are either already or soon-to-be familiar with field school archaeology, let's begin there. Imagine that you have enrolled in a dig in the north-eastern US, excavating a seventeenth-century Native American fortified village. You and your digging partner were assigned what appears to be a rather boring excavation unit. The field director seems excited that you have been finding loads of European-produced ceramics, but you just can't maintain an interest. After all, you have cups and bowls like the ones you found in your own house! You thought that you had signed up to find something new and exciting. As you trowel away at your boring unit on a particularly hot and humid afternoon, you can't help but think of other ways to spend a summer. As you mindlessly peel away the soil, your thoughts of swimming pools and air conditioning distract you from a small glint showing in the corner of your unit. Fortunately, something feels strange to you as your trowel moves over that particular corner, leading you to eventually look down to notice the top of what looks to be a 'mystery object' (one whose colour and texture you don't recognise). You immediately call over the supervisor, who helps to further uncover the object and record its provenience.

You swell with pride as the entire field school gathers around to watch as you carefully remove the mystery object from the ground (Figure 3.2). It has a dark golden-brown colour and – based on the sound it makes when you tap it gently with your trowel – is made of some sort of non-ferrous metal. It is about 5 centimetres long and less than a centimetre across at its widest. It is funnel-shaped like a

FIGURE 3.1 Contemplating the mystery object. Drawing by K-Fai Steele

miniature ice cream cone except there is a hole in the tip and a seam where the two edges come together along its length. In other words, it appears to be a flat piece of 'sheet' metal rolled into a miniature cone, leaving a hole at the tip. Upon close inspection you see a concentration of small dents along its widest edge (where the ice cream would sit). There are also a few scratches and small dents found all across the body of the object. What could it be?

Your know-it-all digging partner unceremoniously rips the item from your hands while exclaiming, 'Ah ha, evidence for cultural continuity!' He explains that indigenous people of the broader area have occasionally used copper – possibly what

FIGURE 3.2 Copper tinkler (metal fragment, 5.3 centimeters at its longest point)

Courtesy of the Royal Ontario Museum

your mystery item is made of – for thousands of years. He is excited to see some evidence for cultural continuity along with the colonial changes apparent in your excavation unit. In spite of the transformations in Native American cultural practices evident at your seventeenth-century archaeological site, like the many European-made ceramics that you could not care less about, he feels that the mystery object shows an important continuation of 'traditional' technologies and long-distance trade networks (likely connecting to the Great Lakes region) during tumultuous times. Unfortunately, the moment of excitement doesn't last forever. Your field director tells you that European traders in the region imported loads of copper and brass to trade with Native Americans during the seventeenth century.[1] Feeling slightly deflated, you begin to see the mystery object as you do the many ceramic sherds that you have already bagged this season: more evidence for European presence and trade relations in the area. You think, 'Tell me something I didn't already know about this site and time period'. Your field director cheers you up by noting that Europeans never traded brass and/or copper in this particular form. In fact, they often traded it in the form of cooking kettles (Figure 3.1). In this sense, your object is new and exciting for the site. One of the indigenous students at the field school also has some interesting insights. He tells you that his aunt has a 'jingle dress' that has more than 100 miniature cones fastened to it and they resemble the object that you found. His aunt wears the dress at Native American gatherings, called 'powwows', for a specific type of dance. As the miniature cones move with the dancers, they bounce off of one another, creating a beautiful jingling sound.

How do archaeologists make sense of objects like your mystery item? In this chapter we explore questions such as this by considering theories of practice and agency. These notions re-wrought archaeological theory beginning in the 1980s and remain highly influential today. In short, they provide useful ways of examining archaeological collections like the one you dug up at your field school; they challenge the functionalist and structuralist approaches laid out in the previous chapter, situating what we discuss below as *cultural reproduction* between thoughts and things. Don't worry if this doesn't make immediate sense to you; we will explain further in the following sections. In the next part, we provide some basic definitions and highlight what we see as the key contributions of theories of practice and agency: their relational perspectives that began to challenge the dualisms highlighted in Chapters 1 and 2. Next, we discuss the respective works of Pierre Bourdieu and Anthony Giddens, two of the most influential practice and agency theorists from outside the discipline. We then move on to examine more closely the archaeological implications of these theories. Here, we highlight major themes and debates that arose as part of the practice and agency turn in archaeological theory. Finally, we return to your mystery object to reassess the situation in terms of these notions we have discussed. As you read through the remainder of the chapter, keep your miniature 'ice cream cone' in mind, and continue to think about how various ideas might shed new light on its significance for your site.

Theorising practice and agency, or what we *do*

Practice theory defies definition in some ways. It is a body of thought first developed in sociology and cultural anthropology. It builds upon Marxist notions of *praxis*, or the ways in which ideas and theories are put into action, and it serves as a general critique of both functionalism and structuralism. Yet it lacks the predictive and law-generating components of other theories employed in archaeology (e.g., cultural evolution, systems theory, structuralism), resembling a loose collection of possibilities rather than a deterministic and universalised model for how societies and cultures work, persist and transform across space and time. Those archaeologists influenced by practice theory focus on the *recursive* connections between *agents* (which might include individuals, groups of people and even things) on the one hand, and *social structure* (which might include other people, communities and things) on the other. The way in which agents and structures interact leads to *cultural reproduction*, or the way in which culture and social structure is maintained and transformed through time.

Let's take this one step at a time. First, agency is the ability to make differences in the world, either through maintaining the status quo or by challenging accepted 'norms' of how to act as part of a larger collective.[2] Through agency you can reinforce certain social patterns. For instance, perhaps you are reading this chapter because you were instructed to do so by your professor. You are exerting agency as you follow the instructions *because you had the opportunity to act otherwise*, but *chose* to read as instructed. You could also use your agency to yell at your professor after being given the instructions, stand up on your desk and set this book on fire. Each of these possibilities comes with a different set of consequences, but that is a completely different matter.

If agency is the ability to make differences in the world, than what precisely do we mean by social structure? That is a very good question and the answer is quite easy. Let's begin by thinking of social structure as anything that helps guide people's choices, actions and beliefs. Remember your field school from above? You learned a certain way of behaving at the archaeological site, including how you dressed, talked, moved your body around the excavation units, addressed fellow students and instructors, excavated and recorded artefacts, and classified the things that you found. The way you learned these things was through social structure, which ranged from explicit instructions from your teaching assistant ('Do this, but never do that!') to implicit patterns like the way you came to address the field director. Perhaps no one told you how to address her, so you made a decision that was likely based on your previous experience with archaeologists and professors and on how you observed others in the field school (perhaps of a similar 'rank' as you) addressing her.

The relationship between agency and structure is vital here. Agency takes shape from structure in the sense that structures influence agents' choices and actions. Because they are recursively connected, however, there exists a 'feedback loop' of sorts (see Box 3.2). This simply means that agency also has the potential to act back and influence structures. On the first day of your field school someone handed you a shiny new trowel to use over the summer. The instructions you received, the trowel itself and your observation of other participants using trowels in the field all served as social structure in that they influenced you – the agent in this case – to act a certain way with the trowel. Can you think of a scenario where you might use the trowel to influence the broader social structure of the field school? Perhaps you thought it would be practical to mark your name on the handle of your trowel using permanent marker and all of the other students – seeing your marked trowel handle – decided to copy you. This is how the recursive feedback loop between agency and structure works, and this is precisely why we refer to theories of practice and agency as relational. They do not privilege *only agency* or *only structure*, but rather study the relationship between the two. In fact, practice theorists would argue that there is no way to treat the two as separate entities since they are both part of cultural reproduction, the simultaneous processes of cultural continuity and change.[3]

Practice approaches seek to locate and study the roles that people, things, mixtures between the two and any other 'social' entities play within processes of cultural reproduction. According to the practice theorists discussed below, the things that people do and the representations they produce are neither mindless behavioural responses that follow broad-scale evolutionary schemes of adaptation nor passive reflections of the cultural laws and regulations nested in actors' heads. On the contrary: they are the active, meaningfully constituted parts of social and cultural reproduction, the dynamic and improvised interplay of individuals and their surroundings, and the arenas in which cultural change and continuity take form.

Taking influence from anthropology and sociology

During the 1970s and 1980s, anthropologist Pierre Bourdieu and sociologist Anthony Giddens each produced comprehensive theories of practice,[4] both of which proved foundational for many archaeological practice-based approaches.[5] Each model focused on the recursive feedback loop between agents and the social structures of which they are part, framing practices (the things we do) as key components of social and cultural reproduction. Although Bourdieu and Giddens used slightly different concepts and terminology in their respective approaches, each thinker set out to explore the roles that individual actors played in rebuilding and transforming social structures through time and space.

Pierre Bourdieu (Box 3.1) began his career as a structuralist thinker. He conducted ethnographic fieldwork in Algeria among the Kabyle. Soon after, he published a frequently cited analysis of the layout of Kabyle households.[6] He found that the households he observed were spatially organised by principles of

BOX 3.1 PIERRE BOURDIEU

Pierre Bourdieu (1930–2002) was a French anthropologist, sociologist and philosopher known best among archaeologists for his theory of practice. He was Professor and Chair of Sociology at the Collège de France. His *Outline of a Theory of Practice*[7] helped to redefine archaeological theory beginning in the 1980s. These illustrations show one of Bourdieu's most famous subjects of study, the Kabyle house; the top diagram shows the make-up of the Kabyle house, the bottom shows some of the ways in which Bourdieu interpreted it based on various dualisms.

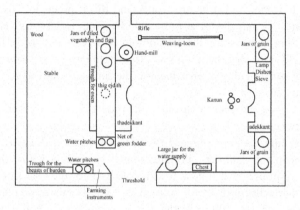

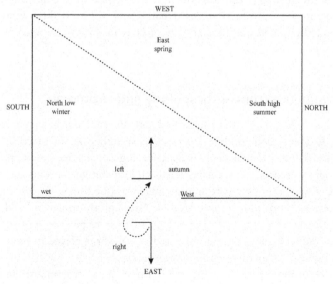

After Bourdieu 1990: 272, redrawn by Vicki Herring

opposition (or sets of dualisms), such as female/male, dark/light and low/high. As discussed in Chapter 2 and later in Chapter 7, structuralism seeks to uncover the principles and rules stored in people's minds (in fact, some structural archaeologists, like James Deetz,[8] used the term 'mindsets'). These thinkers insist on dualisms, or binary oppositions, as the main organising rules for all human meaning. For instance, they would assume that Bourdieu's observations on male/female spatial oppositions in households are direct reflections of cultural laws stored in people's heads. This model, unfortunately, has no way of accounting for the variability of individuals within a culture or for cultural change of any sort.

In contrast to these approaches, Bourdieu wondered precisely how individuals and their actions served to maintain or transform certain spatial household patterns. This interest led him to focus on the things that people do and how those actions relate to the material patterns he observed and the deep cultural logics (inside people's heads) fixated on by structuralists. He came to focus on the dynamic feedback loop between the physical structure of the house and bodily experience of – and actions within – the house.[9] In short, he was interested in how the house shaped the people's actions and how the people's actions shaped the house; a 'two-way street', so to speak. This is different from structuralism's typical focus on how the mindset shapes the house, a 'one-way street'. This contrast is one reason why many consider Bourdieu to be a '*post*structural' thinker.

Bourdieu's *Outline of a Theory of Practice* addressed these issues for anthropology and for social theory in general. According to Bourdieu,[10] cultural reproduction largely takes place unconsciously in the mundane aspects of everyday life (e.g. building and living in a house). The actions that individuals take, the things they make and use, and the representations they produce simultaneously take shape from their observations while also influencing future practices, representations and materials around them (the two-way street mentioned above). For Bourdieu,[11] the stability of social structures and the maintenance of cultural traditions rely largely on an assumed natural order, or unquestioned beliefs in the way things have 'always' worked. The Kabyle house maintains its spatial order and you conduct yourself in a particular way at the archaeological site because these patterns (what he called 'structuring structures') remain unquestioned; there is no conceivable way of doing things otherwise. Of course, there are many different ways to organise a house and act on an archaeological site. The random or arbitrary nature of certain structures is only brought into focus and questioned when an alternative presents itself. This introduces the possibility for practices to become politicised, and for social transformation to occur.

For instance, let's imagine that another local archaeological field school visits your site. This other field school only uses plain unmarked trowels. When they observe your entire field school using individually marked trowels, they immediately become aware of a choice (between plain and marked). This difference can even come to stand as a symbol representing your two different field schools.

Bourdieu[12] used the term *doxa* to refer to this phenomenon. If some component of social life is doxic, it is taken to carry no political connotations since there is no conceivable alternative way of acting.[13] Once questioned and dissolved, however, doxas are subsequently re-established through *orthodoxy* or continually challenged through *heterodoxy*. Archaeology is particularly well positioned to address issues of doxa given its long-view perspective on human history.[14] For example, Stephen Silliman[15] used this concept to interpret colonial interactions between Native Americans and settler-colonists in nineteenth-century California. He framed colonialism and its introduction of new types of material culture as a break in the doxa of pre-colonial North American societies and cultural practices.

Alongside doxa, a critical notion for Bourdieu's theory is the concept of *habitus*, a term he took from Marcel Mauss,[16] who was mainly interested in the ways in which tribal societies exchanged and circulated trade items.[17] Habitus refers to an embodied set of predispositions that tell you how to act and engage with your surroundings. Remember your mystery object from above? How did you decide to finally look down and pay attention to your trowelling? Something didn't feel 'right' as your hand gripped the trowel and peeled back soil.[18] Your *habitus* helped you become aware of this new and unexpected sensation. Previous weeks of experience had encouraged you to move your body in a certain way at the archaeological site; it conditioned you to expect a certain feel when excavating soil with no material culture in it versus soil containing material culture. Connected to – and influenced by – the surrounding structures through our feedback loop, habitus is an individual's embodied predisposition to act in certain ways. The habitus is a durable but transposable set of dispositions generated from a person's life experiences and cultural repertoires; again, simultaneously structur*ed* and structur*ing*.[19] Doesn't this sound a bit like the definition for culture in Chapter 2? Indeed, but it adds a degree of flexibility to processes of social and cultural reproduction and considers the individual body as a key part of these processes. Habitus is 'regulated' and 'tends to produce' regularities, but it is also improvised and context-dependent. In contrast to previous understandings in cultural anthropology, practitioners taking influence from Bourdieu 'assume that society and history are not simply sums of ad hoc responses and adaptations to particular stimuli'.[20] Practice-based approaches thus acknowledge the ever-present possibility for structural transformation while also noting the importance of the physical body.

Habitus has been a very important idea for archaeologists, so let's give one more example to hammer this home. When you sit down for dinner, how do you know which piece of cutlery to use and when? If you have a knife and fork, you probably automatically use them with a particular hand in a particular way. How do you know how to do this? Do you have to consciously think about it each time or does it happen automatically? This is part of your habitus. Now imagine you are having dinner with your partner's family who come from a very different social class. You are suddenly confronted with two or three knives and forks. Like before, do you unconsciously know which to use or do you have to remind yourself to work from outside in? In this case, you are moving outside of your own habitus. Finally, imagine that you are in a foreign place and the cutlery is entirely absent. You need to eat with your hands, but which hand? In some places eating with one hand is normal while using the other is disgusting. It is when we find ourselves in situations like this that we can think about how almost all of our daily lives (much more than just moments when we eat) are based in simple habit, in knowledge of how-to-go-on or, as Bourdieu would say, a feel for the game.[21]

Sharing many qualities with Bourdieu's theory of practice, sociologist Anthony Giddens' (Box 3.2) theory of structuration[22] represents a middle ground between analysis of the world 'out there' (objectivism) and individuals' experiences of that world (subjectivism). Like Bourdieu, Giddens sought to establish a theory of practice that sat between – and linked – these two extremes. He sought to make the study of 'social practices ordered across space and time'[23] the main focus of the social sciences. Like Bourdieu, he identified practices as the areas where society and culture made themselves in relation to social structures; 'Structure is both medium and outcome of the reproduction of practices'.[24] Giddens was primarily interested in how social practices were reproduced across space-time and made increasingly systematic in form. This process by which practices became engrained in everyday life is what Giddens referred to as *structuration*. Structuration occurs largely on the level of what Giddens calls *practical consciousness*, a concept that shares many characteristics with Bourdieu's notions of doxa and habitus. This level of awareness exists between discursive consciousness – when people can actually explain and express their motivations for acting in a certain way and not another – and unconscious motivations, of which individuals are unaware and thus unable to explain. In other words, as people go about their daily lives, much of the work that they do in reproducing social structures takes place beyond the realm of language. Think about every time you go to a lecture, take a seat, sit quietly taking notes while your lecturer babbles on in front of you. Although you may not be doing it deliberately, your agency in going to the lecture and behaving appropriately helps us to sustain the structure of the lecture – which in turn of course is what is shaping your agency.

Giddens also offers a broad definition of agency as the capability to do things: 'Agency concerns events of which an individual is the perpetrator, in the sense that the individual could, at any phase in a given sequence of conduct, have acted differently'.[25] Giddens[26] describes a person flicking on a light switch, perhaps after waking up in the middle of the night to get a drink of water from the kitchen. Let's imagine that when our waker switches on the light, she inadvertently scares off a burglar who was just preparing to break into the house. For Giddens, the waker's agency (turning on the light) is partially responsible for the thief's retreat even though our sleepy almost-victim had no idea of the thief's presence or motives. Agency, then, is much more than intentional action aimed at producing specific kinds of outcomes.

BOX 3.2 ANTHONY GIDDENS

Anthony Giddens is a British sociologist known best among archaeologists for his theory of structuration, first introduced to the discipline by Ian Hodder and his students in the 1980s. He is author of *Central Problems in Social Theory: Action, Structure, and Contradiction*[27] and *The Constitution of Society: Outline of a Theory of Structuration*.[28] He is Professor Emeritus in the Department of Sociology, London School of Economics. This diagram illustrates Giddens' ideas on how agents monitor and understand their own actions.

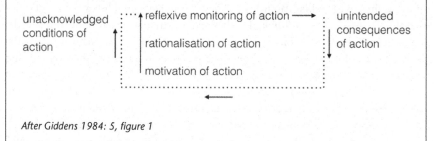

After Giddens 1984: 5, figure 1

Archaeologies of practice and agency

How do all of these ideas fit into archaeological theory? They began to take off in the 1980s, when Ian Hodder and his students at the University of Cambridge started to draw upon the writings of Bourdieu and Giddens. They found these works promising for addressing issues of action, context and history in archaeology. As noted in Chapter 2, such questions had been overlooked or rendered insignificant within the frameworks of processual archaeology and thus came to play an important part in the emergence of postprocessual archaeologies. Hodder's[29] edited volume, *Symbolic and Structural Archaeology*, outlined the potential that practice theory had in archaeology. In the introductory chapter of the volume, he proposed a shift towards structuration (à la Giddens) that would focus on 'the role of material culture in the reflexive relationship between the structure of ideas and social strategies'.[30] This boils down to a new balance between functionalist perspectives of the New Archaeology and the structuralist leanings of early postprocessual thinking. Here, we briefly revisit these two strands of thought to emphasise the differences between them and practice approaches. Can you guess what the main distinction is? Think back to dualisms versus relationships!

As we saw in Chapter 2, the structural-functionalist frameworks of the New Archaeology drew analogies between social groups (of the past) and organic life. Lewis Binford was interested in defining how each part of a social group helped it adapt to its environment (this is the *function*) while also studying how each part related to the others (this is the *structure*), hence the term 'structural-functionalism'. This approach placed heavy emphasis on adaptation and universalised laws governing cultural processes. A major shortcoming was the assumption that change always came from outside of the cultural system. In other words, these approaches had no means to explain how people (individuals or groups) might have altered their ways of doing through time other than for the purpose of adapting to a new environmental stimulus. Can you see the dualism in this approach? Perhaps the most obvious one is its opposition between nature and culture. On one side, nature presents the challenge to people, who need to survive in their respective environments. On the other side, culture is the way that people adapt to – and exploit – their environment.

Archaeologists turned to structuralism to shift the focus away from the environmental determinism of structural-functionalism to consider symbolism and meaning within past human societies and cultures. These archaeologists sought to study archaeological sites in a similar manner to the way that linguists study language and other forms of symbolism. The ultimate goal of early structural archaeologists was to uncover a system of rules (like grammar in language) that governed human societies and cultures in the past (see Deetz[31] for lucid examples of structuralist archaeology). Archaeologists looked to the archaeological site and its material culture as *representations of* past human society and culture. Let's consider an example. Perhaps you know that many human burials (from a variety of time periods across the globe) contain ochre, a red pigment. Based on this observation, a structuralist-minded archaeologist might infer a strong connection between the red colour of ochre and the colour of blood, associated with life. In this sense, the material found in graves is a reflection of one part of a system of meaning: the ochre stands for life within this convention. Can you find the dualism that underlies this approach? Think about the relationship between material culture and culture, or between things and thoughts. Here we find a dualism between the hard, obdurate things we encounter in the 'archaeological record' and past systems of human meaning in the sense that one (the material record) is said to reflect the other (thoughts and symbolic associations). This dualism previews some themes explored in Chapter 6, particularly Daniel Miller's concept of materiality. What we are missing, here, is the recursive connections between thoughts and things, which is where poststructural thinkers like Bourdieu and Giddens become quite valuable.

Thus it is useful to think of the practice and agency approaches highlighted in this chapter as bridging this conceptual gap between structural-functionalism and structuralism. At the start of the new millennium, archaeologist Timothy Pauketat[32] emphasised just this with the notion of *historical processualism*. He framed historical processualism as a reconciliation of processual and postprocessual archaeologies. This approach shied away from archaeology's previous focus on behaviour and evolution to consider the importance of context and history through theories of practice.[33] Pauketat[34] clearly set this new approach apart from those archaeologies only interested in behaviour and evolution. Following thinkers like Bourdieu,

Pauketat framed practice as the key stage on which cultural change and continuity take place. In contrast to earlier processual approaches in archaeological theory based in functionalism and systems theory (structural-functionalism), cultural practices *are* cultural processes rather than *consequences of* cultural processes. At the same time, these practices are about more than just the ideas people hold in their heads (as with structuralism). Though the term 'historical processualism' never fully caught on among archaeologists, practice-based approaches and the cross-fertilisation of elements of both processual and postprocessual archaeologies are a major part of archaeology in the new millennium.

Reconsidering power, cultural interaction and history

Questions of power always loom large in considerations of practice and agency. The difference between agency and power is a matter of degree. This is to say that power is a *specific type* of agency and structure. Remember that agency concerns the ability and choice to act a certain way and to make differences in the world. Power concerns an agent's ability to limit the ways in which *other people exercise agency* in a given situation or an agent's ability to challenge the limitations placed upon them by other social actors. Archaeologists often disagree on the potential that actors have to transform or maintain the social structures around them. On one extreme are those that frame certain social structures as rigidly deterministic; these thinkers portray actors as essentially powerless in relation to their surroundings. On the other extreme are thinkers who treat actors as all-knowing and ever capable of transforming social structures according to their specific goals and intentions.[35] We place the theories of practice and agency reviewed in this chapter on a middle ground between these two extremes. This is because they recognise the interconnections between agency and structure.[36] How people act is important, but it is never simply the exercise of free will over a pliant world. We might wonder, though, about the kinds of people who seem to be exerting this agency. We explore a related set of problems in the next chapter, when we ask critical questions about personhood and identity. Questions about the distribution and nature of power in past societies go hand in hand with questions over what *types* of people had power. As we will show, some archaeologists have uncritically mixed their own western sensibilities in with their interpretations of agency and power in the past. For example, this led to problematic assumptions that males and females in societies around the globe have always had the same types of influence and agency. We see this in egregious interpretations that assume major cultural innovation has always been the domain of men (typically modelled after contemporary understandings of white, western males).

The approaches outlined in this chapter have also proven useful for thinking critically about cultural interaction, a key theme of your field school. Theories of practice and agency offer new means of understanding the dynamism of culture and human agency. For example, Kent Lightfoot, Antoinette Martinez and Ann Schiff[37] used a practice-based approach in their analysis of cultural admixture in interethnic households at Colony Ross, a nineteenth-century Russian fur-trading settlement in Northern California. Couples comprising Native Alaskan men and local Kashaya Pomo women occupied most of the analysed households. Lightfoot and his colleagues[38] found that domestic routines in the households usually followed patterns found readily in the local Kashaya Pomo village, whereas the overall village layout closely resembled settlement patterns found only in Native Alaskan villages. In this instance, both Kashaya Pomo women and Native Alaskan men reproduced their respective 'traditions' within their daily routines. In this case, it was women who organised the household, and men who initially laid out the village settlement pattern. The fusion of two sets of cultural traditions in single households led to hybridised patterns that combined elements of each group's respective habitus.[39] Timothy Pauketat[40] frames the insights that practice theory offers issues of cultural continuity and change (or history) in terms of *traditions*. In contrast to earlier generations of archaeologists who treated traditions as conservative and resistant to change, Pauketat[41] views traditions as practices brought from the past into the present. Instead of approaching traditions as the constant variables of culture, he takes a contextual approach, framing traditions as arenas of cultural reproduction. As individuals and groups 'replicate' the traditional practices of their ancestors, they always introduce some degree of change. For example, they might bring these 'old practices' into new temporal, spatial and social contexts[42] as with the archaeological findings at Colony Ross.

One of the most extended examples of the application of practice theory in archaeology is John Barrett's *Fragments from Antiquity*.[43] Barrett examined how ideas like Giddens' structuration theory could help us understand the changing nature of society in British prehistory, specifically between the Early Neolithic and the Middle Bronze Age (4000–1500 cal BC). Barrett traced how Early Neolithic funerary practices created communal burial chambers that could be returned to repeatedly. With these practices emerged a shared notion of ancestry. In the Late Neolithic, this engagement with ancestors led to the production of more elaborate monuments, such as henges or stone circles. These new monuments had consequences in that they created through their architecture the possibility for some people to rise to preeminence. For example, when people constructed the enormous Silbury Hill – the largest prehistoric person-built mound in Europe – around 2500 cal BC (Figure 3.3), or when they erected stone avenues leading to the entrances to the nearby Avebury henge monument at about the same date (Figure 3.4), they did not mean for hierarchies to emerge. Nevertheless, the shape of the avenues meant that the processions that marched down their length needed to be led by someone, and the shape of Silbury meant only a fraction of those who built it could stand on its top. This wasn't a conscious decision by the architects of these sites, but rather a way in which agency (people building a monument) changed the structure of society (creating the possibility for hierarchy and new forms of agency).

In turn, Barrett examined how the creation of these hierarchies led to new forms of single burials (like the Amesbury Archer we discuss in Chapter 6), often under round barrows. Rather than communal burials, where people returned to

FIGURE 3.3   Silbury Hill, Wiltshire, England

Photograph by Emily Banfield (reproduced with permission)

FIGURE 3.4   The West Kennet Avenue, which guides people towards the Avebury
henge monument, Wiltshire, England

Photograph by Emily Banfield (reproduced with permission)

bury everyone in the same monument, individual burials created new possibilities for agency. You could dig into the round barrow and bury someone there, creating a link between that person and the barrow's founder. Or you could bury someone nearby and create a new barrow, a different kind of relationship. Or you could go off and bury someone somewhere completely new. These possibilities, Barrett argued, did not exist in the Neolithic. As a result, new kinds of ancestry emerged. Now people were connected via linear descent from specific people, rather than to a generalised body of ancestors everyone shared. With these ideas of descent came ideas of ownership. In the Middle Bronze Age, this led to new kinds of land tenure involving fields and permanent settlements. Nobody intended this when they first built henge monuments or buried the dead in new ways; it emerged through the recursive interaction of structure and agency over two millennia. Although there are many ways we might refine this argument with the new data that has emerged in the last 20 years,[44] this remains one of the most sophisticated and elegant accounts of the period.

Conclusions: some final thoughts on the mystery object

In light of practice theory, how might you interpret your new find (Figures 3.1, 3.2)? We know that the raw material used to produce this item likely came from a kettle, brought from Europe from the seventeenth century onwards for trade with North America's indigenous peoples. We also know, however, that indigenous people of the area had a much deeper history with copper; it was used to make objects that functioned as grave goods and items of personal adornment for thousands of years prior to the arrival of European colonists. Indigenous understandings of copper and its uses thus existed well before this particular kettle made its way to your site. As copper kettles appeared in North America, they presented a new and foreign use of the same raw material with which Native peoples were already familiar. Based on archaeological finds, it seems that Native people quickly put their 'traditional' ideas of how to use copper into new conversation with 'foreign' copper trade vessels. Native practices transformed kettles into various items, including your mystery object, typically referred to as a 'tinkler cone' or 'tinkling cone' in archaeological circles. The practices that created this new class of object existed between thoughts (or mindsets) and things (or the material world). They demonstrate the dynamic nature of cultural reproduction, including changes and continuities that are inseparable. A version of this 'new' artefact of the seventeenth century, which mixed indigenous understanding of copper and European copper artefacts, is still used today by indigenous people of North America, as your indigenous colleague reminded you.

Okay, so practice and agency theories advocated for a relational approach to archaeological theory that began to challenge dualisms. Are there any shortcomings or unresolved issues with these approaches? Of course! Otherwise, we could simply end the book here. We see practice and agency approaches as the very beginning of a series of related critiques outlined in the remaining chapters. Do they really get us out of the dualisms we were critical of in Chapters 1 and 2, though? Rosemary Joyce and Jeanne Lopiparo[45] point out the interpretive dangers of treating structure and agency as a dualism, or 'as an alternation of moments of the exercise of agency in an otherwise continuous flow of structure', rather than as a constant and seamless process. Indeed, we might wonder if starting with two opposed categories is a good way of getting out of a dichotomy, even if we emphasise the relationship between them.[46] In fact this approach certainly leaves particular dualisms in place. Agency in the approaches we have seen in this chapter is really a 'humans-only' concept within practice theory. Humans have agency; the rest of the world is structure. This means that these approaches privilege human beings – they are what we call anthropocentric. Later in this book we will examine theories that challenge this, and ask difficult questions about the basic qualities of being a human. In the next chapter we begin this process by looking at how archaeologists have thought about gender, identity and personhood.

Notes

1 See Howey 2011 for a recent discussion of trade copper.
2 Barrett 2001; for an excellent recent discussion of agency in archaeology see Robb 2010.
3 Practice theorists would argue that this is not a dualism (Chapter 1), but rather a 'duality' (Giddens 1984), because practice and agency are two sides of the same coin. Whether this is convincing, and whether the difference between a dualism and a duality is meaningful, goes beyond the scope of this book. Because the words are so similar and can cause confusion, we will avoid the term duality from here on in outside of the endnotes.
4 In addition to these theories, a third and surprisingly underused model of practice comes from the work of sociologist Michel de Certeau (1984). His concept of tactics emphasises the recursive relationship between individuals and social structures, acknowledging the roles that individuals play in manipulating and shaping the system while still addressing the limitations and unintended consequences of practice.
5 See also de Certeau 1984; Sahlins 1985; Butler 1993.
6 Quoted at length in Bourdieu 1977 and reprinted in Bourdieu 1990.
7 Published in French in 1972 and translated into English in 1977.
8 Deetz 1977.
9 Bourdieu 1977: 90.
10 Bourdieu 1977, 1990.
11 Bourdieu 1977: 72.
12 Bourdieu 1977: 164.
13 Silliman 2001: 194.
14 Loren 2001; Silliman 2001; see also Smith 2001 for a critique of doxa in archaeology.
15 Silliman 2001.
16 Mauss 1973 [1935].
17 Cipolla 2017.
18 Cf. Edgeworth 2012.
19 Bourdieu 1977: 78.
20 Ortner 1984: 148.
21 Bourdieu 1990: 6.
22 Giddens 1979, 1984.
23 Giddens 1979: 2.
24 Giddens 1984: 5.
25 Giddens 1984: 9.
26 Giddens 1984: 10.

27 Giddens 1979.
28 Giddens 1984.
29 Hodder 1982b.
30 Hodder 1982a: 1.
31 Deetz 1967, 1977.
32 Pauketat 2001b.
33 Pauketat 2001b: 73.
34 Pauketat 2001b: 86.
35 See Joyce and Lopiparo 2005: 366.
36 Jones 1997: 89–90; Giddens 1984; Dobres and Robb 2000; Joyce and Lopiparo 2005.
37 Lightfoot, Martinez and Schiff 1998.
38 Lightfoot, Martinez and Schiff 1998: 209–15.
39 Interactions such as these also bring to light questions of identity, explored in further detail in Chapter 4. For now, it is important to note that practice-based approaches often focus on the ways in which individuals and groups construct and transform their identities through the material world. An excellent example of this approach is Sian Jones' (1997) work on ethnic identity, material culture and symbolism (see also Loren 2001). For further examples of practice-based approaches to colonialism see Silliman 2001 and 2009.
40 Pauketat 2001a.
41 Pauketat 2001a: 2.
42 Based on this general premise, Stephen Silliman (2009) argues that cultural continuity and change are inseparable, forever fused to one another within larger processes of cultural reproduction.
43 Barrett 1994.
44 Notably Whittle, Healy and Bayliss 2011.
45 Joyce and Lopiparo 2005: 365.
46 Which, as we saw earlier, practice theorists (e.g. Giddens 1984) refer to as a duality rather than a dualism.

4

SITUATING THINGS IN SOCIETY

Identity and personhood

Introduction: who were they and who are we?

What makes people different from one another? Were people in the past just like us, perhaps lacking the comforts of modern living and thus with a few more immediate needs regarding food, clothing and shelter? Or did they have different concepts of who they were? In this chapter we explore these critical questions of identity. Let's start with a deceptively simple puzzle. In a Bronze Age barrow, two people were buried. One was placed in the barrow as a whole body – an inhumation – in association with a pot just behind the person's head, a number of barbed and tanged arrowheads, a stone bracer, and a copper dagger (Figure 4.1). The other is a cremation in an urn, accompanied by no other grave goods. While the whole body is present in the former case, the low weight of the cremated bones in the urn suggests that only part of the body was included. What kinds of differences can we detect between these two burials? Is one high status and the other low status? Biologically, if the inhumation is male and the cremation female, could this pattern relate to gender differences? What might the ages of those bodies have to do with how they were buried? These are the kinds of conundrums archaeologists are faced with all the time. In addition, we face a second kind of puzzle. As hinted at above, we must ask how past conceptions of identity match up with the ones we have in the present. Did Bronze Age people divide their society up into gendered groups that match up neatly with biological sex, or were other gendered identities possible? Perhaps more fundamentally, archaeologists have started to ask whether past communities even had the same concept of what it meant to be *a person*, of what we call 'personhood'. In the modern world we tend to consider ourselves individuals, gifted with free will, who enter into and leave different

FIGURE 4.1   Encountering a burial. Drawing by K-Fai Steele

relationships throughout our lives. What if very different ideas of personhood existed in the past?

In this chapter we examine how archaeologists began developing more complex approaches to gender and identity, often drawing on relational theories. We first examine how gender archaeology developed in the 1980s and 1990s as a challenge to sexist assumptions about the roles of men and women in the past. Next, we look at how this initial movement changed, especially through its engagement with the work of feminist theorist Judith Butler, to question even whether notions of biological sex can be seen as 'natural'. Butler draws on the notion of performativity to frame identity as something that is emergent through our relationships with the ideals held by society, rather than something that is inherent in who we are. These ideas form a connection with the issue of personhood, explored next. Here we discuss how anthropologists question whether western ideas of the 'individual' can be applied to other groups around the world today, and in turn how archaeologists have used these ideas to think about identity in the past. Rather than thinking of identity as linked to a bounded sense of self, these authors have suggested that it may emerge from the relationships people have with each other and with the world around them. Finally, at the end of the chapter, we link these ideas of performative and relational identity back to the human body itself.

From practice to identity

As we saw in Chapter 2, from the very beginning of postprocessual archaeology in the late 1970s, feminist archaeologists played a critical role in raising new questions about identity, especially gender, in both the past and the present.[1] Considering the work done in archaeology at that time, feminists showed how everything from the language used to describe people in the past through to the kinds of research questions that received funding were fundamentally *andro-centric*, or in other words, they privileged men. Men were much more likely to get big grants for fieldwork, while women were more likely to get smaller grants to look at pottery and other finds, what Joan Gero (Box 4.1) scathingly called 'archaeological housework'.[2] In recounting the past, it was men who were portrayed as doing all the big exciting things like building monuments, leading conflicts and driving economic change, while women were typically interpreted as stuck in the background, making things like pottery. Similarly, when it came to hunting and gathering, not only was it men who did *all* the hunting, hunting was also often valued by archaeologists as much more impor-tant than gathering! In contrast to this, feminist archaeologists began to develop more systematic investigations into how women played crucial roles in mul-tiple past societies. In the last chapter we saw how archaeologists in the 1980s and 1990s began thinking about practice. This was central to many investiga-tions of gender, as archaeologists became increasingly interested in how certain ways of acting in the world emerged through particular structural conditions. For archaeologists interested in gender, this meant we could begin to explore not just what people were doing, but what kinds of people were doing it. As Ruth Tringham put it, people in the past up until this point had been 'face-less blobs',[3] and archaeologists needed to give them back a sense of identity. It is worth noting here that while the impact of feminist archaeology has done much to combat these issues over the last 30 years, many of these problems continue right up to the present.

Such considerations quickly went well beyond the issue of finding women in the past to broader questions about gender, including masculinity.[4] From there, they extended to a whole host of other questions about identity. Throughout the 1990s, a range of studies examined questions of age, sexuality and ethnicity.[5] Since the interest in Marxist archaeology in the 1980s (encountered briefly in Chapter 2), social class has also been a critical focal point, and this could now be incorporated alongside these other facets of identity. Such considerations of the complex, multi-layered and 'intersectional' nature of identity also helped develop the topic of agency that we encountered in the last chapter. More simplistic ideas of agency as simple 'free will' or 'choice' could be shown to reflect specific kinds of agency that were perceived to exist for certain people in the present. Imagine the kinds of choices presented to you by advertising: choose your own car, your own career path and your own lifestyle! This kind of agency, based around a

BOX 4.1   JOAN GERO

Joan Gero (1944–2016) was Professor Emerita of Anthropology at American University and one of the leading figures in feminist archaeology. She was an expert both in Andean archaeology and in the relationship between archaeology and modern social and political conditions. One of her most important publications is *Engendering Archaeology*[6] (co-edited with Margaret Conkey). This photograph shows an archaeological excavation. Take a closer look at it; what do you notice about the gender roles on display?

Photo by Dan Addison

specific kind of capitalist consumerism, is not only historically specific; it is also, as feminist archaeologists have shown, quite specifically gendered.[7] It is the kind of gendered agency stereotypically associated with the choices white, western, middle-class men are perceived as having in the modern world. Thus simply discussing agency in this sense allowed a kind of androcentrism (male dominance) in by the back door. In contrast, the emphasis on multiple forms of identity allowed for various types of agency to emerge in differing contexts. In differing periods of the past, alternative material worlds were produced by different kinds of people, and in turn these allowed for varying forms of gendered agency. Just like agency and structure in practice theory we saw in the last chapter, the emphasis here on social relationships and action allowed for a more nuanced and specific version of the past to emerge.

This move to think more about gender and identity in the past has been incredibly useful. One of the main things it has succeeded in doing is challenging many of the assumptions we hold implicitly about what is normal or natural. In this sense it is what we call anti-*essentialist*. As we saw in Chapter 2, essentialism is when you take one element of a society (usually our own) and treat it as if it is eternal, universal and unchanging. The assumption here is that we know exactly what it means to be human – the human *essence* – in all times and places. In the most egregious cases this has meant archaeologists presuming that in all societies men were the ones with power, wealth and agency. Susan Shennan's[8] 1975 interpretation of the Bronze Age cemetery of Branč in Slovakia illustrates this problem perfectly. She noticed that most of the richest burials at this site were females, but rather than arguing that this meant women were rich and powerful in that society, she suggested that this was a sign of men giving wealth to their wives and daughters.[9] The larger number of rich female graves – compared with their male counterparts – was a sign of polygyny, that men had multiple wives.[10] Rich female infant burials indicated not that women could inherit wealth, but that they were in arranged marriages. Fundamentally, whatever the evidence, it needed to show that men were the ones with wealth and power. This idea clearly did not come from the Bronze Age, but instead was an uncritical assumption imported from the present to the past.

A good example of how these ideas can be challenged comes from the work of Sharisse and Geoffrey McCafferty.[11] They examined a Mesoamerican Mixtec burial from Monte Albán (Figure 4.2) in the highlands of southern Mexico. There, during the Late Postclassic period (c. 1400–1521 AD), a particular burial was deposited, potentially in mummified form (individual A). Although other bodies were present, this burial, the most elaborate of them all, seems to have been the central focus.[12] Along with the human remains, over 500 objects were deposited, many of them made from precious materials. At the centre of all this was individual A, whom the initial excavator and subsequent textbooks had always identified as male. Yet, when the McCaffertys came to examine the grave goods found with this person, they discovered that many objects were associated with spinning, including spindle whorls, bowls and 34 carved eagle and jaguar bones they interpreted as miniature weaving batons.[13] Given that the iconography and wider burial record of this period always associated spinning with women, why had this person been interpreted previously as a male? The obvious next

FIGURE 4.2 The site of Monte Albán, Oaxaca, Mexico

Prisma Bildagentur AG/Alamy Stock Photo

move was to examine the skeleton itself, but the data were ambiguous. Bones that are comparatively easy to sex on skeletons (like the pelvis) were missing, and the person had suffered from pathological conditions that made sex harder to resolve with the bones that did exist. Strangely, though, a mandible that was found with the body (and potentially in the right position) was identified as female, but rejected as part of individual A because it didn't fit the narrative of this person being male.[14] McCafferty and McCafferty examined the material evidence and the body and together they clearly showed that the most likely explanation was that this person was female, a fact that archaeologists had missed for 60 years.

Performing sex and gender

These kinds of critiques were undoubtedly very important in the context of the 1980s and 1990s where the pervasive male bias of archaeology fell under serious critique for the first time. Fairly quickly, however, archaeologists realised that there may be more to it than this. Was it simply a case of identifying 'female' material culture like spinning items, and using those objects to suggest where women could have been in the past? Isn't identifying something like spinning as 'female' quite a worrying thing to associate all women with in the past? Doesn't that sound like essentialism? What if the body did turn out to be male but was associated with 'female' material culture? What might that tell us about gender?

Anthropological research from around the world shows many examples of societies who use complicated gender spectrums that go far beyond the simple binary system. For instance, some Native American societies have two-spirit genders, for people who identify as neither male nor female.[15] In India the Hijra,[16] a group of people who are often 'biologically' male but take up different gendered identities, play important roles in certain ceremonies. In Oman we find the Xanith,[17] young men who take on a temporary gender during adolescence, and in the Balkans the sworn virgins, women taking on aspects of male identity.[18] In many societies there are people who do not identify as either male or female, who act as a third gender, or even a fourth. In our own society we have both transsexual and transgendered people. Indeed, in some circumpolar groups anthropologists have identified up to 10 gender categories.[19] This means that while it is critical to challenge the way in which high-status burials are gendered as male, or how status itself is understood in male terms (as our two examples above show), there is more to interpreting the past than just this. Indeed, a simple male/female binary is just another example of the dualisms we have been critical of thus far.

Many archaeologists pursuing these lines of thought draw on work from thinkers like Judith Butler. Inspired in part by French philosopher Michel Foucault, Butler has been a huge influence on how identity, especially gender, has been thought about across numerous disciplines. Her work played a significant role in the development of queer theory, which not only problematises sexuality, but also seeks to explore the possibility for complex and different identities in the past and present.[20] Butler's work is immensely rich – and immensely complex – but in many ways the key elements of her thought that have been employed in archaeology can be set out in a relatively straightforward manner. Butler is highly critical of the notion that while gender is a cultural construction, sex is a biological absolute that exists outside specific historical situations.[21] This dichotomy (sex versus gender) maps neatly onto the distinctions we have already criticised between nature and culture. It suggests that one part of identity – sex – is dictated by one set of forces that are neither historical nor social. We will return to this issue in more detail below. For Butler, the notion that the world is primarily characterised by two biological sexes ignores the historical *heteronormativity* of our current society. Heteronormativity assumes that the vast majority of people are not only male and female, but also heterosexual. This is not inevitable, Butler argues, but the outcome of particular kinds of power relationships that are produced and reproduced in the modern world through what Butler terms 'performativity', a concept absolutely central to her work. Performativity is 'that which produces what it names'. Don't be intimidated; this isn't as complicated as you might think.

BOX 4.2 JUDITH BUTLER

Judith Butler is Maxine Elliot Professor of Comparative Literature at the University of California, Berkeley. Her work is best known for its engagement with queer theory. She developed a radical critique of the dominant understandings of sex, gender and sexuality in western society. Although she has published multiple books on a range of subjects, she remains most famous in archaeology for her work on gender performativity, most notably *Gender Trouble: Feminism and the Subversion of Identity*[22] and *Bodies that Matter: On the Discursive Limits of 'Sex'.*[23] The image here is not of Butler but rather the famous drag queen Ru Paul. We have selected this because drag is a very important concept for Butler; it reveals for her how we all perform gender through our dress and actions. The reason some people are threatened by drag is because it reveals that all of our gendered identities are much less stable than we would like to believe.

Image: https://commons.wikimedia.org/wiki/File:RuPaul_by_David_Shankbone_cropped.jpg

Imagine, for instance, that you are at a 'traditional' Christian wedding; at the front of the church the vicar is going through all the usual turns of phrase. At the final moment, she turns to the couple and says, 'I now pronounce you husband and wife'. This statement does not describe their transformation but *actually creates it*. The words themselves make the statement true.

For Butler, this idea of performativity is at the heart of how identity operates. Rather than being born with a particular identity already present within us, we constantly create our identities through performativity, and in particular by using and referring to what she calls differing 'regulatory ideals'.[24] These are the basic concepts we have of what it is to be male and female (in relation to gender). On one level, they are very stereotypical things that we might easily critique (e.g., men like action movies and women like romantic comedies), but they also refer to much more subtle differences: that women wear skirts, that girls should be quiet and boys loud, that men sit with their legs apart and women with their legs together. Each day when any of us has our hair cut to a particular length, dresses in ways that are deemed appropriate for our gender or puts on makeup (or doesn't), we are in the process of living up to these regulatory ideals. Because these actions are performative, though, they don't only live up to these ideals, they help *create* and *reinforce* them, a process Butler refers to as citation. By repeatedly acting appropriately for your gender you are helping to ensure these ideals remain in place for others. When people say that someone is 'acting like a little girl', they are helping to ensure that certain kinds of behaviour are associated with and appropriate for one particular kind of person (a young lady) and not others (an adult man). You can probably spot some links here between these ideas and some of the ones we discussed in terms of practice theory in the last chapter.[25]

Butler's approach means that ideas of difference between genders, sexualities and so on are historically specific. More than this, though, the eternal existence of categories of male and female, or heterosexual and homosexual, can be called into question. In other words, the past might be made up not just of powerful women, but of genders and identities that do not match up to any of those that we see around us in the world today; if our concepts of identity are regulatory ideals rather than the outcome of biological processes, then very different possibilities for gender and identity emerge.

Archaeologists like Rosemary Joyce (Box 5.2 in Chapter 5) have drawn on Butler's work to explore how gender may have been produced and materialised through practices in Mesoamerica.[26] For example, by examining both historical records and material culture, Joyce has looked at the way in which Aztec children were taught to perform differing kinds of identity.[27] Children's bodies were materially shaped through clothing and ear and lip piercing at differing moments in their upbringing, especially at specific lifecycle rituals. Often this would include giving children parts of adult clothing to wear, or giving them bodily ornaments they would only come to use in adulthood.[28] They would learn to move in specific ways, and have their hair cut in a particular fashion. These acts of shaping the body helped to teach children about how to perform differing forms of gendered identity and helped to materialise them, physically, on and through the body. Interestingly, these different ways of shaping the body were not simply split between girls and boys, but also included a third gender: those who would go on to be celibate religious figures.[29] Three different kinds of gender emerged through the performances of both adults and children in this context. Elsewhere in Mesoamerica among the Classic Maya (250–900 AD), Joyce examined how monumental sculptures of men and women acted as regulatory ideals stressing how to dress and move the body (much like adverts do for us today), but also emphasised how – for upper-class men and women – there were many ways in which they could act in a similar fashion, blurring gendered boundaries.[30]

Performing personhood

The notion that identity, including gender, is not limited to the historical categories we currently recognise has also opened up wider questions for philosophers, anthropologists and more latterly archaeologists.[31] In particular, the question of personhood has become paramount. Personhood, as we mentioned in the introduction to this chapter, is the question of what it is to be a person.[32] *Stereotypically*, western people perceive themselves to be bounded individuals. We are given our own names, we own personal possessions and we understand ourselves as having free will. We have a single gender assigned to us at birth that is an essential part of our identity. Privacy and bodily boundaries are important, and anything that crosses the boundaries of the body is at best a little embarrassing and at worst a serious violation. So we have private cubicles in toilets, bedrooms and bathrooms are not on display at the front of houses, we use tissues to mask coughs and sneezes, and so on. This notion of being an individual – literally something that is indivisible – is at the heart of who we conceive ourselves to be.[33] We tend to think of ourselves as unique like snowflakes – no two are exactly the same! Being an individual links to notions of personal responsibility and agency. If you commit a crime, of course, you expect to go to jail for it, not your friends and family, because you, *individually*, are responsible. This notion that people are unique individuals is so pervasive that we rarely question it; the 'snowflake' approach to personhood underwrites many aspects of our society. Yet archaeological and historical studies have shown that this understanding of personhood is a relatively recent phenomenon. Archaeologists like James Deetz[34] and Matthew Johnson[35] have traced different conceptions of personhood that operated in Britain and America as recently as the late seventeenth and early eighteenth centuries.[36] Instead of the private spaces for using the bathroom that we expect today, or houses that demarcate public and private spaces, family groups shared the same chamber pot, ate from the same trencher in the middle of the table and lived in far more open-plan housing.[37] This in turn produced very different understandings of who they were. Similarly, this work has been paralleled by a string of anthropologists going back to Marcel Mauss[38] in the 1920s, who have traced even more substantial differences in how personhood is conceived around the world today.

BOX 4.3 MARILYN STRATHERN

Marilyn Strathern is a British anthropologist and most recently William Wyse Professor of Social Anthropology at the University of Cambridge until her retirement in 2008. She has published prolifically on notions of kinship, gender and medical anthropology. Her books include *The Gender of the Gift,*[39] *Partial Connections*[40] and *After Nature,*[41] among many others. The image here is a bilum string bag from Melanesia. These bags, which Strathern discusses,[42] are made by women but used by both genders, and are exchanged in ways that construct relationships between people.

Image: The original uploader was Richard Ames at English Wikipedia (https://en.wikipedia. org/wiki/Bilum#/media/File:Bilum.jpg)

Although anthropologists and historical archaeologists had been discussing these ideas separately for some time, it was not until the 2000s that wider archaeological discussions of personhood really took off. In particular archaeologists became intrigued by the work of one specific anthropologist: Marilyn Strathern (Box 4.3). Strathern is an anthropologist interested in two differing contexts: Melanesia (that is, the island of New Guinea and the surrounding area) and Britain. In her famous book *The Gender of the Gift*,[43] Strathern used the anthropology of New Guinea to question whether ideas of individuality were really as universal as some people had claimed. She examined how people in New Guinea do not perceive of themselves as bounded individual entities that enter into relationships (with the world, with each other and so on) but rather *emerge out of these relationships*.[44] So people are composed of relationships from the very start. These are relationships between their parents, but also the relationships they have with their spouses and children, friends and in-laws.

For the people Strathern had worked with in Melanesia, all of these relationships were exchange relationships of different kinds. People formed these relationships by giving each other objects or animals – especially domestic pigs – or bodily substances like semen and breast milk. When something was given away, people were creating a relationship, and as people are composed of relationships, they were both adding to the person they were giving it to but also subtracting something from themselves. So when mothers breastfed their children they gave part of themselves to the child and in so doing created both the relationship and themselves as a mother and the child as their child. This *also* applies to objects and animals. When a person gives away a valuable object like an axe, they give away part of themselves. In this case, people are not indivisible individuals, but rather partible *dividuals* whose identities are fundamentally *relational*; that is, based in relationships. This notion that the body is partible and dividual rather than whole also has a significant effect on how gender is understood in these societies (thus the title of Strathern's book). Rather than each person possessing a singular gender, gender emerges in particular relationships depending on kinds of exchange. This means that someone who – by western standards – might be considered male could in fact be female in the context of a particular exchange relationship and vice versa. If gender is fluid and contextual in present-day Melanesia, rather than fixed from birth, this clearly suggests that identities in the past might also be very different from those we normally imagine.

One of the critical points from Strathern's work for archaeologists is her idea that personhood need not be limited to human beings (in the manner it is in our society). This works in two ways. First, for all things (whether human or otherwise), personhood has to be attained; it is not part of you as an essential aspect the moment you are born (as in the Christian idea of soul). Instead, because it comes from relationships, you have to form and maintain many connections to be a person. Thus being a person is not only available to human beings but also to things ranging from objects to houses to clans. So among the Sabarl people of New Britain in Melanesia, Debbora Battaglia has explored how their axes are understood as containing many of the same elements that people do.[45] The axe blade has *hinona*, which is both a vital substance and the term for genitals. The axe as a whole has different elements named after different parts of the human body. It is not that people in this area confuse humans and axes. They know which is which! Instead it means that being a person, and having the things that lead to personhood, is not limited simply to our species. This matches a pattern anthropologists have written about in other societies. For example, among the Native American Navajo, personhood can be extended to *Ts'aa* ceremonial baskets, and children are taught that the earth, mountains, sky and thunder are 'living kin'.[46] This does not mean that they are the same as *humans*. But they are all people because like humans, mountains, for example, are made in the image of holy people; they share a sense of personhood through their common origin.[47] In Chapter 5 we will see how Alfred Gell draws on these ideas to develop notions of object agency in anthropology, and in Chapter 10 we will consider what happens to our understandings of the world when nonwestern ideas like this are taken seriously.

All very well, you might say; it's great for anthropologists who can go around and ask people what they consider to be a person to analyse the different kinds of personhood that exist around the world today. But how do we get at these things archaeologically? Since the turn of the millennium, archaeologists have been increasingly interested in tracing how different kinds of relational personhood may have existed in the past both in European prehistory and in other contexts such as Central and South America.[48] John Chapman, for example, has used ideas from Strathern to think through the reasons archaeological objects are so often found in fragments.[49] The traditional explanation has always been to think of this in terms of either accidental breakage in the past, or through the effects of *taphonomy* (all the processes that happen to archaeological objects once they get into the ground). Chapman, both alone and in conjunction with Bisserka Gaydarska,[50] has challenged this idea. He asks whether the breakage, or fragmentation, of objects may actually be a deliberate strategy. Why would people do this? Drawing an analogy with Strathern's work in Melanesia, Chapman argues that people may be using these objects to create relationships and thus to forge their identities. So at the end of a meal a pot would be broken and different people could take parts of it away with them, thus creating what Chapman calls enchainment.[51] Just as in Melanesia, where the exchange of objects creates a sense of dividual personhood, so the fragmentation of objects in Neolithic Europe created dividual identities, Chapman argues. He then contrasts this with a different sense of personhood that emerged in the Copper Age, as rather than enchaining relationships through fragmentation and division, people sought to accumulate more and more items together in hoards and rich cemeteries.[52] This, Chapman argues, indicates the emergence of a different form of personhood.

Chris Fowler and Joanna Brück developed similar approaches to personhood by looking, respectively, at the treatment of human bodies in Neolithic and Bronze Age Britain.[53] Fowler, for example, has looked at Neolithic burials on the Isle of Man to see how differing conceptions of personhood may emerge.[54] In contrast to the individual grave plots of the modern cemetery, treatment of Neolithic bodies in the Isle of Man suggests other conceptions of personhood. He shows how people and things were mixed together on cremation pyres in the Early Neolithic.[55] Similarly, he looks at how parts from different people were rearticulated with one another after death. Drawing on comparisons with anthropologists' work – especially Strathern's – as well as Judith Butler, Fowler argues that partible, dividual conceptions of personhood were being cited through these different practices, producing understandings of identity very different to ones we are familiar with today.[56]

Joanna Brück[57] offers similar arguments for Middle and Late Bronze Age practices in Britain. Archaeologists typically think of the Bronze Age in Europe as a period when 'individuality' become prominent; in other words, archaeologists often think that a sense of identity celebrating difference and status came into being at this time.[58] Brück, however, looks in detail at the way in which objects and bodies were treated and argues that rather than the emergence of individuals, personhood at this time was much more fragmented, fluid and relational. In particular she looks at how pottery, metalwork and human bodies went through processes of transformation, often involving fire. Pottery had to be forged in the fire, as did metalwork. Similarly, human bodies were often cremated, ending their existence in fire. In each case, elements of these substances could be reused or recycled later, from fragments of human bone being included in deposits, to pottery being crushed and used as grog or metalwork being melted and recycled. Substances were mixed together in parallel ways, potentially carrying with them a genealogy of relationships. Brück powerfully argues that human reproduction and fertility could be conceived like this as well.[59] Rather than bounded individuals, then, Brück argues that people and things emerged out of complex circulations of relationships and substances that continued after their deaths.

Archaeologists have not accepted these interpretations uncritically. To begin, many people have been suspicious of the contrast that Strathern (and thus many archaeologists) draws between Melanesian people and people in the west. Do people in the west really always conceive of themselves as bounded individuals? Remember, we used the term 'stereotype' above. Similarly, do people in Melanesia always consider themselves to be dividuals? As the anthropologist Edward LiPuma[60] has pointed out, things are a little bit more complicated than that. In fact when you consider yourself, we are sure that you can probably identify lots of aspects of yourself that are 'relational'. If you have a brother or a sister you are a sibling because of that relationship; you cannot be a parent unless you have a child (biologically or otherwise); you cannot be a spouse unless you are married to someone. Similarly there are moments in Melanesia where people act and conceive of themselves as individuals,[61] and other kinds of individuality may have existed in the past.[62] Archaeologists like Matthew Spriggs[63] have also criticised the way in which Melanesia has been used as an analogy by archaeologists without attending to its own historical specificities. In a similar way, Andrew Jones[64] has queried whether the widespread use of a single analogy has meant that Neolithic and Bronze Age Europe has increasingly come to resemble Melanesian societies.[65]

Whether archaeologists should use analogies from ethnographic contexts has been a matter of much debate in the discipline,[66] and clearly it is very important to avoid over-reliance on particular comparisons that reduce the range of our interpretations rather than opening up new ways of thinking.[67] Nonetheless, it remains the case that personhood has become a critical category of analysis for archaeologists interested in identity. The criticisms directed at these developments, while powerfully aimed at the application of these ideas, have not refuted the central point: that personhood in the past was almost certainly different to personhood in the present. It is historically and socially contingent, in other words. It is also difficult to see how these ideas could have emerged in archaeology without the use of ethnographic sources to stimulate the imagination.[68] Fundamentally, discussions of personhood have also done much to spearhead the broader focus on thinking about the past in terms of relations. Whereas in the 1990s, the term personhood was largely unheard of in archaeology, today it is one of the most widely debated aspects related to identity.

Embodied identities

The final issue in this chapter takes us to the body itself. Much of the archaeology of gender and identity has done a wonderful job of challenging sexist interpretations. It also did a lot to bring about really new understandings of whole categories of identity, like personhood, when thinking about the past. In another sense, however, they left other ideas imported from the present into the past intact. In other words, they can still be thought of as essentialist. For example, these approaches have tended to concentrate on the way in which cultural identity is separate from the biological, or if you like, culture is separate from nature. In other words, dualisms remain in place here, and this is especially true when it comes to the issue of gender and sex.

Many archaeologists tend to investigate gender within a simple philosophical compromise. As the narrative goes, biological sex is fixed and unchanging, while gender is a socially constructed category that varies between cultures. This compromise has successfully allowed archaeologists to explore cemeteries, examining the biological sex of the skeletons in question, and also looking at grave goods included with the burial to see how they helped produce different senses of gender. This compromise seems to work out in the modern world as well. We are familiar with the idea that biological sex is the product of the distribution of chromosomes; men have XY and women have XX. Gender, on the other hand, emerges from the kinds of clothes we wear, the way we have been taught to act, the fact we live in a patriarchal society that means that women get paid less than men for doing the same jobs, and so on. This distinction between sex and gender has allowed both gender theorists and archaeologists to get on with important work in both the present and past, challenging gender inequalities and gender essentialism. Even those archaeologists who have drawn on Judith Butler – who, as we saw, has been very critical of this dichotomy – tend to downplay this aspect of her research in favour of ideas of gender (rather than sex) performativity.

The trouble is, of course, that this compromise is just that – a compromise. In the previous two chapters we have shown how archaeologists have become increasingly critical of dualisms; that is, the idea that we can understand the world by dividing it up into binary oppositions (mind and body, culture and nature, or domestic and wild). Thinking about the past in these terms, especially if we do so uncritically, is another form of essentialism. The dichotomy of sex and gender is a great example of the dichotomy between nature and culture.[69] On one hand, we seem to have something determined by material facts on the ground – the (at this scale at least) continuity in the human genome – and something that emerges in different ways at different places and times – how we conceptualise and imagine gender. In this mode of thinking people are either reduced to their biology (what really matters are issues like reproduction or child rearing – note how these terms are pretty gendered already) or the physical reality of the body gets written out of existence (and what really matters is what people think about gender).

This latter issue tends to be the problem with accounts that draw on the work of Butler. Such approaches have done a brilliant job of destabilising our assumptions about identity. They also provide a very helpful vocabulary for examining how bodies act and produce a sense of gender. However, there is little room in these accounts for the physical body itself, for the blood that flows in veins, for the way in which practices transform the muscles, bones and synapses of our body.[70] In the last few years, however, archaeologists have tried to address these questions in more detail. Joanna Sofaer, for example, has looked at how the physical structures of the body are 'plastic' in some senses.[71] That is, the way in which you carry things, whether you take part in strenuous activity, whether you play a musical instrument changes you – not just your idea of yourself but the very structures of the body. To give just one example, the upper arm bone (the humerus) of a tennis player can be 30 per cent thicker on their dominant side than the same bone on the other arm.[72] Archaeologists are drawing on these kinds of understandings to think about how the body itself has a history; not just how people understood it and thought about it in terms of gender and identity, but how its very physical structures and possibilities create the potential for new ways of thinking about the past.[73] This also allows us to think about whether the boundaries of the body are simply those of the skin, or can also encompass the material things we engage with.[74]

Conclusions: identity beyond our assumptions

Since the 1980s archaeologists have developed increasingly complex understandings of identity in the past. Drawing on feminist thought, queer theory and anthropology, they have developed understandings of the people in the past that celebrate rather than suppress the variability of ethnicity, sexuality, gender and personhood. At the heart of this has been the recognition that identity is a *relational* concept and that we need to look at the relationships between people, objects and places if we want to understand these issues in the past. Recognising the variability of identity in the past is important, not just because it allows us to more accurately describe and understand past worlds. As feminist archaeologists of the 1980s showed, when we fail to discuss these ideas we end up leaving the past just like the present – we essentialise. In this essentialism we tend to make inequalities in the present seem timeless and unchanging, *natural* if you like, and thus impossible to change. In recognising the critical role of relations, these studies of identity have played an important part in making archaeological theory focus on how things and people emerge out of relations, rather than pre-existing them and beginning as clearly separate from one another. As we will see in the next few chapters, this has become an issue of increasing concern.

Where does this leave us with the two Bronze Age burials? Drawing on the work of Brück[75] – who we encountered earlier – we can think about how both of these reveal different kinds of relationally constructed identities. The whole body with its grave goods need not be understood as a high-status individual man with his possessions, but rather a person composed of different relationships, ones revealed in the grave *gifts* that others placed around the body. These now reveal the complex relationships this person had in life. A notion of gender here does not emerge solely from the biological body, but from the relationship of that material body to the pot, to the arrowheads and so on. These are not just *reflections* of that identity. Instead they played a critical role in creating it, in how that identity was performatively produced by both the living and the dead. The cremation burial can reveal the partibility of the body, how different parts could be buried in differing places. In so doing it can be seen as revealing how people themselves are made up of different elements from different places, and how places in turn are made through the actions of different people. The urn in which the cremated remains were contained formed a new body, a new person, born in fire as the old body perished. From simple ideas of status and gender to complex, relationally produced ideas of personhood enfolding material things, our ideas of identity have changed markedly from where we started; the past was different and so were the people in it.

Notes

1 E.g. Conkey and Spector 1984; papers in Gero and Conkey 1991; Gilchrist 1999; Sørensen 2000.
2 Gero 1985: 344.
3 Tringham 1991: 94.
4 E.g. Treherne 1995.
5 On age see Sofaer Derevenski 1997; on sexuality see Voss 2008b and papers in Schmidt and Voss 2000; on ethnicity see Jones 1997.
6 Gero and Conkey 1991.
7 Gero 2000.
8 Shennan 1975.
9 Shennan 1975: 285–6.

10 Shennan 1975: 285.
11 McCafferty and McCafferty 1994, 2003.
12 McCafferty and McCafferty 1994: 144.
13 McCafferty and McCafferty 1994: 146.
14 McCafferty and McCafferty 1994: 150.
15 Whelan 1991; Holliman 1997, 2000.
16 Nanda 1999.
17 Bolin 1996.
18 Grémaux 1996.
19 Jacobs and Cromwell 1992.
20 For more on queer theory see Halperin 1996. In archaeology see Casella 2000; Voss 2008b.
21 Butler 1993.
22 Butler 1990.
23 Butler 1993.
24 Butler 1990: 43.
25 McNay 2000.
26 E.g. Joyce 1998, 2000, 2001; Perry and Joyce 2001.
27 Joyce 2000.
28 Joyce 2000: 478.
29 Joyce 2000: 474.
30 Joyce 2001, 2008.
31 The best introduction to personhood in archaeology is Fowler 2004a; for more recent reflections see Fowler 2016.
32 Fowler 2004a, 2010.
33 On the history of this see Thomas 2004: chapter 6.
34 Deetz 1977.
35 Johnson 1996.
36 Though they do not use the term 'personhood'.
37 Robb and Harris 2013: 182.
38 Mauss 1990 – first published in 1925.
39 Strathern 1988.
40 Strathern 2004.
41 Strathern 1992.
42 E.g. Strathern 1992: 86, 2013: 102–7.
43 Strathern 1988.
44 Strathern 1988: 13.
45 Battaglia 1990: 133.
46 Trudelle Schwarz 1997: 9.
47 Trudelle Schwarz 1997: 11.
48 E.g. Fowler 2004a; Gillespie 2001; Robb 2009; Whittle 2003.
49 Chapman 2000.
50 Chapman and Gaydarska 2007.
51 Chapman 2000: 5; Chapman and Gaydarska 2007.
52 Chapman 2000: 47.
53 Brück 2005, 2009, 2006; Fowler 2001, 2004a, 2004b, 2008, 2010.
54 Fowler 2001.
55 Fowler 2001: 152.
56 Fowler 2001: 158.
57 E.g. Brück 2006.
58 See Cipolla 2013a for a related argument in colonial North America.
59 Brück 2006: 307.
60 LiPuma 1998.
61 As Strathern (1988: 15) herself recognises.

62 Wilkinson 2013.
63 Spriggs 2008.
64 Jones 2005.
65 Similar criticisms have been made of the kinds of analogy that other archaeologists have used including by Binford, who we met in Chapter 2 (see discussion in Wylie 2002: chapter 9).
66 For a good example see the debate between Parker Pearson and Ramilisonina (1998) and Barrett and Fewster (1998).
67 Brittain and Harris 2010.
68 Thomas 2004.
69 As pointed out by Donna Haraway (1991), an author we will meet again in Chapter 9.
70 Sofaer 2006: 66.
71 Sofaer 2006.
72 Sofaer 2006: 72.
73 Robb and Harris 2013.
74 Malafouris 2013; Merleau-Ponty 1962; Robb and Harris 2013.
75 E.g. Brück 2009.

5

SECRET LIVES OF THINGS

Object agency and biography

Introduction: a museum visit

Think back to a recent visit to a museum (Figure 5.1). What drew you there in the first place? Perhaps it was a specific piece of art from the Renaissance, a massive rearticulated dinosaur skeleton (blasphemy in a book on archaeological theory!) or Incan archaeological collections. Maybe you went to complete an assignment, or simply tagged along with a friend who was interested in one of the things just listed. In any case, try to formulate your 'true' motivations. As you entered the museum, what did you see first? What couldn't you see? As you checked in at the front desk, did museum staff provide you with any instructions on how to find your way around? Did they give you a map? Once inside, how did you find the overall organisation of the different sections of the museum? Did you ever question how things had been laid out? At the first exhibit area, other than the objects of focus (art, fossils, artefacts), what other material culture was present? For example, were there picture frames, display cases, interpretive signs, lighting or benches? On your way out of the museum, did you stop at the gift shop? Where was it located in relation to the exit? Take a moment to think back on your experience some more, and do your best to answer the following question: how did the material world of the museum (that is, nonhuman aspects of the museum) influence you? How free were you to move through and engage with the spaces of the museum? What nonhuman elements constrained your movements and engagements, and how?

In this chapter, we explore if and how nonhumans have agency and biographies. As you'll recall, we discussed agency in Chapter 3, when we explored the reflexive relationships between individual agents and the structures that influence them. To reiterate, these 'structures' consist of anything that encourages or limits certain types of choice or action, ranging from the choices or actions of other people around us ('monkey see, monkey do') to the official laws on record in government offices. Here, we push the argument in a new and subtle direction,

FIGURE 5.1 A museum visit. Drawing by K–Fai Steele

asking what if, like those individuals mentioned in Chapter 3, nonhumans had agency too? Remember, with much of the recent agency scholarship in archaeology, the term 'agency' does not necessarily include any assumptions about the intentionality of actors in the past. Instead, as you'll recall from our discussion of Anthony Giddens' work (Chapter 3), agency refers to *the ability to make differences in the world*, intentionally or not. In this regard, it certainly seems reasonable to ask if and how objects have agency. Object agency comes in many flavours. A bright pink flower amid a sea of white flowers draws our attention. A familiar image 'nudges' us to remember a childhood experience or friend, or the hard reality of a professor's shut door during study week stops you from barging in and asking her more questions! So we must ask how that agency influences *our* agency and *our* understandings of the world. By the way, was the museum gift shop located in such a position that you had to move through that space to exit the building? This is a common ploy used in museums to 'remind' and influence visitors (especially those of us with small children) that they can and should buy some mementoes through which to remember their visit. This is what anthropologist Alfred Gell[1] might have referred to as 'secondary agency' that was distributed from the people who made the decision to position the gift shop in such a way. For Gell, humans use the material world to distribute their personhood and agency. We explore these concepts and more throughout this chapter.

In the next section, we step back and examine the work of Alfred Gell in more detail, particularly his notions of distributed personhood and his two types of agency. We then explore the work of other anthropologists like Arjun Appadurai and Igor Kopytoff, both of whom inspired archaeologists to ask questions on the 'biographies' and 'life' histories of objects. Finally, we conclude with a return to your museum visit. Without trying to make you too paranoid, we point out the ways in which you might have been 'encouraged' by the nonhuman components of the museum. As we will see in this chapter, thinking about object's agency and their biographies has been a popular way of trying to bridge the dualism between people and things or humans and nonhumans.

Object agency

So do objects have agency? We can begin to address this question in direct reference to the anthropological writings of Alfred Gell (Box 5.1). Gell's[2] *Art and Agency: An Anthropological Theory*, published posthumously, built upon the work of Marilyn Strathern (Chapter 4) and further investigated relations between persons and their nonhuman surroundings. Gell's ideas translate easily from the study of art, in particular, to broader considerations of the material world. The first thing to note is that Gell's book contains some contrasting and contradictory ideas about object agency. This might be because he died before completing a fully polished draft of the book.. Therefore, some of this ambiguity might be caused by the various chapters in *Art and Agency* representing the ways in which Gell changed his mind about agency as he continued to think through these problems. The second thing to note is that despite this variation, archaeologists tend to read in Gell's work a singular theory of how agency operates between humans and things rather than several contrasting ideas on this topic.[3] We will explore these different understandings below.

Although Gell recognised that agency results from a wide variety of human action, ranging from intentional to completely unintentional, his theory of art operates on a very specific definition of the term: 'Agency is attributable to those persons . . . who/which are seen as initiating causal sequences of a particular type, that is, events caused by acts of mind or will or intention, rather than the mere concatenation of physical events'.[4] At the start of his book, he uses this specific definition because he is primarily interested in how *humans understand* agency. He first argues that humans typically recognise agency as a force stemming directly from the choices and actions of other humans. This is an important clue to reading the first sections of Gell's book: *agency is only agency when a human recognises it as such.* Now that we have teased out Gell's stance on agency (at least in the first part of his work), it is also worth figuring out what he meant by 'art'. Gell[5] saw art as 'a system of action, intended to change the world rather than encode symbolic propositions about it'. Here we see an interesting break within the study of symbols and meaning that shifts attention away from what, in Chapter 7, we will refer to as symbolic or conventional signs to indexical signs. This entails an important shift in emphasis from early postprocessual approaches influenced by structuralism (Chapter 2), where meanings assigned to objects were often seen as arbitrary, to the practical effects that materials might have in the world regardless of human perception and intention.[6] As we discuss later in this book (Chapter 7), this could be thought of

BOX 5.1 ALFRED GELL

Alfred Gell (1945–97) was a British anthropologist who taught at the London School of Economics and Political Science. His fieldwork focused on the cultures of Melanesia and India. Gell's seminal book, *Art and Agency*,[7] was published one year after his death. In this work, he established several key ideas concerning agency, including a relational approach. Heavily discussed among the archaeological community is Gell's example of how his car possessed 'secondary' agency (in contrast to Gell's 'primary' agency as a human).

Photo by Oliver Harris

as a shift from the study of how things acted as symbols in the past – materially 'standing for' some concept for people – to the study of how signs or symbols actually shape the world through their material properties. Gell[8] was mainly interested in theorising how, in certain contexts, art objects could stand in for persons and their agencies. In other words, he intended to study how art objects acted as social agents. We can easily broaden this project out to consider how material culture in general might possess agency of a sort.

Drawing upon the writings of Marcel Mauss[9] and his considerations of gift exchange in tribal societies, Gell argued that material culture had the potential to serve as extensions of people. This is because, in Gell's[10] language, art permits observers to 'abduct' agency. This simply means that observers of an art object recognise that the object resulted only from the agency of some other person, who may or may not be present with the art. Gell provides a general example: while walking along the beach, we encounter a stone with some peculiar chipping along its edges.[11] Applying Gell's early logic to this case, the stone shows us agency *only* when we recognise the possibility that another human might have shaped or used it. This agency is lost, however, on the other beachgoers who are too busy slathering on sunblock, building sandcastles or preparing for a dip to notice this subtle artefact. When a newcomer accidently steps on the rock, they may very well blame themselves for being so careless, perhaps also sputtering a few curse words. On the other hand, our injured beachgoer may attribute the agency to the onlookers, for knowing the dangers of that sharp rock and not warning them before they stepped on its edge. In both of these scenarios on our fictive beach, the stone works as an agent *in relation to humans*, either past or present. In this model, however, the humans have control of the lion's share of agency; they remain the puppet masters, and it is our personhood that becomes distributed. A dualism between people and things certainly remains here.

This is the point in the argument where we really begin to see some distinctive elements of Gell's approach to the agency of objects. As indicated above, all of these ideas fit together in what we call an anthropocentric, or human-centred, model of agency.[12] This simply means that Gell saw humans and their understanding of the world around them as the key ingredient for agency. We can see this in his notions of primary and secondary agents.

> I am prepared to make a distinction between 'primary' agents, that is, intentional beings who are categorically distinguished from 'mere' things or artefacts, and 'secondary' agents, which are artefacts, dolls, cars, works of art, etc. through which primary agents distribute their agency in the causal milieu, and thus render their agency effective.[13]

So, for Gell, agency existed only in the *relationships* between different agents of these two main types (primary-primary, primary-secondary). He used the relationship he had with his car as an example. If the car broke down on a dark street in the middle of the night, Alfred, like our injured beachgoer above, might curse at the car or even give it a stiff kick. Again, Gell saw this scenario as a crucial set of relations between primary and secondary agents, with the primary agent always at the centre. He wrote:

> My car is a (potential) agent with respect to me as a 'patient', not in respect to itself, as a car. It is an agent only in so far as I am a patient, and it is a 'patient' (the counterpart of an agent) only in so far as I am an agent with respect to it.[14]

With this quotation we also see early evidence for Gell's relational approach to agency, meaning that he understood agency as a phenomenon that comes about from relationships, a point we explore in much further detail in later chapters.

An alternative to the anthropocentrism of this model is the way that Gell discusses agency in the later parts of his book. In his discussions of Maori house styles, for example, he notes the ways in which the physical house and its relationship to other houses past and present exert a subtle type of agency over the people who built and used it.[15] Archaeologist Chris Gosden (Box 10.1 in Chapter 10) correctly notes these inconsistencies:

> Although he doesn't explore the conceptual implications of this idea, Gell's view that artefacts form a world with its own logics somewhat independent of human intentions is vital in demonstrating that there might be many cases in which forms of abstract thought and mental representation take the shape suggested by objects, rather than objects simply manifesting pre-existing forms of thought.[16]

Gosden takes influence from Gell (among others) to track the ways in which collections of artefacts influence people over long trajectories of time. For instance, a child born in a particular type of house, situated in a settlement that is composed of a number of houses that all fit within the accepted stylistic range for that community would grow up thinking about houses in a particular way. The relationships between all the houses that person has experienced will then shape how they see the world and how they recreate it (cultural reproduction à la Chapter 3). We deal with a set of approaches that are similar to Gosden's (working under the heading 'materiality') in Chapter 6. For now, it is important to note that even though Gell explicitly defined agency in one particular way at the start of his book, his discussion of various examples in the second half actually contradicts those solely anthropocentric models. Again, the key contribution here is Gell's idea of relational agency and distributed personhood.

From this perspective, the beauty of the material world lies in its ability to stand in for human agents. For example, we might theorise the door to your house or apartment as an extension of the architect, builders and even you every time that you use it. The architect who designed your building probably had a good understanding of where doors are usually located, how they function and what is needed for them to function efficiently. Based on these factors, and probably in consultation with several other people, the architect used their agency to situate your door (in relation to other features) on a set of blueprints that were handed to the builders. The builders used their agency – in relation to the 'real world' of building materials, other features of the build and general working conditions – to construct the door. They probably did so, however, in relation to the architect's distributed agency, which was in the form of blueprints. In this sense, the material state of the plans somehow transmitted the architect's agency, redistributing it in their absence.[17] The same general idea applies to the nails and screws that hold your door in place. They are redistributing the agency of the builder, who no longer has to stand in your house and hold up your door as they did when initially constructing your house. (Perhaps doornails aren't as *dead* as Charles Dickens thought!)

Likewise, the door continues to function as a 'conduit' for your agency in that you probably close it or even lock it to prevent other people from entering when you are away from home or sleeping. If it was not possible to distribute agency through material things, as discussed by Gell, it is hard to imagine what our world would be like. The human lineage has been using things to distribute its various forms of agency now for at least 2.6 million years, and probably much longer.

Enchanting the collector

Archaeologist Rodney Harrison[18] provides a fascinating application of Gell's ideas to an archaeological and anthropological problem concerning Australian Aboriginal heritage. His discussion focuses specifically on one type of artefact: Kimberley projectile points (Figure 5.2). These bifacial points were made from a variety of different raw materials, including stone (e.g., chert and quartzite), glass and even ceramic (usually telegraph insulators). They were made using a technique known as pressure flaking, when a soft hammer is strategically pressed along the edges of the artefact to shape it. Kimberley points were made in the Kimberley region of Western Australia (Figure 5.3). White collectors traded for – and circulated – large numbers of Kimberley points in the late nineteenth and twentieth centuries. Indeed, Kimberley points are often used in museum exhibits to represent all or at least much of Australian Aboriginal history and heritage. Harrison attributes Kimberley points' prominent place in such heritage representations to their aesthetic beauty and the technological expertise that is necessary for their manufacture. However, he also points out that this is a misrepresentation in many ways since Kimberley points were not 'typical' examples of Australian Aboriginal stone tool production, but rather unique examples from a limited geographical region of Australia, produced directly for white consumption in the late nineteenth and early twentieth centuries. This quality is what makes Kimberley points 'artefacts of colonial desire' from Harrison's[19] perspective.

Drawing upon Gell's writings, Harrison argues that Kimberley points exercised agency in their various connections to collectors, members of the general public interested in Australian Aboriginal heritage, trade partners with Kimberley point makers and even archaeologists. Going back to our discussion of Gell above, these artefacts served as secondary agents in relation to the primary agency of their makers and collectors. They allowed the toolmaker to distribute their agency and personhood across space-time like the doornails in your house. Yet these were not the only agents involved. Harrison recognises the agency of the consumers in these transactions, which included collectors and other types of trade partner. Here, he employs Gell's ideas on technologies of enchantment.[20] These are instances where we become nearly transfixed by another's skill and proficiency. For instance, have you ever looked at a painting and simply found the level of technical detail nearly impossible to grasp? Gell would tell us that you had been enchanted! He discussed the ways in which art captivates its audiences. As described by Harrison, 'the technical proficiency of the painting defies our

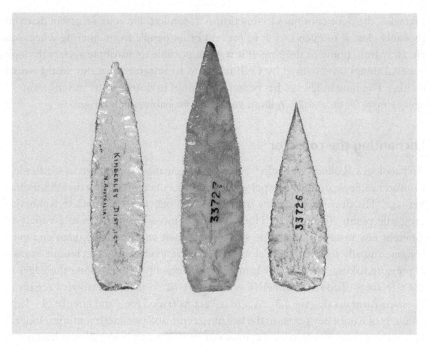

FIGURE 5.2 Kimberley points, glass, Australia

Photo courtesy of the Royal Ontario Museum

imagination or, more accurately, our ability to conceive a resemblance of our agency to the agency which originated the artwork'.[21] Harrison views nineteenth and twentieth-century consumers of Kimberley points as captivated by the technological complexity of the tool manufacturing process. There must be some recognition of the makers' agency since they were the ones actually producing these artefacts (and the agents in possession of all of that technological expertise); however, Kimberley point agency does not work in the same way without a specific set of colonial consumers.

This is an interesting example, but how do we know for sure about the agencies that artefacts exercised in the past? This is a difficult question to address. In Harrison's case, he used a combination of archaeological interpretation, documentation concerning collecting and trading activities, along with contemporary indigenous knowledge. Could we apply these arguments and perspectives to archaeological contexts that are not associated with other lines of evidence such as documents, oral histories and oral traditions? For instance, could we discuss the agency of Acheulean handaxes (Figure 5.4) recovered from a one-million-year-old deposit? The answer is yes, but not in exactly the same way that Harrison does. For such an ancient site, we must remain open to the idea that humans and their material surroundings shaped and influenced one another. For instance, the fact that all

FIGURE 5.3 Map showing the Kimberley Region of Australia

From Wikimedia: Derivative of File:Northern Territory locator-MJC.png based on File:Kimberley_region_of_western_australia.JPG and File:Regions_of_western_australia_nine_plus_perth.png

FIGURE 5.4 Biface handaxe of chordate form, circa 1.65 million to 100,000 years BP

Photograph courtesy of the Royal Ontario Museum

Acheulean tools meet certain stylistic criteria for paleoanthropologists and archaeologists who study a vast expanse of time in different regional contexts shows that those tools likely shaped previous human understandings of both the raw material and the artefacts. Over the long term, the relationships between Acheulean tools embedded themselves in human understanding of the world and therefore effected change. For instance, when a member of the species now called *Homo ergaster* knapped stone, previous and current experiences of tool types – how they looked, functioned or performed in the past – influenced the shape of new 'generations' of tools. Of course, as we will see in Chapter 8, raw materials and their unique qualities also play an important role in shaping the final product.[22]

Object biography

As time passes and the house door described above transforms with age, how do we account for the different types of relational agency it takes on or loses? We know that the door started out in some other form, perhaps as a tree or as minerals in the earth. Each of these possibilities comes with a distinct set of potentials for agency. We also know that the door will likely take on new meanings, uses and relationships after it parts company with the rest of your house. This could be as simple as switching it to a new house. Or, more radically, it might be repurposed into a coffee table or picture frame. Eventually it will be discarded and possibly take on a new role in the complicated ecology of a landfill. Archaeologists interested in the dynamic nature of artefacts often frame their analyses as object biographies.[23] Intellectually speaking, this set of approaches came before studies of object agency and certainly influenced some of the questions on agency highlighted above. We could trace this interest in 'biographical' approaches to processual studies of the use-life of artefacts, but we must remember that there are some important distinctions.[24] Studies of the use-life of artefacts tend to view humans as working *on* the object world (similar to the *hylomorphic* models we will discuss in Chapters 8 and 10), with agency flowing only one way, i.e. from humans to things. In contrast, approaches that study object biographies tend to look at the co-development of humans and things alongside one another as they age and transform together. Archaeologists taking this approach draw upon the work of anthropologists Arjun Appadurai[25] and Igor Kopytoff.[26] Kopytoff[27] famously described his biographical approach as follows:

> In doing the biography of a thing, one would ask questions similar to those one asks about people: What, sociologically, are the biographical possibilities realised? Where does the thing come from and who made it? What has been its career so far, and what do people consider to be an ideal career for such things? What are the recognised 'ages' of periods in a thing's 'life,' and what are the cultural markers for them? How does the thing's use change with its age, and what happens to it when it reaches the end of its usefulness?

Although he makes no mention of agency here, we could reframe these general questions using Gell's ideas on the agency of artefacts.[28] Both Appadurai and Kopytoff are interested in the ways in which things become commodities (defined by Appadurai as anything that is exchangeable) and fall in and out of this state as they age and move through different social contexts.[29] As archaeologist Lynn Meskell[30] (Box 6.2 in Chapter 6) points out, this original interest in exchange places emphasis on humans and the meaning and intentionality they invest in objects rather than on the 'experiential and sensuous dimension of materiality'. As we will see in the next chapters, this critique of anthropocentrism remains at the heart of archaeological theory in the new millennium. However, it is also worth pointing out that some thinkers would even characterise Meskell's critique of object biographies as anthropocentric because 'experiential' and 'sensuous' aspects of material things still place human values and understandings on a pedestal.

Tracking colonial 'lives'

We could certainly take a biographical approach to the Kimberley points discussed above. From that perspective we could easily trace their shifting meanings and life histories as they aged and came into contact with new sets of people ('primary' agents), including Rodney Harrison. Laura Peers[31] provides another compelling example of how such an approach would work. She provides a biography of the S BLACK bag (Figure 5.5), an object currently housed in the Pitt Rivers Museum, Oxford.

An associate of the Hudson's Bay Company collected the bag in the 1840s in Western North America,[32] but it was probably made slightly earlier in time, perhaps in the 1830s. Bags such as the one in question have a deep antiquity for indigenous peoples of the American west. Starting around 1800 in this region, indigenous women began decorating such bags with floral motifs that were inspired by textiles, ceramics and other decorated objects acquired through trade with white trappers and traders.[33] This particular example is made of black wool and decorated with embroidery, beads and tassels.[34] On one side of the bag is a floral design with the text, 'S BLACK'. On the reverse side there is a heart design. This particular type of bag is referred to as an 'octopus bag' because of the four hanging 'tentacles' along the bottom edge. Earlier bags of this general type were made from the whole skin of a small-sized mammal.[35] The dangling tabs were originally made from the skin covering the four limbs of the animal used to make the bag.

This specific bag, being made of wool, only mimics the original shape of the animal skin bags. The original bags took their shape from the 'natural' world, i.e. the physical shape of certain mammals. After that, the shape of octopus bags – initially based on the physical shape of the animals being used – became engrained in social memories and practices. New bags like our S BLACK bag were constructed to look like the original animal skin bags even though the makers could just as easily have made bags in a variety of shapes. Here we see a type of agency that things like mammals and their skins have over people, but it is not quite the

FIGURE 5.5 Photograph of the S BLACK bag

Copyright Pitt Rivers Museum, University of Oxford, accession number 1893.67.183

same as the primary/secondary agency model that Gell explicitly endorses in *Art and Agency*. It is much more subtle and it resembles some of the approaches to materiality explored in the next chapter.

So who owned this particular bag and what is its story? The 'S BLACK' on the bag almost certainly refers to Samuel Black, an Aberdeen-born trader who became associated with the fur trade around 1802, and rose to the status of chief trader during the 1820s. Black was married twice. If he followed the typical pattern for fur traders at this time, it is likely that his wives were both métis (mixed indigenous and European heritage). The actual identity of the maker of the S BLACK bag remains a mystery, though Peers argues that it was standard practice for wives and daughters to make bags like this one for husbands or fathers. The early part of the S BLACK bag's life thus ties to the long-term indigenous history of the area and to colonial entanglements, including the exchange – both forced and voluntary – of materials, ideas and genes. As opposed to the close relationship that Black likely had with the maker of the bag (possibly referenced with the heart design on the reverse side), Black also had an antagonistic relationship to other indigenous people. This idea is supported by the fact that an indigenous person shot him dead in 1841. Shortly after his murder, a member of the Hudson's Bay Company collected the bag, possibly as a token by which to remember a colleague and his violent death.[36]

In the next phase of the bag's life, it transitioned from a memory (or mnemonic) device for a biographically known European individual and his death to a representation of North American indigenous cultural traditions, seen as evidence for 'primitive' and 'exotic' ways of life. This is a major change that warrants serious attention. It went from representing one particular (European) fur trader to standing for indigenous culture in general! This sounds similar to our discussion of Kimberley points above. In both cases, things transitioned from representing a complex and long-term set of colonial and culturally plural interactions to representing *only* indigenous cultural traditions. According to Peers, the collection that includes the S BLACK bag came to be seen as an associated set of 'symbols of the anonymous, timeless, "primitive" societies which produced them and of the courage and fortitude of the "civilised" people who worked with them'.[37]

Then, in 1880, the bag was accessioned by the Pitt Rivers Museum where it transformed into a museum artefact. This transition only cemented the S BLACK bag's new status as representing Native North Americans for British viewers and researchers. The value of the bag was seen in its potential connection to 'pure, authentic, localised' tribal history rather than the complicated and plural colonial interaction that led to its manufacture.[38] In 1999, Peers reassessed the biography of the bag to problematise and correct some of these interpretations, restoring some emphasis on the S BLACK bag's connection to the plural fur-trading society of nineteenth-century Western North America.

As with the Kimberley points above, we are reminded that one must exercise caution when trying to associate a particular time period and/or 'culture' with specific artefact types.[39] Part of the challenge of such a project has to do with the nature of object agency and the ways in which it might differ from human agency. In a recent edited volume, Rosemary Joyce (Box 5.2) and Susan Gillespie[40] make this very point and build upon and critique early versions of object biography in archaeology. They note that the 'biographical' approach assumes that objects live similar lives as humans.[41] In a metaphorical sense, it is assumed that they are born, they age and they die, perhaps when they are placed into the archaeological context where we find them. Joyce and Gillespie[42] argue that the notion of object 'itineraries' opens up more (and better) possibilities for exploring the agency and movement of objects. In her chapter, Joyce[43] considers marble vases produced in Honduras between 500 and 1000 AD. She demonstrates that, in the past, the vases in question were part of complicated sets of objects. They shared important relationships with other things, including polychrome painted ceramics, stone bowls and mortuary or commemorative funerary contexts. In contrast, today the vases are valued as singular art objects. If we were to gloss over or lose sight of part of this complex itinerary, which spans up to the present, we also limit how much the vessels can tell us (as with the Kimberley points and the S BLACK bag). For instance, by treating the vases only as singular pieces of art, we are making them into 'quasihumans'[44] even though they were clearly 'relational agents' in the past (possessing a different type of agency than the kind we associate with humans alone).

BOX 5.2 ROSEMARY JOYCE

Rosemary Joyce is professor of anthropology at the University of California, Berkeley. A leader in archaeological theory, she has published numerous influential books, papers and edited volumes on Mesoamerican archaeology, gender and the body. In her recent edited volume with Susan Gillespie, *Things in Motion: Object Itineraries in Anthropological Practice*,[45] she discusses itineraries of Honduran vases like this one.[46]

Image © Trustees of the British Museum

Conclusions: back to the museum

Are you feeling tentative about our claims in this chapter? Does it sound as if we are uncritically embracing a return to the 'pots equal people' approach associated with culture history archaeology and outlined in Chapter 2? We certainly did not argue that Kimberley points or the S BLACK bag 'stood' for aboriginal Australian or Native American culture. In fact, we argued against such notions to show how these things shaped and influenced a variety of people during their respective 'itineraries'. This is quite different from pots = people! What about the concepts of agency and structure from Chapter 3?[47] Could it be that we are conflating agency (sometimes thought of as the usual domain of people) with structure? Of course, we also pointed out in Chapter 3 that structure and agency are part of the same process of cultural reproduction. This means that we cannot and should not try to separate an object's agency from its structure. The two go hand in hand. Instead of reverting back to pots = people or making agency/structure into a dualism, in this chapter we continued to acknowledge (as with Chapters 2 and 3) the ways in which people and things interact with one another and become enmeshed or entangled.

What about that museum visit mentioned in our introduction? Did this chapter supply you with any new ways of thinking about your experience? We would suggest that without the museum and its material contents, you would not have made the trip. We further suggest that the museum's designers and builders used the fabric and layout of the structure to influence your movement in very specific ways. As you found your way to the Andean section of the archaeology museum, for instance, you arrived by interacting with many nonhuman entities, including that handy map, the stairs and the corridors. You were discouraged from handling the Andean pots by the glass case they sat in, and by the museum guard, properly uniformed and stationed next to it. The lighting and text present alongside the Andean artefacts allowed the curators to show you what they wanted. The relationship of these artefacts to other collections also forced their typology on you. To give one example, some anthropology museums have been critiqued for the ways in which they organise different archaeological assemblages in terms of rigid cultural-evolutionary frameworks. Classically, they would use the hierarchy of tribe–chiefdom–state to create a physical hierarchy, sometimes using different floors of the museum as proxies for various stages along cultural-evolutionary trajectories.

On the bright side, museum directors and curators do not have *complete* control of the ways in which the materiality of the museum shapes your experience and understanding of the world. This is partially related to the fact that different people see and experience the same material world in a variety of different ways. However, it also has to do with the stubbornness of the material world; it does not always conform to the way that humans would like it to act. Here lies the main weak point in Gell's approach to object agency: he assumed that humans are the usual starting points for agency, and this leaves certain dualisms intact. This is a hypothesis that will factor prominently into the remaining chapters of this book. Next, in Chapter 6, we challenge this idea by focusing on the ways in which things act back upon us in ways that we can't fully comprehend.

Notes

1 Gell 1998.
2 Gell 1998.
3 For instance see different uses of Gell in Gosden 2005 and Robb 2010: 505.
4 Gell 1998: 16.
5 Gell 1998: 6.
6 Cipolla 2013a.
7 1998.
8 Gell 1998: 7. See also Hoskins 2006.
9 Mauss 2011[1990].
10 Gell 1998: 13.
11 Gell 1998: 16.
12 Hoskins 2006: 75.
13 Gell 1998: 20.
14 Gell 1998: 22.
15 Gell 1998: 215.
16 Gosden 2005: 196.
17 In Chapter 8 we will see how we can take these ideas of design further to become less anthropocentric.
18 Harrison 2006.
19 Harrison 2006.
20 Gell 1992.
21 Harrison 2006: 67.
22 And see Malafouris 2013: 169–77 for an excellent discussion of the complex agencies involved in knapping a handaxe.
23 See papers in *World Archaeology* 1999, edited by Gosden and Marshall.
24 Gosden and Marshall 1999: 169.
25 Appadurai 1986a; 1986b.
26 See also Meskell 2004.
27 Kopytoff 1986: 66.
28 In fact, Gell has a chapter in Appadurai's edited volume.
29 Cipolla 2017.
30 Meskell 2004: 57.
31 Peers 1999.
32 Peers 1999: 289.
33 Peers 1999: 289.
34 Peers 1999: 288.
35 Peers 1999: 291–2.
36 Peers 1999: 296.
37 Peers 1999: 297.
38 Peers 1999: 298.
39 Hayes 2011, 2013.
40 Joyce and Gillespie 2015a.
41 See also Domańska 2006.
42 Joyce and Gillespie 2015b.
43 Joyce 2015.
44 Joyce 2015: 35.
45 Joyce and Gillespie 2015a.
46 Joyce 2015.
47 Some archaeologists have been very sceptical of the notion of object agency. For example see Lindstrøm's (2015) recent attack on the subject (and Sørensen's (2016) withering response!).

6

THINGS MAKE PEOPLE?

Considering materiality, phenomenology, experience and entanglement

Introduction: making the Amesbury Archer

Discovered near Stonehenge, the archaeological find known as the 'Amesbury archer' is the richest Copper Age, or Beaker, burial known in Britain.[1] The 17 flint barbed and tanged arrowheads associated with the burial give the archer his present-day moniker. Also recovered from the burial were five Beaker pots, three copper knives, an anvil stone and other tools used for metalworking and flint knapping, boars' tusks, wrist guards and gold ornaments that were likely worn in someone's hair. Since they do not seem to have been attached to the archer's body when he was buried, perhaps the latter came from a mourner who removed them and placed them in the grave. Analysis of the skeleton shows that he may well have come from a mountainous area of central Europe. There is also evidence for trauma and wear on his skeleton, indications that he lived a difficult life. For instance, his left kneecap was missing, potentially lost in a painful injury.

Considering this brief summary, first think about who the archer was based on the archaeological finds. Regardless of the many interpretive dangers associated with analogy, you might compare him to a character or set of characters from movies or television. We know that he came from far away and suffered through some tough injuries. Similar to Frodo Baggins, maybe? Possibly, but don't forget his trusty arrows. So, perhaps more like Katniss Everdeen? Maybe you think of him as an outdoors type or survivalist. Bear Grylls? Remember the metalworking tools? He was a master of cutting edge technologies too. Doctor Temperance Brennan? Whoever you end up with in your interpretation of the archer, take a moment to scrutinise how different qualities of your version of the archer's character relate and depend upon the things that he possessed. You could also do this exercise for any of the characters mentioned above. What qualities of each character depend upon the things that they possess and use?

FIGURE 6.1 An archer without arrows. Drawing by K-Fai Steele

We can begin with a close consideration of the archer's nickname. What makes an archer, the person or the things (Figure 6.1)? An archer is typically defined as a person who shoots with a bow and arrow. Many would likely add in something concerning the skill involved in using them. In other words, not just any person plus a bow and arrow equals an archer. So, how does someone acquire archery skills? Practice makes perfect, of course! You can only become a skilled archer through careful and prolonged engagement with bows and arrows. The point is that the category 'archer' depends upon both things and people. More important than that, archery skills are only achieved through a close *relationship* between the two, or what Ian Hodder[2] recently discussed as an entanglement. The archer must learn the 'feel' of the bow and arrow to achieve a level of proficiency. For now, we can think of this as 'muscle memory', which only results from the relationship between thing and person in this case. The same goes for Frodo and his ring, Katniss and her bow, Bear and whatever landscape in which he happens to be demonstrating his mastery, or Dr Brennan and her impressive forensic technologies. The relationship between people and things is intimate. We all know of course that people make things, but what these examples show us is that things make people too. In fact, for the purposes of this chapter, the phrase, *people make things and things make people*, is our new mantra.

Does this sound similar to the themes discussed in Chapter 5? Remember, in the last chapter we focused largely on the ways in which things (that is, nonhumans) functioned as agents. Alfred Gell might have thought of his car as an agent when it broke down on a dark road, but with his particular approach, the car was only an agent when he considered it so. He was far less concerned with the physical properties of the car and their effects on him. Tires wear away, mufflers erode and brake lines atrophy, regardless of what humans know about or think of these processes. If you want the car to work properly, you deal with these constraints. Chapter 5 also explored the ways in which nonhumans channel human agency and perception. The physical layout of the museum encourages you to move through and view it in a certain way. In either case, Chapter 5 still had humans and their agency on centre stage. This chapter takes a more subtle approach. We consider archaeological approaches that view people and things as co-dependent on one another as in the archer example above.

In the following section, we consider a core concept for this chapter: 'materiality'. We then move on to explore influential thinkers from outside of the discipline, including Hegel and Miller. After that we proceed to discuss some related approaches that have emerged through phenomenology in archaeology, via the work of philosophers like Heidegger and Merleau-Ponty. We then consider how elements of phenomenological thinking have inspired greater interest in human experience – in the senses, memory and emotion. After each of these sections we will give a brief archaeological example or two, before turning to the latest version of these kinds of theories offered by one of the great figures of archaeological theory who we met in Chapter 2: Ian Hodder. What we find is that studies of materiality, including theories of objectification, phenomenology and entanglement, critique dualisms in important ways without fully transcending them. Don't worry if this doesn't make complete sense just yet; we will take it one step at a time.

What is materiality?

Archaeologists have come to rely heavily on the term *materiality* in the new millennium.[3] If you were to look up this term in the dictionary, you would find something about the quality of being material.[4] Daniel Miller[5] (Box 6.1) – an anthropologist who specialises in the study of mass consumption and material culture – notes that the term has a number of different uses, ranging from the colloquial to the deeply philosophical. On the one hand, we sometimes use the term to refer to the *quality of objects*, what things *are*.[6] This idea lines up nicely with the dictionary definition just noted and it assures us that we can intellectually strip away the meanings that humans give to things to get at the 'sheer' material qualities of objects: the hardness of the stone projectile point, the pliability of the wooden bow, the stubbornness of the sinewy bowstring. The qualities of these items have advantages and limitations for humans. They dictate what humans can do with them.[7]

On the other hand, there are notions of materiality that recognise the messy and complicated relationships between things and humans. They might even go so far as to argue that these two categories are inseparable in important ways. These applications seek to understand the mutual constitution of humans and things. Remember our mantra from above? They aim to investigate how subjects make

BOX 6.1 DANIEL MILLER

Daniel Miller is Professor of Anthropology at the University College London (UCL). Miller's innovative research on material culture has helped to make UCL world-renowned for material culture studies. Miller has published numerous books and edited volumes dealing with consumption, materiality and objectification including *Modernity: An Ethnographic Approach*,[8] *The Comfort of Things*[9] and *Stuff*.[10] His recent work looks at the impact that things like web cameras and social networking have on our lives.

Photo by Simon.zfn (own work) [public domain], via Wikimedia Commons

objects and how objects make subjects. In this context materiality can be seen as an umbrella term for a number of different approaches that we will cover in this chapter including objectification, phenomenology and entanglement.

Dialectics and objectification

To say the least, *dialectics* and *objectification* are not the most user-friendly terms in the world. Never fear! We will be sure to tie everything back to themes introduced earlier. In fact, we recommend that you pause here to review Chapter 3 once again; many of the ideas introduced there, such as the 'feedback loops' of practice theory (see Box 3.2), will pop up again below. The notions of dialectics and objectification tie back to the respective works of philosophers George Wilhelm Friedrich Hegel

(1770–1831) and Karl Marx (1818–83). Drawing on the work of these two thinkers, materiality theorists look at how nonhumans come to have person-like qualities, including agency.[11] This should sound similar to some of the notions explored in Chapter 5. Like the studies and arguments discussed in that chapter, studies of materiality typically focus on identity and social relations.[12] Daniel Miller has written extensively on these subjects, including a 2005 edited volume simply titled *Materiality*. Taking influence from practice theory, Miller introduced his notion of the 'humility of things' in his 1987 book, *Material Culture and Mass Consumption*. He argued that the less we notice things and the constraints they place upon us, the more powerful they become in influencing the reproduction of society and culture. This idea bears a striking resemblance to Bourdieu's *habitus* and Giddens' *practical consciousness*, not to mention some of the ideas proposed by Gell. For instance, the frames and cases of the museum discussed at the start of Chapter 5 are powerful in the subtle guidance they thrust upon visitors. They lead visitors to experience the museum in very specific ways.

Miller sees the study of material culture, such as those museum cases, as a subset of the larger study of human culture, and he has conducted a huge amount of ethnographic work to explore how people and things relate to one another. One example from his ethnographic work in Trinidad[13] helps to highlight the fact that not all people see the world as westerners do. For instance, westerners often use the term 'superficial' to describe someone who is vain and only interested in cosmetic things, perhaps expensive cars or clothes. This insult assumes that the 'surface' (how a person looks, or the material aspects of the person) somehow conceals a deeper reality of that person. Think of how often you are told 'don't judge a book by its cover'! Miller's work shows that this disregard for the superficial dimension of people is considered very strange in Trinidad. Instead people can and should be judged for how well they dress, how cool they are. The surface here is what is real. After all, Miller's informants argue, if something like dressing well is something you can achieve, doesn't this reveal directly who you are as a person? The depths of a person, for them, are where secrets and lies are kept. This is a challenge to the western divide between material (superficial appearances) and immaterial (what 'really' lies beneath your material possessions). Material culture here isn't a surface gloss that hides who you really are – it is what directly reveals who you really are. Thus things can play a critical role in a society, and Miller attempts to think about this through his ideas of objectification.

Before we get to the ins and outs of this, however, we must first deal with dialectics. A dialectic pattern has three parts: a thesis, an antithesis (or contrast) and a synthesis (or 'middle ground' for our purposes). People start with a general idea about their world (thesis). As they interact with new surroundings, they begin to draw new comparisons and contrasts between themselves or their ideas about the world and what they actually experience (antithesis). The antithesis in this case could be anything from other 'types' of people or 'foreign' material patterns. A new understanding emerges that helps people comprehend what they *are* in terms of what they *are not*. These emergent understandings lead people to see themselves and reproduce their worlds in new ways (synthesis). Have you ever travelled to a new country? How did that experience make you feel about your own nationality and self-understanding? Experiences of new countries often influence visitors to see their own home countries in a new light. This is how the dialectic works. Remember your marked trowel from Chapter 3 and the rivalry it eventually caused between field schools? That situation could also be seen as a dialectical process. The context of the field school led you to innovate and mark your trowel, which eventually led to a world where marked and unmarked trowels stood for field school rivalries.

Miller builds his insightful theories of material culture on the back of Hegel's *The Phenomenology of Spirit.*[14] During the Enlightenment, Hegel argued against the very dualities on which we focus in this book. He made the point that, philosophically, humans and the material world are inseparable. In other words, he was opposed to the notion of agentive human subjects versus passive nonhuman objects. Instead, Hegel argued that everything people do is shaped by their understanding and reflection upon the material world, which they or other humans created. This sounds like a feedback loop! According to Hegel, this loop – part of the process he called *objectification* – had a particular sequence fuelled by the notion of contradiction. As summarised by Miller:[15]

> Everything that we create has, by virtue of that act, the potential both to appear, and to become, alien to us. We may not recognise our creations as those of history or ourselves. They may take on their own interest and trajectory.

In short, objectification is the way that humans make, use and observe material things that continually force them to reconsider who they are and how they relate to the rest of the world. This is similar to the way travel in a foreign country allows you to see your own country in a new way.

Archaeologist Lynn Meskell's (Box 6.2) writings on 'object worlds' of Ancient Egypt[16] demonstrate how some thinkers use theories of materiality and objectification to try and transcend dualisms. She considers theories of materiality in Ancient Egypt, examining the complicated relationships between humans and nonhumans as they relate to three iconic aspects of that 'culture': statues, mummies and pyramids. Statues of gods were treated as human. They were not seen as a *representation of the god*, but *as the god's body.*[17] Meskell writes of how statues were 'born' in Ancient Egypt rather than 'made'. Akin to humans, divine statues were also washed, dressed and fed. Mummies too straddled the line between subjects and objects, often shifting back and forth in different contexts.[18] The process of mummification transformed the body of the formerly living subject into object form, but this boundary (between subject and object) was soft and permeable. This is true even in the modern western world. After all, the mummy that unexpectedly comes alive is the star of many Hollywood productions. The living dead in mummy form literally haunts some of our dreams. Finally, the pyramid (Figure 6.2) was a material

BOX 6.2 LYNN MESKELL

Lynn Meskell is Professor of Anthropology at Stanford University. She has published numerous important books, articles and chapters on social archaeology, materiality and cultural heritage. Her book, *Object Worlds: Material Biographies Past and Present*,[19] focused on Ancient Egyptian senses of materiality.

Photo by Lysippos (own work) [CC BY-SA 3.0 (http://creativecommons.org/licenses/by-sa/3.0)], via Wikimedia Commons

thing used to transcend the limitations of human subjectivity. As a massive and imposing monument housing the deceased, the Egyptian pyramid broke dualisms between dead and alive, absence and presence, immaterial and material. Through these three forms of objectification, statues, mummies and pyramids exhibited agency, making the people that made them.

As we will see in Chapter 8, a growing number of scholars associated with terms such as *symmetrical archaeology* and *new materialism* feel that the general framework of the dialectic simply recreates the dualities it seeks to eradicate.[20] These thinkers voice some serious concerns that materiality studies assume an inherent and absolute difference between subjects and objects.[21] Material culture theorists like Miller are aware of these critiques, and argue just the opposite. Miller stands by the notion that the dialectical theory of objectification is:

not a theory of the mutual constitution of prior forms, such as subjects and objects. It is entirely distinct from any theory of representation. In objectification, all we have is a process in time by which the very act of creating form creates consciousness or capacity such as skill and thereby transforms both form and self-consciousness of that which has consciousness, or the capacity of that which now has skill.[22]

This essentially boils down to our example of the archer above. The 'representation' that Miller mentions relates to the core set of dualisms that haunts archaeological theory. We will explore this problem specifically as it relates to symbols and meaning in the next chapter, but for now it is important to remember that many materiality studies argue against a dualistic model of representation. As opposed to 'standard' approaches in archaeology, they are no longer interested in segregating the material from the immaterial. For instance, they don't necessarily find merit in thinking about the archer described above in terms of things (bow, arrow, bowstring) on the one hand, and their meanings or representations (a notion of a skilled archer, a memory of Robin Hood or William Tell) on the other. In fact, some thinkers engaged in discussion of materiality recognise that nothing is fully immaterial.[23] From mountains to ghosts or from things to thoughts, all entities have a material component ranging in durability and effect from electronic pulses in a brain to the sheer blunt-force trauma of a fist to a face.

FIGURE 6.2 Pyramid of Khafre (Giza) behind the Great Sphinx

Phenomenology

Phenomenology presents another useful way of thinking about the mutual constitution of people and things, and in archaeology it has often been integrated with discussions of materiality.[24] The phenomenological work done by prominent philosophers in the nineteenth and twentieth centuries, such as Edmund Husserl, Martin Heidegger (Box 6.3) and Maurice Merleau-Ponty, forms the basis for the approaches developed by archaeologists such as Christopher Tilley[25] and Julian Thomas.[26] The great phenomenological slogan is, Being-in-the-world. As Thomas describes, 'Phenomenology deals in world disclosure, in which an engagement with a particular entity leads us into an expanding web of relationships'.[27] This sounds similar to Miller's use of Hegelian dialectics, but let's push a bit further before we jump to any conclusions. We'll start with a very brief historical overview of the philosophy behind these ideas before looking at their more recent application.

BOX 6.3 MARTIN HEIDEGGER

Martin Heidegger (1889–1976) was a German philosopher known for his writings on phenomenology. He was Professor of Philosophy at Freiburg University, a post held previously by Edmund Husserl. Heidegger's seminal book, *Being and Time*, is still regularly cited today, including among archaeologists. He used a humble thing, a hammer, to illustrate the various types of human–thing interaction.

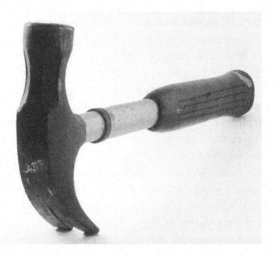

Photo by Malene Thyssen, http://commons.wikimedia.org/wiki/User:Malene from https://commons.wikimedia.org/wiki/File:Hammer2.jpg

---

The first major figure in phenomenology, a German philosopher named Edmund Husserl (1859–1938), was primarily interested in human perception of the world and thus focused on issues related to human consciousness. He sought to move beyond the dualism of idealism versus materialism (or immateriality versus materiality), arguing that human perception was not just a matter of humans experiencing the material world. Instead, he complicated this narrative, asking how things were revealed to individuals.[28] Ian Hodder[29] recently described phenomenology as the study of the 'thingly nature of being'. Phenomenologists see reality as more complicated than just an external material reality approached from a detached and theoretical (human) assessment of that world.[30] In this sense, phenomenology addresses some of the weak points in objectification theory according to its critics. It does not begin with any simple assumptions about subjects or objects. Despite this, Husserl's work was still mainly focused on human consciousness, and on what humans can perceive. However, other thinkers developed his ideas to focus more sharply on the qualities of the world around them.

The 'thingly' dimension of phenomenology is perhaps best illustrated in the works of Husserl's student, Martin Heidegger. Heidegger's work is associated with the term 'dwelling', because he saw the world as not just humans laminating their understandings and symbols over their hard material surroundings, but rather a synthesis (of sorts) of humans and the world: the study of how people dwell, or of their Being. Heidegger's great book *Being and Time* is one of the most important attempts in the twentieth century to critique and escape from the kinds of dualisms we have encountered in the chapters so far. Heidegger argued for critical variations in experience from context to context. The world is not experienced universally as people (subjects) encounter things (objects). On the contrary: humans are inseparable from their world.[31] We are always already *dwelling* within it, we are always Being-in-the-world. Thus there can be no separation between nature and culture, because humans never exist in a state that is prior to their involvement in the world. Being 'unfolds as one interacts with the world over the course of life'.[32] For instance, before you were even born, you were interacting with objects (including your mother's body and outside stimuli such as people's voices) and participating in relationships with them, no matter how simplistic.

Critically, Heidegger found important variation in human–thing relations, distinguishing between 'present-at-hand' (when an observer looks at a thing and contemplates it) versus 'ready-to-hand' (when the thing is engaged in some form of use). His classic example is a hammer and how it might fade in and out of a person's consciousness as a project develops. The hammer moves into the status of 'present-at-hand' when the person contemplates it as an object, perhaps when starting to plan out the project. As the work progresses, the hammer slips into the status of 'ready-to-hand' because it is no longer a singular object, but rather one part of an 'equipmental totality',[33] or a set of relations between the person, the hammer, the nail, the wall being hammered upon and more. Perhaps our carpenter begins contemplating the hammer again (present-at-hand) when the hammer doesn't work as expected, when they are simply marvelling at how well made it is, or more likely when they are cursing it after having smacked it into their thumb. It is also possible that they are forced to contemplate the object in such a way when it is missing.[34] This type of more 'philosophical' assessment between subject and object is the primary focus of objectification, which places less attention on doing and dwelling than phenomenology. This example shows that the hammer (and any thing or set of things, for that matter) can become known to – and intersect with – people in a variety of ways. Heidegger traced the term 'thing' back to its etymological roots, and noted that it came from the old German term 'ding' which meant a gathering. This was critical as it showed, Heidegger argued, how all things were in fact gatherings of relationships. Rather than just an object – 'a hammer' – apart from the world, things, like people, emerge from relationships where the starting point is neither fully human nor fully nonhuman.[35] In this sense, phenomenologists' emphasis on 'things' over 'objects' acknowledges an inter-dependence between human and nonhuman entities, perhaps more so than with the notion of objectification or materiality.[36]

The third philosopher who has influenced archaeological uses of phenomenology has been the French thinker Maurice Merleau-Ponty (1908–61). Merleau-Ponty built upon Heidegger's work, while adding new emphasis on bodily engagement with the world. In particular, he was interested in how humans dwell in a world through their senses. Archaeologists embraced his notion that humans 'grasp the unity of our body only in that of the thing, and it is by taking things as our starting point that our hands, eyes, and all our sense-organs appear to us as so many interchangeable instruments'.[37] For Merleau-Ponty, sensations were not isolated sense-events; they were best understood as a person's immersion, or being, in the world.[38] Remember, our archer only gains skill by engaging the world through her senses. Merleau-Ponty also recognised the critical issue that this emphasis on how our senses reach out into the world blurred the boundaries between bodies and things, just as we saw at the end of Chapter 4. Looking at the way in which blind people used their sticks to reach out into the world, Merleau-Ponty argued that it made little sense to think of the boundaries of our body as being identical to the edge of our skin. Here the divides between people and things become even more difficult to spot.[39]

Unlike Miller's work, which as we saw has been something of a tangential inspiration to archaeologists, phenomenology has been much more directly applied. The most famous application of these ideas has come from Christopher Tilley in a series of engagements beginning with his 1994 book *A Phenomenology of Landscape*. Tilley drew on the work of the different phenomenological philosophers above, especially Merleau-Ponty, to critique the way in which archaeologists had studied landscape up until that point. Archaeology, Tilley argued, primarily approached landscape through maps and measurements from a bird's-eye view. This was not the experience that people would have had in the past. Instead, Tilley argued that you could better understand landscapes by visiting them in person and experiencing them through all of your senses. Here you can see the emphasis on Being-in-the-world. Tilley, as good as his word, took himself off to different sites and landscapes and recorded his experiences. For example, he walked the 9.8km

Dorset Cursus, a Neolithic monument made of two parallel ditches that crosses a chalk plateau known as Cranborne Chase in Dorset, England (Figure 6.3).[40] As he moved along it, Tilley noted the undulation of the ground, the way in which features in the landscape appeared and disappeared, and the manner in which other monuments appeared or were encountered as he progressed. This new perspective allowed him to generate innovative interpretations of how the monument could have been experienced and understood in the past.

Almost immediately, however, Tilley's work came under attack. On the one hand, archaeologists like Andrew Flemming[41] assaulted the accuracy of his interpretations. He argued that Tilley was simply wrong about what you could see and what you could experience at different sites. Various archaeologists like Vicki

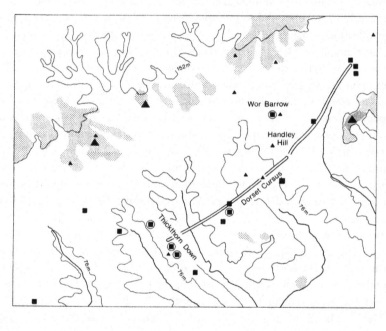

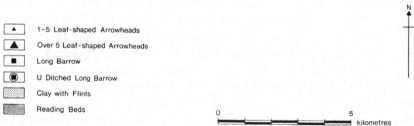

FIGURE 6.3 A bird's-eye view of the Dorset Cursus (a view that Tilley complemented with his on-the-ground explorations)

After Barrett, Bradley and Green 1991, fig. 2.4 © Cambridge University Press

Cummings[42] have since responded to this and found other ways of recording and verifying phenomenological experiences at monuments. Tilley[43] has also provided his own response to Fleming's arguments. More importantly, from a theoretical perspective, was the criticism of Joanna Brück.[44] First she argued that while Tilley might have accurately described his own experiences, they would not be the same as someone of a different gender, or someone who was pregnant, or someone who was differently abled. Even more significantly, she pointed out that Tilley's claim to have shared experiences with people in the past rested upon an explicit claim that the experiences were similar because of a 'common biological humanity'.[45] In other words, they were the same because of our shared nature, despite differences in culture. Can you see what the problem is here? Phenomenology was created to challenge dichotomies, yet here we find that Tilley's phenomenology rests precisely upon the most intransigent of all modern oppositions: nature and culture.[46] As we saw in Chapter 4, though, the body is not something simply natural or eternal; it is something that emerges in different ways in differing historical contexts. While there is an important material element to it, this cannot be reduced to a pre-cultural, universal nature without returning to dualisms.

Tilley's approach has been enormously influential, and often when people in archaeology mention the word phenomenology this is what springs to mind. In many ways it has much in common with other forms of more traditional landscape archaeology, which have often involved visiting sites in person, as Matthew Johnson[47] has noted. However, it would be a significant mistake if one was to presume that this was all phenomenology has to offer archaeology, or indeed this is the only way in which it has been applied. Not only has Tilley developed and added to his arguments in a number of publications, but other archaeologists such as Julian Thomas (Box 6.4) have drawn on Heidegger's work in particular to try and think in more detail about the relationships between people and things. For example, Thomas uses Heidegger's ideas that things are gatherings of relationships to examine artefacts from Late Neolithic Britain.[48] Thomas was critical of the way in which artefacts in Late Neolithic Britain had either been used to identify cultural affiliation (in the manner of culture history that we discussed in Chapter 2) or seen as evidence for a ranked and hierarchical society (drawing on notions from processual archaeology that again we saw in Chapter 2). Rather than seeing these items as bounded 'objects', he examined how these 'things', in the sense that Heidegger defined, helped to create a particular kind of world. Things like antler maceheads, jet belt sliders and polished knives gathered different relationships to them, relationships with the people that had made and used them, the places they had come from and the meanings they revealed.[49] Rather than being solely a 'symbol' either of identity or power, these things disclosed a particular kind of world to the people of Neolithic Britain. This is a quite different kind of phenomenological analysis to Tilley's – these insights do not come from handling the artefacts or experiencing them for oneself. Instead they emerge by thinking about the kinds of Being-in-the-world that are possible within particular sets of relationships with material things, what kinds of Being are revealed against a background of this 'equipmental totality'.

BOX 6.4 JULIAN THOMAS

Julian Thomas is Professor of Archaeology at the University of Manchester. He specialises in the British Neolithic and his publications include *Time, Culture and Identity*[50] and *Archaeology and Modernity*.[51] He draws on Heidegger to think about how material things, like this discoidal knife, can best be thought about *as gatherings of relationships, rather than as bounded objects with essences.*

Image © Museum of London

As we will emphasise in Chapter 8, some theorists still critique phenomeno-logical approaches as anthropocentric, or human-centred.[52] The focus remains on how humans are affected by nonhuman things. In particular in Tilley's work the emphasis falls on how humans experience landscape. Nonetheless, these two examples do not exhaust the ways in which phenomenological philosophy has influenced archaeologists both directly and indirectly.[53] We will encounter Heidegger's influence again especially when we look at Tim Ingold's work in Chapters 8 and 9, and some of Bjørnar Olsen's work in Chapter 10. We're getting ahead of ourselves here, though. One of the consequences of the emphasis on phenomenology and materiality has been a growth in archaeology's interest in how human beings experience the world around them. It is in this fascinating direction that we now turn.

Experiencing the world

When Tilley published *A Phenomenology of Landscape*, it marked the start of an increasing emphasis on archaeologists investigating how people experienced the world, and in particular how they experienced engaging with material things – with materiality. Some of this work followed an openly phenomenological bent. Tilley,[54] for example, went on to write a book in 2004 that focused explicitly on the materiality of stone, considering how people experienced the textures, colours and shapes of this form of substance in different parts of Europe during the Neolithic and Bronze Age. Within this and other work, a critical issue has been embodiment; that is, not only how people have under-stood the body (the kinds of issues around gender and the body we discussed in Chapter 4) but also what it was like to have a particular kind of embodied experience of a particular time and place in the past. These kinds of concerns have led to the development of two overlapping issues. First, a number of archaeologists began to emphasise the way in which the senses play a critical role in how people engage with the world around them. This has run in paral-lel with discussions of other elements of human experience, things that might at first glance be even more ephemeral, such as memory and emotion. Let's set out some examples of each of these in turn.

Archaeologists have been interested in vision for a long time, or at least cer-tain elements of it. What can you see from this monument? Are these two sites inter-visible? More recently, however, archaeologists have begun to think about senses beyond this, including hearing, touch, smell and taste. Vision is a very important sense in the modern world today;[55] after all, how often have you heard someone say 'I'll have to see it to believe it', or in our more social media-savvy age, 'photo or it didn't happen'? When we think about the reality of our daily lives, however, this ignores the way we are constantly relying on all the other senses as well. Indeed, while many people survive in the world without a sense of sight, it would be difficult to imagine how you could operate without a sense of touch. These reconsiderations have challenged the emphasis on vision that has developed over the last few hundred years, and raised the possibility that we need to broaden our understandings of the rich sensory experiences of the past. Robin Skeates,[56] for example, has looked at how we can understand the prehistory of Malta very differently when we put the different sensory experi-ences people would have had in the past at the forefront. Similarly, Cummings[57] examined how Neolithic monuments in Wales were constructed of stones that were made up of very different textures, exploring how touch may have been as important to experiencing these sites as what they looked like. It might seem very speculative to consider these kinds of embodied sensory experiences when thinking about the past. What these archaeologists have stressed, however, is that it is not necessarily about recapturing the *same* experience that others had, but rather attending, once again, to the materiality of the world, the way in which these things bring certain kinds of experiences to the foreground. So whether a rock is smooth or rough is a quality of the materiality of the rock, rather than simply an experience shared between past and present.[58]

In parallel with these discussions, archaeologists have also developed an interest in memory and emotion as elements of experience central to people's past lives. These approaches have not tried to 'remember' what people in the past thought, or feel what they felt, but rather to consider the importance of these elements of people's lives, and how that importance might help us understand some of the remains we encounter today. Authors have explored how treatment of the medieval dead intertwines with different practices of both remembering and forgetting, for example.[59] The importance of memory can also be shown in longer-term historical practices. For example, histories of deposition at the North American site of Cahokia can show memories extending over two generations.[60] At Hambledon Hill, a Neolithic monument in Southern England, we can see longer-term patterns than this. At the main enclosure at this site where the remains of 44 dead people were discovered, only two individuals were buried whole.[61] These were two children, from the same part of the site, both of whom were buried under flint cairns with grave goods. Both were also suffering from the premature fusing of the skulls. The evidence for memory here is that the two children were buried at least 170 years apart. People remembered where the previous child had been buried and in what form over many generations – there are no other burials like this at the site.

Alongside memory, emotion has become an increasingly important element in understanding people's experiences of the past. This may feel like a step too far – surely emotions are the most ephemeral of all things? How can we possibly think about what people in the past were feeling? This is doubly problematic when you think about the fact that anthropologists have shown that emotions are not even necessarily universal among people – the kinds of emotions people feel vary around the world today. The founder of this field of investigation, Sarah Tarlow (Box 6.5),[62] has acknowledged these issues, and stresses that thinking about emotion is not about recovering individual experiences, but rather about exploring the importance of emotion in particular contexts. She has examined how thinking about emotion adds to our understanding of funerary practices in historical contexts. More recently, other archaeologists have tried to think about how the power of emotions may have been central to how people experienced certain kinds of places, or why they treated the dead in the way that they did.[63] In some cases archaeologists have gone on to think about how specific emotions like anxiety and fear may have been at play.[64]

BOX 6.5 SARAH TARLOW

Sarah Tarlow is Professor of Historical Archaeology at the University of Leicester. Author of *Bereavement and Commemoration: An Archaeology of Mortality*, among numerous other books and articles, Tarlow specialises in the archaeology of death and burial, and is best known for her innovative writings on the archaeology of emotion. Her first book focused on cemeteries in the Orkney Islands such as the one pictured here.

By Bob Jones [CC BY-SA 2.0 (http://creativecommons.org/licenses/by-sa/2.0)], via Wikimedia Commons (from https://upload.wikimedia.org/wikipedia/commons/2/2a/St_Magnus_Kirk_ and_graveyard_-_geograph.org.uk_-_1302651.jpg)

For many people looking at experience, whether the senses, memory or emotion, the materiality of objects is critical. Memories can be stimulated by objects – think about what it is like when you see something that used to belong to a loved one, or you find an old school book, or see a photo of a friend. Memories and feelings return unbidden because of the way a smell, a taste, a texture or a sight affects you. These areas are thus explicitly intertwined with one another. As people make and use things, memories are formed that the smell, the shape and the texture of the item can later evoke in the person – people make things and things make people. In perhaps the most sophisticated engagement with the senses, memory and emotion to date, Yannis Hamilakis[65] has explored how these different sensations emerge out of the connections and relations with the material world. His work goes further than any other in thinking about how feelings and memories are not located in the human body alone but rather in our relationships with the world around us. As such, his work and its use of the important notion of 'assemblages' has more in common with some of the themes we discuss in Chapter 8 when we consider new materialism.

Entanglements

The final element of the range of approaches we discuss in this chapter comes from one of the most famous archaeological theorists of all, Ian Hodder. He has combined aspects of objectification, phenomenology and more in *Entangled: An Archaeology of the Relationship between Humans and Things*.[66] Central to Hodder's theory[67] are his notions of human to nonhuman relations, *dependence* (plural *dependences*) and *dependency* (plural *dependencies*). Dependence is an enabling relationship through which humans use things to accomplish new tasks. For example, Heidegger hammering a nail into his wall would be a perfect example of dependence, or a human's reliance upon the hammer. Of course, we must remember that this relationship is contingent upon the hammer working as Heidegger (and almost any person) expects it to. If the wooden handle breaks in two, if the iron head detaches from the handle, if the weight of the tool is too heavy for one to lift and swing easily, the whole relationship breaks down and Heidegger can't hang his painting or mend his broken fence. This notion harkens back to our materiality mantra: people make the hammer and the hammer makes the people (or at least has the potential to help them accomplish new tasks), so long as the hammer operates properly according to its human designers and users. This contingency relates to the second form of dependence explored by Hodder: dependency. Dependency is a constraining relationship between humans and things. As humans interact with things, they become 'involved in various dependencies that limit their ability to develop, as societies or individuals'.[68] Hodder discusses a bottle of whisky and the dependencies it asserts over an alcoholic or recovering alcoholic.

It is important to note that both dependence and dependency are relational terms. The advantages and disadvantages that things offer/assert upon people are not inherent in things themselves. Hodder[69] defines entanglement as *the dialectic relationship between dependence and dependency*. This involves complex webs of relationships between: humans and things; things and things; things and humans; humans and humans. People are caught, ensnared in webs of entanglement (similar to the ways in which phenomenologists theorised dwelling). Hodder is adamant that his entanglement theory is distinct from the other theories explored in this chapter because of the emphasis he places on the 'object-nature' of things. This has to do with the 'material properties of things'.[70] Does this sound familiar? Yes, think back to the definition of materiality introduced at the start of the chapter. The material properties of things serve to entrap people.

The things themselves produce part of the entanglement. Hodder illustrates this with the example of buying a house that is a listed historic property, and thus subject to historical preservation legislation. The house's material properties are such that the roof wears down through time and begins to leak. The buyer must replace the roof, meaning they must have a good paying job or some other means to pay for the new construction. For the house to continue to function according to the buyer's interests and the cultural conventions that dictate how humans and 'historic' houses interact, the buyer is entrapped, partially due to the 'sheer' materiality of the house.

To explore this in an archaeological context, Hodder turns to Çatalhöyük (Box 2.3), a Neolithic tell in Turkey that he and his team have been excavating for many years. The houses at this site that were occupied between 7400 and 6000 cal BC were built out of clay. Just as in the example above with the house buyer in the modern world, this act of construction entangled people and clay into relationships of dependence and dependency. Hodder[71] examines how the decision to build the walls out of clay, and the specific properties of the clay they used, trapped people into a series of relationships with their material surroundings. The particular clays people were using were very prone to swelling and shrinking and thus to collapse. This meant people had to work to prop up the walls with posts, continually re-plaster the walls and so on. As they chopped down trees to make posts, trees disappeared from the landscape, so people had to make thicker walls and use different clays dug from deeper sources. This new clay was sandier and could be moulded in new ways, allowing for new and more complex technologies to emerge that took more time and labour. By making the decision to build their first houses out of clay, Hodder brilliantly shows how the people at Çatalhöyük became trapped by the materiality surrounding them.

In Chapter 8, we will learn of a set of radical orientations to archaeological theory that question whether this type of 'sheer' materiality could ever be singled out within complex mixtures (what we will later call 'hybrids' in the terms of Bruno Latour) of human and nonhumans. For now, we will simply note that Hodder[72] critiques the extreme anti-dualism of the arguments we will encounter later, arguing that their insistence on hybrids and networks goes too far. According to Hodder, some phenomena, like the end of the Ice Age, are completely independent of humans. Others, like your leaking historic roof, ensnare humans because of their physical properties (e.g., the gradual decay of wet wood), which operate separately from humans. Hodder's theory of entanglement explores how humans and things are entrapped in complex webs of dependence and dependency. He focuses on the importance of the object-nature of things, in contrast to those thinkers making heavy use of objectification, phenomenology or some combination thereof. Despite his protestations, therefore, elements of Hodder's entanglement theory share qualities with the symmetrical and new materialist ideas we will encounter in Chapter 8. Yet he still frames humans and nonhumans as distinctive in some ways. He explicitly argues that we can best understand this within a dialectical relationship where human–nonhuman relationships are primary.[73] This is why we discuss the heart of Hodder's theory here rather than in later chapters of the book.

Conclusions: person makes arrow, arrow makes person

What similarities and differences can you pick out from a general comparison of theories of objectification, phenomenology, experience and entanglement? All four approaches concern themselves with the complex set of relations that exist between humans and their worlds. Let us return to our friend the archer to think about each of these in turn.

We have seen already how, for those interested in objectification, the critical issue is that as people engage with things, they transform themselves. So here the possibility of being an archer emerges with the use of a bow and arrow, with the repeated acts of practice that allow a person to acquire the necessary skills. Each use of the bow will change the person, just as it changes the bow itself (wearing the bowstring down or altering the flexibility of the wood). From a phenomenological perspective, especially of the sort that Julian Thomas has argued for, we could think about how the bow allows new forms of Being-in-the-world to come into existence. The bow allows new kinds of relationships to be formed between the archer and the thing they are shooting at. While using the bow, the phenomenologist might point out, you don't really think about the bow itself – you think about your target, or perhaps if you are a skilled archer like a skilled driver of a car, you don't really think at all. Here the bow is ready-to-hand, and as such it gathers together the relations between the person, the bow, the arrow and the thing they are shooting at, and allows the person to exist in a new way.

Those interested in experience would agree with a lot of this, but they would also point out that we could think about how the freshly oiled bowstring might have smelt; how it could evoke memories of previous hunts and the person who taught you to use a bow. The memories here aren't in the head of the person using the bow, but emerge *relationally* again from the way in which the bow evokes a response in the person through its impact on the senses. Finally, Hodder might look at the way in which the bow entangles a person into new kinds of relationship. By using the bow you might become the person your family relies on to get food. This means you need to spend more time knapping flints for arrows and looking after your bow; more time out in the landscape. Here the bow and the person are caught up in relationships that were not intended or planned for, but have consequences nonetheless. Which of these approaches you select may depend as much on the kinds of questions you want to ask of your archaeological material as the nature of the theories themselves.

In all of these examples the issue of materiality is critical and the relationship between people and things has come to the foreground. Even more than with Alfred Gell and the object agency we discussed in Chapter 5, we now see how people and things are active players in the world, and that there are different ways of approaching this. However, interesting questions remain. Are the meanings associated with the material properties of things still something that human beings apply to the world around them? Should we be focused on dialectical relationships between people and things? Or could we think about the world in broader terms; could we think about whole networks or assemblages of relationships that include human beings, but do not place them always in the centre? These are the important questions archaeologists have started to ask themselves in the last few years, and it is to these that the next chapters turn.

Notes

1 Fitzpatrick 2011.
2 Hodder 2012; see also Hodder 2016.
3 Boivin 2008; Gosden 2004; Hicks and Beaudry 2010; Hodder 2011, 2012; Jones 2012; Knappett 2005, 2014; Meskell 2005; Meskell and Preucel 2006; Miller 2005; Tilley et al. 2006. See also Ingold 2007a; Webmoor and Witmore 2008.
4 You would likely also discover that the term originated in law, specifically in accounting. In that context, materiality refers to the importance of line items as they relate to different economic transactions and decisions; for example, if a client misses a monthly payment of 50 GBP to a bank worth one billion GBP, the problem is classified as 'immaterial' because, by itself, the missing payment could not impact the bank and its employees' abilities to make sound business decisions.
5 Miller 2005: 4.
6 Miller 2006: 60.
7 This idea also connects nicely with materiality's origins in accounting. Depending on how they relate to humans – helping, hurting or somewhere in between – things represented by line items on a receipt, tax record or probate inventory have different relative values.
8 Miller 1994.
9 Miller 2008.
10 Miller 2010.
11 Hodder 2012: 30.
12 Miller 2006: 60.
13 Miller 1995, but see also Miller 2005.
14 Hegel 1977.
15 Miller 2005: 8.
16 Meskell 2004, 2005.
17 Meskell 2005: 54–8.
18 Meskell 2005: 58–62.
19 Meskell 2004.
20 Webmoor and Witmore 2008; see also Pinney 2005.
21 See also Pinney 2005 for a critique of objectification as what Latour (1993) would call 'purification' (see Chapter 8).
22 Miller 2005: 9.
23 Miller 2005.
24 E.g. Tilley 2004.
25 Tilley 1994.
26 Thomas 1993.
27 Thomas 2006: 48.
28 Thomas 2006: 44.
29 Hodder 2012: 27.
30 Hodder 2012: 27.
31 Hodder 2012: 28.
32 Hodder 2012: 28.

33 Thomas 2006: 46–7; Hodder 2012: 27–30.
34 See Fowles 2010.
35 Hodder 2012: 27–30.
36 Ingold 2012.
37 Merleu-Ponty 1962: 322.
38 Fisher and Loren 2003; Loren 2003, 2007; Thomas 2004: 48.
39 See Malafouris 2013 for a full exploration of the impact of this on archaeology.
40 Tilley 1994: 170–201.
41 Fleming 2005, 2006.
42 E.g. Cummings 2009: Chapter 6.
43 Tilley 2012.
44 Brück 1998, 2005.
45 Tilley 1994: 74.
46 Although do look at Tilley's (2012: 474) response to these accusations.
47 Johnson 2012.
48 Thomas 1996: chapter 6.
49 Thomas 1996: 159.
50 Thomas 1996.
51 Thomas 2004.
52 Hodder 2012: 28.
53 Thomas 2015a: 1288.
54 Tilley 2004.
55 Cf. Thomas 2004: 178–9.
56 Skeates 2010.
57 Cummings 2002.
58 Cf. Hamilakis 2012: 6.
59 Williams 2003.
60 Pauketat 2008: 79.
61 Harris 2010; Mercer and Healy 2008.
62 Tarlow 1999, 2000, 2012.
63 E.g. Harris 2009, 2010; Harris and Sørensen 2010; Nilsson Stutz 2003; Sørensen 2015.
64 Fleisher and Norman 2016.
65 Hamilakis 2013.
66 Hodder 2012; see also Hodder 2016.
67 Hodder 2012: 17–18.
68 Hodder 2012: 18.
69 Hodder 2012: 88.
70 Hodder 2012: 95.
71 Hodder 2012: 66–7.
72 Hodder 2012: 93.
73 Hodder 2012: 94.

7

MEDIATING THE WORLD

Archaeological semiotics

Introduction: signs in a lonely forest

If a tree falls in the forest and no one is there to hear it, does it make a sound? As you can see in Figure 7.1, our trusty trowel looks thoroughly perplexed! The answer to this classic philosophical question has everything to do with how you understand the world. It all depends upon your particular take on what reality 'is' and how it relates to human observation and understanding. On the one hand, the empiricist insists that, yes indeed, there is a world 'out there' just waiting for us to discover, record, measure and interpret. On the other hand, a 'constructivist' might focus on the ways in which the world is only known through our subjectivity as human beings.[1] Think back to the last chapter where we discussed knowing the world through our senses. Remember how we cautioned against making any assumptions about the *universal* nature of human experience and understanding? If you enjoy this sort of debate, you can look forward to Chapter 10, where we expand such arguments to think critically about ontologies and the possibility for multiple worlds out there instead of just one. For now, let us get back to that poor old tree. Sound or no sound?

If your answer is, 'yes, the tree makes a sound, even when there are no people to hear it', the implications are that human perception has little to do with shaping the world, of which people are only one part. Reality is simply there for humans to observe when they can. On the other hand, if the answer is, 'no, there is no sound unless a human is there to process and interpret it', this implies that human perception plays a large part in creating reality. Therefore what we see, hear, smell, taste and feel is by and large a product of our own unique cultural perspectives. Since people have no way in which to understand the world other than through their own perception, reality is culturally constructed. We have been referring to this type of perspective as anthropocentric because it frames humans (*anthropos*) and human perspectives as more important than the other animals, plants, rocks and soil that make up the forest in this example.

With the first option, humans and nonhumans start on a more equal footing when it comes to making up and participating in the real world. In contrast, the second option frames humans as the centre of the 'real world' in the sense that all reality perceived by humans is shaped, processed and organised in terms of culture. This question grows even more complicated when we recognise that other living beings like the plants and animals in the forest also perceive and interpret the sound in their own ways, but we will set that question aside for now and pick it up again in Chapter 9, where we will even explore 'semiotic' relationships between the sun and a sunflower.

In the last chapter we explored how people make things and things make people. In this chapter, we explore how semiotics – the study of signs – might shed light on these feedback loops of cultural reproduction and human–thing entanglement. In this sense, we maintain our focus on the role of dualisms in archaeological theory, while investigating a relatively new set of approaches to these problems. As we will see, according to some thinkers, semiotics sheds new light on the ways in which archaeologists think about the past and the things that they dig up in the present.[2] Hold on a minute, though – we haven't even explained what a *sign* is! As with the other chapters, we need to proceed with caution. Let us begin with a broad definition for signs as *any type of stimulus that invokes a response by a living thing*.[3] This means that the sound that a tree makes when it falls *could* be a type of sign, just as the printed words on this page, autumn leaves blowing across a field or the nervous twitch of a student in a university examination are also potential signs. Each of these examples has the potential to elicit some type of response, but only if

FIGURE 7.1 Contemplating our tree. Drawing by K-Fai Steele

'read' by a person. The potential responses range from moving your body to avoid being hit over the head by the tree, to connecting the characters T-H-E-O-R-Y to that concept discussed in class last week when your professor brought up the topic of materiality (Chapter 6); and from understanding that you might need a scarf when you go outdoors to keep the chill off to flashing a reassuring smile to the nervous student to help them remain as calm as possible.

So why exactly do some archaeologists find semiotic theory interesting and useful? It is true that most of the examples covered thus far are rarely studied in archaeological circles. After all, when was the last time you read an archaeological account of trees falling in the forest? This is a very fair point, but could we conceptualise the things and patterns that archaeologists find and interpret as signs? For example, we could apply the semiotic theories explored in this chapter to think about how archaeologists look at a charred feature that sits in the middle of a ring of small postholes and interpret it as the remains of a hearth that once sat in the middle of some sort of domestic structure. We could apply these concepts to think about how people in the past used and understood signs. How did its users understand that domestic structure? What meanings and understandings were associated?

Oftentimes, archaeologists thinking about semiotics tend to focus only on representation, or how certain stimuli are thought to represent other concepts. This we might call a *standing-for relationship*; for example, how the characters T-H-E-O-R-Y represent the concept of 'theory' or how a certain flag represents a nation state. As explained below, some semiotic approaches include much more than the study of this type of representation. However, we shouldn't get ahead of ourselves, so let's begin with small steps. Don't get us wrong; there is much to *fear* about semiotic theory, not least its seemingly warm embrace of loads of esoteric terminology that only your professor seems to get. If we give it a chance, however, we can link these new ideas up with the arguments set forth in earlier chapters. In the following two sections, we briefly compare the two most prominent thinkers in semiotics: Ferdinand de Saussure and Charles Sanders Peirce, neither of whom was an archaeologist. In making this comparison, we introduce some terminology that will help us unpack basic semiotic theory for archaeologists. We will maintain a close eye on this terminology so as not to lose you in a theoretical and terminological haze. Our comparison will also help us to draw your attention to some important contrasts between Saussure and Peirce.

Do you recall our discussion of early postprocessual archaeologies from Chapter 2? This was when archaeologists, sick and tired of thinking about adaptation to environments, began delving into the world of past meanings and symbols. This was a world fraught with dualisms, as we will show with our discussion of Saussure, who inspired structuralism. We contrast the structural semiotics of Saussure and early postprocessual archaeology with the work of Peirce and his followers. Here we emphasise the recent uptick of archaeologists making use of Peirce's writings, often as a means of escaping the dualisms of structuralism while still maintaining a focus on meanings and symbolism. For some, Peirce offers a way to have their 'symbolic' cake and eat it too; that is, without choking on our old friend dualisms. As we saw in the last chapter, many archaeologists turned towards theories of materiality and away from discussions of meaning precisely because they felt that the latter ignored the 'thingly' nature of the world. Accounts that draw on Peirce seek to create space for meaning within an account that also makes room for materials and their relations.[4] It thus comes as no surprise that interest in his ideas has grown since the emergence of materiality studies.[5] After our introduction to Peirce, we look to some examples of his ideas in recent applications of semiotics in archaeology, considering new ceramics in the Black Sea and hybrid architectural forms in Southern Africa.

With a brief return to our fallen tree in the lonely forest, we conclude the chapter, setting us up to move on to a new and radical movement in archaeology theory that seriously challenges the assumed distinctions that semiotic archaeology makes between living and non-living matter.

Two sides of Saussure

The linguist Ferdinand de Saussure (Box 7.1) is a central figure in semiotic theory. It helps to remember that, for our purposes, Saussure's linguistic analysis shares many similarities with structuralism (Chapter 2). Structuralism doesn't necessarily focus only on language, but its roots tie directly to Saussure,[6] whose main interest was language and how it represents concepts. He understood signs as composed of two main parts: the *signifier* and the *signified* (Box 7.1, Table 7.1). For our purposes, the signifier is the stimulus (usually the sound of a word or words that the listener hears). The signified is the corresponding concept conjured in the listener's mind (i.e., whatever is being represented by the signifier). Saussure wondered how it was possible that when English speakers heard the utterance 'dog' or read the characters 'D-O-G', it brought to mind a set of furry four-legged creatures ranging in size and shape from a chihuahua to a mastiff. Certainly, in this case, there is no 'natural' connection between signifier and signified. In other words, the sound that you make when you pronounce 'dog' bears no resemblance to the four-legged creature. Adding to these complications is the fact that people who do not speak English simply do not make this connection. When German speakers observe the same set of four-legged creatures that English speakers know as 'dogs', the Germans think, 'hunde'.

Saussure pointed out that this is because *nearly* all linguistic signs or words are composed of a signifier and signified that share an *arbitrary* relationship that is established through *cultural convention* (Box 7.2). In other words, the only reason that you, the reader of this text, associate the characters 'D-O-G' with the same class of animals that we the authors do is because at some point in your life someone told you to make the connection. As a child, you probably failed to pick it up right away. However, as you explored the world and pointed to different things around you while speaking the word 'dog', your family either encouraged you or corrected you to the point where you remembered what could acceptably be classified

BOX 7.1 FERDINAND DE SAUSSURE

Ferdinand de Saussure (1857–1913) was a Swiss linguist who held a professorship in the history and comparative study of Indo-European languages at the University of Geneva.[7] In 1906, he began teaching a course on general linguistics, which became the basis for his *Cours de linguistique generale*,[8] still used today by linguists across the globe. This diagram shows the structure of a sign according to Saussure; the two parts are the signifier (the stimulus) and the signified (e.g., an image conjured by a stimulus).

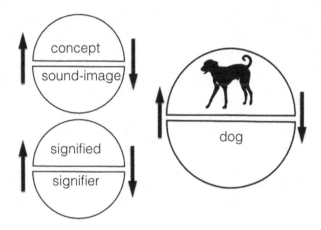

Dog illustration by Amada44 (own work) [public domain], via Wikimedia Commons; illustration by Craig Cipolla after Saussure 1986: 6

as dog and not–dog. This example reminds the second author of the time when his two–year–old daughter, confronted with an exceptionally large black and white Great Dane on the street, looked earnestly at him for a bit before offering her form of greeting: 'Mooooo'. There is always room to adjust our understanding of the categories, of course! This is how cultural convention works. And this is the usual way that people learn to interpret and use language. With only a few exceptions, linguistic signs elicit uniform responses across massive parts of the human population because the people and culture around us tell us how to connect words to their socially and culturally acceptable concepts.

Do you smell a rat? Ah yes, it must be dualisms again. Saussurian semiotics operates using a number of dualisms, including signifier/signified, sound/concept and – an old favourite – material/immaterial. As we will discuss in Chapters 8 and 10, this type of approach to meaning and symbolism has lately received a fair share of critique. We have been told that it tends to 'marginalise' material things only as empty vehicles for human meaning.[9] This indeed is one of the reasons that archaeologists became so interested in the kinds of materiality we met in the last chapter. In this sense, it appears that the Saussurian or structuralist approach also artificially separates out humans – by virtue of their fantastical representational capabilities – from the rest of the world. This is certainly true to a degree, but Saussure did recognise some ways in which the world 'out there' shapes human signs and systems of meaning (although it is fair to say these did not play a major role in his work). The best examples are *onomatopoeic* words such as 'buzz' or 'oink'. For these types of signs, the signifier connects to the signified in a non-arbitrary manner. We do not necessarily make the connection because people and culture guide us. Instead the connection is made because of resemblance between signifier and signified; what we will later refer to as an *iconic* relationship. Thus, the experience of hearing the utterance 'buzz' actually resembles the experience of hearing a bee buzz by your ear. Above, did you immediately know what animal with which the second author's daughter confused the dog? This is because the utterance or signifier, 'Moooo', resembles the actual sound that cows make (signified). These examples are quite interesting when we apply them back to the quandary of our lonely forest example raised in the introduction. This is because they begin to challenge the distinction set out there between empiricism (focused on the reality 'out there' independent of human perception) and constructivism (focused on how humans construct reality through a cultural lens). We might say that most language represents concepts in an arbitrary way (constructed), while onomatopoeic words take influence from the world 'out there' that is partially shaped by human perception and interpretation.

This is because the differences between arbitrary relationships (cultural convention) and relationships of resemblance (iconic) are not exclusive of one another. This is best illustrated when studying variation in onomatopoeic words between speakers of different languages. For example, an English speaker will report that a bee makes the sound 'buzz' or 'bzzz' while the German speaker mimics the same bee as 'sum'.[10] How can the same exact reality – the bee droning – resemble two very different utterances? Perhaps human perception is more arbitrarily and culturally constructed than we previously thought, but we will leave this issue until the end of the chapter.

There is one last shortcoming of Saussurian-inspired approaches that we must point out here: their ability, or lack thereof, to understand and account for change. This issue sounds like something that would raise warning flags for archaeologists! Language is always changing as we put it to use and refer to new things in our world. After all, if we had a time machine, it is safe to assume that even though we would be able to communicate quite effectively with our pre-4 February 2004 selves, before the invention of Facebook, we had no linguistic means of referring to Facebook 'pages', 'likes' and 'pokes'. Yet our language is flexible and fluid enough that it has adapted. Similar to the flexible and creative process of cultural reproduction outlined in Chapter 3, as people put language to use in new contexts, they are constantly introducing change. This has to do with the difference between what Saussure referred to as *langue* and *parole*. For our purposes, langue is the dictionary definitions of words and the grammatical rules that link them, while parole is the way in which words are actually used and transformed as part of speech. These new concepts sound similar to structure and agency (Chapter 3). The reason why we need to constantly publish new dictionaries with amendments is because of the change introduced when we actually put language to use in new contexts (e.g., the world before Facebook and the world after). Like practice, agency and structure explored in Chapter 3, language is dynamic and ever changing. Unfortunately for us, Saussure was largely interested in the *langue* side of the equation. In other words, he was interested primarily in the structures of language that people must learn to communicate with one another rather than the 'living' language that is constantly in a state of transformation. Since, in Chapter 3, we learned that practice and structure are part of the same process, and therefore cannot be artificially separated, this deficiency of Saussurian semiotics should give us pause.

Perhaps an example with material culture might help. Since we have been referencing Chapter 3 already, think back to Bourdieu's Kabyle households (Box 3.1). As you'll recall, he found a fascinating spatial pattern in the houses. They were organised by principles of opposition like female space/male space, dark/light and low/high. A structuralist might focus only on these organising relationships. The female section of the house sits in a particular relation to the male section of the house similar to the way that the dark section of the house exists in relation to the light section of the house. By observing these material patterns, the structuralist would seek to reconstruct the mental 'template' that generated them. They would assume a direct, reflective relationship between the two. This means that structuralism looks at the material world as a reflection of thoughts and concepts in people's heads. The linguist deals with the material world (the materiality of spoken language consists of vibrations in the air) to figure out what it represents (the immaterial, mental template) in the same way that a structural archaeologist might use the materiality of the Kabyle house.

TABLE 7.1 Summary of terminology discussed in relation to Saussure and structuralism

Term	Basic definition
Signifier	Sound or image that links to a concept (the signified); one part of a sign
Signified	Concept conjured by signifier; one part of a sign
Cultural convention	Cultural cues that establish an arbitrary relationship between signifier and signified (together they make a sign)
Icon	Sign with signifier and signified linked through resemblance rather than cultural convention
Langue	Linguistic structure; 'dictionary' definitions; the rules of grammar
Parole	Linguistic practice; language as used in speech (transformative)

Pierre Bourdieu recognised a problem with this approach, didn't he? He sought to figure out how it was that these patterns were reproduced though time, from generation to generation, and argued for the importance of practice and how it conditions human bodies to act in certain ways. But his practice theory leaves room for change. In contrast, Saussurian semiotics, like the structuralism that it inspired, has no way to account for change or for the fact that many of us now know and understand the thing called 'Facebook'. Thinkers like Bourdieu and Giddens asked us to look at the relationships between practice/agency and structure. Drawing on the work of a second key thinker in semiotics, Charles Sanders Peirce, our next section considers ways of avoiding structuralist dualisms while maintaining a focus on symbolism and meaning in general.

Three cheers for Peirce

Archaeologists began seriously experimenting with the semiotics of Charles Sanders Peirce about 15 years ago.[11] If this topic piques your interest, you can read more on the history of semiotics in archaeology and anthropology in Robert Preucel's *Archaeological Semiotics*.[12] Since presenting an in-depth history of the field is well beyond the scope of this book,[13] here we simply focus on a bare-bones summary of Peircian theory as it relates to contemporary archaeological theory.[14] It is worth noting that Peirce was far from a popular writer, in the sense that his work is filled with jargon and neologisms that tend to discourage new readers. Having recognised this point, it is also important to note that many of his terms and concepts that we do not explore in this chapter are absolutely necessary to obtain a complete understanding of his approach to semiotics.

Compared to Saussure and his conception of the two-part sign (signifier and signified), Peirce[15] (Box 7.2) thought of all signs as composed of three parts: Sign, Object and Interpretant[16] (Table 7.2). Similar to Saussure's signifier, the Sign is the focus of someone's or something's perception.[17] The Object is the meaning of the Sign that exists in the world 'out there', external from the interpreter. Finally, the Interpretant is the meaning of the Sign that is conjured by the interpreter.[18] The Interpretant is also a potentially new Sign in the sense that the interpreter may react to the observed Sign–Object relation in some way that has meaning for another observer. It is through the Object that humans and other living entities are able

TABLE 7.2 Peirce's triadic sign

Term	Basic definition
Sign	Something perceived by an interpreter
Object	Meaning of Sign; exists outside of interpreter
Interpretant	Meaning of Sign; connection between Sign and Object made by interpreter; potentially becomes a new Sign

BOX 7.2 CHARLES SANDERS PEIRCE

Charles Sanders Peirce (1839–1914) was an American philosopher and a founder of pragmatism.[19] He was a lecturer at Johns Hopkins University. Peirce's prolific writings cover a vast variety of topics, including semiotics.[20] His essays, *What is a Sign?*,[21] *Of Reasoning in General*[22] and *The Categories Defended*,[23] are excellent starting points for new readers. This diagram illustrates the structure of a sign according to Peirce; note the three-part system, which sits in direct contrast to the Saussurian sign from Box 7.1. The bracket connecting Sign to Object represents the link that exists between Sign and Object for a specific interpreter.

Illustration by Craig Cipolla after Bauer 2013

to recognise, experience and interpret Signs. As we illustrate next, Objects relate to Signs in three major ways, one of which is through regularity or cultural convention such as the case with many linguistic signs discussed in the previous section (e.g., 'dog' conjures the notion of a specific set of furry four-legged creatures).

As we are beginning to see, a reoccurring theme in Peirce's writings is the number three. Just like the sign itself – made up of Sign, Object and Interpretant – Peirce[24] saw three types of connection between Sign and Object, which we can call *sign modes* (Table 7.3). Because we have already introduced Saussure and his focus on the conventions of language, it makes most sense to begin this exploration of Peirce's work with a discussion of *symbols*.[25] The Sign and Object of a symbol are connected through cultural convention, created and reiterated for an interpreter through social regularities. Symbols include the type of sign in which Saussure was most interested: language. In archaeological interpretation, symbols are perhaps the most difficult type of sign to understand because they are arbitrarily and culturally constructed.

Next is the *icon*,[26] composed of a Sign and Object connected through physical resemblance (Table 7.3). Onomatopoeic words are an excellent example since the Sign (e.g., the utterance 'buzz') resembles the Object (a droning bee) for some interpreters. Archaeological typologies are also good examples of how iconic signs work. For example, when an archaeologist finds flint tools in an Upper Palaeolithic deposit (Figure 7.2), the Signs would be the freshly dusted-off lithic artefacts and the Object would be the general types assigned to those tools by the interpreter.

FIGURE 7.2 Upper Palaeolithic flints from various sites in the UK and Europe

Photograph courtesy of the Royal Ontario Museum

Because the Signs (the new artefacts) resemble their Objects (types based on different characteristics of various Upper Palaeolithic flints), the archaeologist is confident of what they have found. However, we should note that the Objects in this case exist beyond the individual archaeologist's understanding, since it is really up to the wider archaeological community and their relationship to all other things known as Upper Palaeolithic flint artefacts.

We turn last to the trickiest sign mode, the *index*,[27] or indication. This is when the Sign and Object are linked through a spatiotemporal connection for an interpreter (Table 7.3). The classic example that Peirce used is the weather vane on a windy day.[28] To gauge the wind direction (Object), the farmer looks out the window at the orientation of the weather vane (Sign). Here, the Object is physically pushing the Sign in a certain direction. Indexical signs are everywhere, including in language. For example, when you say, 'come here', the sign 'here' shares a spatial and temporal link with the intended Object, or the spot where you are speaking from at that very moment in time. In summary, Objects exist in the external world beyond the interpreter, either as a physical presence in the case of icons and indexes or as a general regularity, as is the case for symbols.[29]

Now that we have covered the basics of the three sign modes, it is time that we deal with the overall triadic structure of Peirce's system. As we mentioned above,

TABLE 7.3 Peirce's sign modes (ways a Sign connects to an Object)

Term	Basic definition
Icon	Sign and Object linked by physical resemblance to one another for an interpreter
Index	Sign and Object linked by physical connection in space-time for an interpreter
Symbol	Sign and Object arbitrarily linked through cultural convention for an interpreter

this structure allows for a more dynamic perspective on the use and transformation of signs in society. This is because the Interpretant is also a new Sign created by the observer of a Sign–Object relationship. In contrast to Saussure, and his primary interest in langue (structure) rather than parole (practice), here we get a glimpse of the forward-looking quality of the Peircian semiotic. As illustrated in Box 7.2, every Sign serves as mediator between the Object behind and the Interpretant ahead.[30]

The most widely used example of Peirce's semiotic process comes from the linguist Richard Parmentier.[31] He offered the example of a golfer looking to judge the direction of the wind. Having left his weather vane at home, the golfer inconspicuously tears a few blades of grass from the ground and throws them in the air, observing their movement as they fall. Here the direction of the wind (Object) shares an indexical connection with the movement of the grass blades as they fall (Sign). Someone or something has to make the connection: the golfer in this case, who hits the ball in a certain way (the Interpretant[32]) based on their understanding of the wind and the results of their little grass experiment. And as we mentioned, Interpretants have the potential to serve as new Signs. Perhaps a second, less experienced golfer approaches the first and simply decides to hit the ball in the same direction as the first golfer (old Interpretant/new Sign). The way in which golfer 1 hits the ball based on his grass experiment is a new Sign for golfer 2 (new Interpretant), iconically connected to its Object, perhaps the notion of 'being a competent golfer' (Figure 7.3).

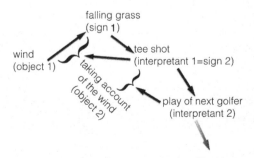

FIGURE 7.3 Diagram of the semiotic process

Illustration by Craig Cipolla after Bauer 2013: 16. See also Parmentier 1994; Peirce Edition Project 1998

Archaeological semiotics

Alexander Bauer[33] uses Peirce's ideas on semiotics to interpret a curious pattern of Early Bronze Age material culture found along the coastal regions of the Black Sea (Figure 7.4). Bauer notes that deposits dating between 3300 and 2100 cal BC in the region often included new types of material culture, not previously used in the area but bearing close resemblance to assemblages collected from all across the region during that time. In other words, communities across the coast of the Black Sea began constructing and using similar types of architecture, pottery and metalwork. They also began organising space in their settlements and using resources in similar ways.[34] Bauer is particularly interested in the manufacture and use of a unique type of handmade, dark burnished ceramics (Figure 7.5) that appeared at approximately the same time across the entire region.

Here we have a very clear archaeological pattern to interpret, so how does Peirce help? As Bauer[35] frames the question, 'how might we confront the apparent sameness or "iconicity" emergent in Early Bronze Age pottery in the Black Sea, and how might have emerging social relationships across the region at this time been signalled and in part constituted by these similarities'? Interestingly, there is no clear geographical origin point for this new type of pottery. In other words,

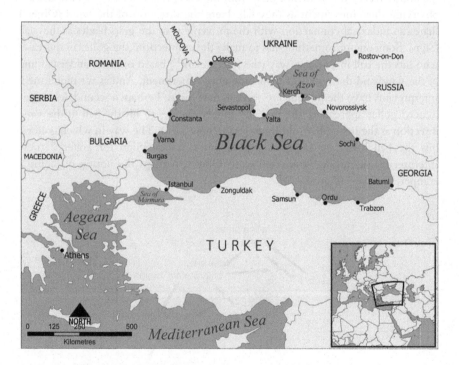

FIGURE 7.4 Map of the Black Sea region

it is not the case that a single group invented the pottery type and then shared it through either direct communication or trade with neighbouring communities, allowing the new ceramic type to diffuse across the landscape. Additionally, Bauer notes that there is no evidence for major trading activity between the various communities that shared the new pottery type.

From a Peircian standpoint, this archaeological problem is not about people changing the world intentionally through agency (see Chapter 3), but rather about how *the results* of various forms of agency were viewed and interpreted by the wider community of ceramic users or observers. This focus moves us beyond questions of human intention to consider practical outcomes of agencies, both human and nonhuman (Chapters 5 and 6). Bauer primarily concerns himself not with *why* the new pottery appears but with *how* this appearance impacted the broader societies that created and used it. Here, he argues, the new pottery type situated the community of users in the social world that it was simultaneously helping to create.[36]

In Bauer's interpretation, the way in which the new pots 'stood' rather than just 'stood for' was important in this case. The material qualities of the new pottery that popped up in any one community on the coast at this time physically resembled (iconically) the pots used by all other communities across the coastal region. As you'll recall from above, iconic sign modes involve material qualities that in some way force themselves on interpreters through physical resemblance. In this case, a person from one community, having knowledge of what ceramics look like 'at home' (Object), might – through travel or trade – encounter a pot (Sign) from a 'foreign' community that lives across the sea. For the interpreter, this is an iconic sign mode, perhaps conjuring up thoughts (indexically) about similarities between

FIGURE 7.5 Black Sea ceramics

Photograph courtesy of Alexander Bauer

his or her home community and the far-off community (Interpretant). Eventually, perhaps by realising that inland communities use distinct types of pottery, the iconicity of pottery types across the coastal region might transform into symbols of social identity, pointing to (or creating) some sort of distinction between insiders and outsiders for interpreters. Do you remember the marked trowels at your field school from Chapter 3? This is a similar situation.

Zoe Crossland (Box 7.3),[37] another leader in archaeological semiotics, uses Peirce's triadic framework to interpret new architectural forms and settlement patterns that emerged in nineteenth-century Southern Africa (Figure 7.6). She explains that the new spatial patterns had something to do with the arrival of European Christian missionaries, who brought with them foreign ideas and expectations of how to live along with explicit motivations to change the ways in which local indigenous populations both lived in – and saw – the world.

BOX 7.3   ZOE CROSSLAND

Zoe Crossland is Associate Professor of Anthropology at Columbia University. Crossland is known for her innovative use of Peircian semiotics in archaeology. In her recent book, *Encounters with Ancestors in Highland Madagascar: Material Signs and Traces of the Dead*,[38] she examines how standing stones in Madagascar like the one pictured here mediated relationships between the living and the dead via complicated material semiotic interactions and entanglements.

Standing stone on pathway leading to the fortified site of Ambohitrandriananahary, visible in the background. Imerina, Highland Madagascar 2003. Photograph by Zoe Crossland, reproduced with permission

Prior to missionary intervention, indigenous settlements in the region were laid out in concentric patterns made up of a circular arrangement of house compounds with a main court and the chief's ward located in the centre.[39] Surrounding the chief's ward were the other wards of the settlement, with all wards surrounded by agricultural fields, then pastureland and finally uncultivated land.[40] Houses were circular in plan, reproducing the larger pattern of the very wards they composed. Most houses were constructed in an expedient fashion to help facilitate easy relocation in times of environmental stress, for example when grazing grounds became worn-out and fallow.

In contrast to these patterns were the missionaries' traditions of permanent, square or rectilinear houses and settlement layouts. As part of their efforts to convert indigenous peoples to Christianity, missionaries encouraged them to reject their own traditions of architecture in favour of rectangular-plan houses. As Crossland notes, these introduced forms of architecture 'embodied British values of privacy and the divided and gendered taskscape of the domestic home'.[41]

As the missionary project continued in Southern Africa, new forms of architecture emerged. However, the resulting archaeological patterns are quite complicated. This is where Peircian semiotics comes in handy. We can start by

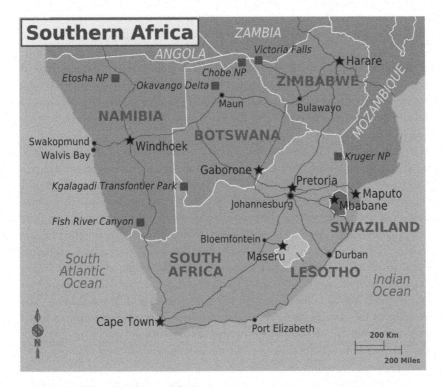

FIGURE 7.6 Map of Southern Africa

By Nick Roux and Shaund (own work based on a map of Africa) [public domain], via Wikimedia Commons

considering the shift to rectilinear architectural forms as a strategy for changing indigenous perspectives. For the missionaries, their 'type' of buildings certainly acted as exemplars of how to live in a good Christian way. Missionaries sought to push these ways of building into indigenous settlements and homes, making them part of the everyday lives of indigenous populations. Crossland[42] aptly notes that we can interpret these missionary actions, in Peircian terms, as Signs with different connections to the same Object: one is iconic, the other indexical. In their attempts to reproduce the spatial patterning of British settlements, new missionary structures in Southern Africa were icons of remembered houses and settlements in the missionaries' homeland. Likewise, they were icons of the missionaries' ideal vision for indigenous living. However, missionary architecture was only iconic for those observers who had memories of England and 'civilised' life. A suite of indexical signs were required to communicate to local indigenous people the set of iconic sign relations present in missionary buildings. Indexical sign relations are about experience rather than representation (see Table 7.2). For example, closed doorways physically made sections of the buildings private by restricting movement, while other material presences encouraged or even forced certain types of practice. The way in which a teacup's shape encourages you to pick it up and hold it in a certain manner or the way in which the teacup is offered in one part of a building and not another index certain types of practice. In other words, one had to physically experience the space and its indexicality for it to function as an icon of new ways of 'civilised' living; that is, for it to function as intended by the missionaries. Unfortunately for them, the local indigenous population – lacking previous experience with such spaces – learned about them through their own cultural perspectives rather than from the perspective of the missionaries. This problem of translation left plenty of opportunities for indigenous 'ways of doing and seeing' to persist in spite of the missionaries' goals.

These interactions often resulted in hybrid cultural formations that were simultaneously new *and* old. Even in cases of acceptance and conversion on the part of indigenous people, this hybridity is clearly evident. Traces of the 'old' ways of doing were hard to replace. For instance, one chief that converted to Christianity and rejected some of his traditional practices also used his new status as converted, which included new control of local churches, to extend his political influence into new regions.[43] Thus, we see a hybrid between introduced religion and traditional political structures. The chief built a new church with (introduced) heavy stone architecture at the centre of his ward. In adopting this new form of building, however, the chief also made the settlement more permanent and far less flexible. The materiality of the new building restricted the settlement's ability to move when resources became scant. In this case, the chief and the missionaries actually did once 'move' the stone church a distance of 80 miles to gain access to fresh resources and, in turn, preserve the settlement's coherence.

Crossland[44] frames the chief's situation in semiotic terms. His position at the centre of the society was made observable both indexically and iconically through his new building projects. The stone architecture served as an index of his invest-ment in place, while its location in the centre of the settlement was an icon of his place in society. By constructing such a powerful structure at the centre of the settlement, the chief also restricted his ability to use the very sign relation he had innovated. In other words, the materiality of the structure and the significance of its location made it difficult to use in new contexts. Yet the chief was some-how able to move the structure 80 miles to the centre of his new settlement! The ability to manipulate this stubborn sign also became an index of the chief's enhanced power and control.

With each of these examples, we see how a Peircian approach shifts the focus on agency (Chapter 3) from the agent or sender of the sign and their intentionality to the wider community of observers situated around that agent or sender, something we might refer to as *semiotic consequences*. In other words, both Bauer and Crossland demonstrate how the wider community of observers and interpreters might have made sense of the signs in question based on their cultural background and mat-erial surroundings, regardless of the intentionality of the senders. In this sense, this approach looks at processes of becoming in the relationships between people, things and hybrids of the two. On the Black Sea coast, resemblance (through iconicity) of ceramics made by various communities had the potential to translate into a symbol of identity. Both the pots and the people in this equation played key roles. It wasn't just a matter of a potter creating a new pot to achieve certain goals. The potters, the pots and the wider community were entangled in ways that were beyond the control of any one entity. In Southern Africa, missionary architecture and settlement patterns meant different things to different observers, with very dif-ferent cultural backgrounds and experiences with the material world. Using Peirce, Crossland demonstrates the multivalent and ambiguous nature of certain signs, particularly in cases of culturally plural contexts. She also shows, however, the semiotic repercussions of new signs appropriated by chiefs in the area, specifically how the obdurate and stubborn nature of new stone churches challenged chiefs' abilities to maintain their status in the traditional way. Remember that the chief had to go through loads of trouble to move his new, heavy-duty church! Each example brings us well beyond mere issues of representation to consider semiotic mediation and semiotic consequences that have to do both with culture and the broader material world. This approach is not only about 'reading' and 'decoding' conventions.[45] It also has to do with simply *being* in the material world, which sounds similar to the phenomenological approaches explored in the last chapter. Keep Peirce's concepts of Objects and Signs in mind. These are not Signs because human interpreters made them so; they force themselves into interpretation; they exist out of necessity and often through their material conditions. However, since the Interpretant emerges out of interpretation by a living entity, this approach maintains a set of assumptions about the different capacities of living and non-living things. We will explore some critiques of this approach in the next chapter with our consideration of symmetrical archaeology and new materialism.

Conclusions: back to the forest

Now that we have covered all of the basics of a Peircian semiotic approach, we ask that you put down this book and consider how Peirce or Peircian-inspired archaeologists might address the philosophical question posed at the start of this chapter. Would a falling tree in the lonely forest make a noise or not?

Back already? So, what do you think? Peirce would probably start with the fact that all of the sensuous aspects of the tree falling are *potential* Signs, whose *potential* Objects certainly exist in the world 'out there'. Our very ability to discuss this example illustrates the fact that many humans have a wide range of understanding of the general process of trees falling, either through direct physical experience and observation or through other modes, such as reading an account or viewing video of falling trees. These are all *potential* Objects that we could easily connect to a new experience with a falling tree (Sign). Since there is no interpreter to make this connection in our example, however, the sign remains incomplete, and there is no sound in this particular example. Having stated this point, it is important to note that a Peircian position sits uneasily between the two caricatured positions stated at the outset of this chapter. Remember, a straightforward 'yes' vote emphasises the importance of the world beyond human perception, while a straightforward 'no' vote situates human perception as a key component in shaping the world. In the end, Peirce understood the importance of both the material world 'out there' and human perception and interpretation though semiotic mediation. This is exemplified in our earlier discussion of onomatopoeic words. Systematic variation in the ways that humans of different language groups verbally reproduce sounds of 'nature', such as the bee droning, further shows that the divide we often assume between nature and culture is a false one. It demonstrates that human representation and understanding *and* the world beyond it influence one another in important ways.

As we have illustrated in this chapter, Peirce understood signs as operating within both the materially and culturally constituted world. Unlike Saussure and his structural semiotics, Peirce offers archaeology a theory that accounts for signs and semiotic mediation well beyond representation, while also providing a framework for understanding the multivalent and dynamic nature of signs in society. Living things that have the ability to interpret signs are key parts of the semiotic process according to a Peircian approach. As evinced in the broader literature concerning biosemiotics, humans are far from the only living things that interpret signs. We will briefly explore this theme in Chapter 9. For now, it is simply important to note that Peircian semiotics emphasises the importance of humans and other living things as driving the process of semiotic mediation and cultural reproduction more broadly (Chapter 3). In the next chapter, we will encounter a new approach in archaeology that focuses on things in the hope of creating a 'symmetrical' framework that makes no assumptions about the ontological status of living versus non-living entities.

Notes

1 We will return to this distinction and how it can be thought about in terms of that tricky word ontology in Chapters 10 and 11.
2 Agbe-Davies 2015; Bauer 2013; Cipolla 2008, 2013b; Crossland 2014; Knappett 2005; Preucel 2006; Preucel and Bauer 2001.
3 Peirce 1998 [1894].
4 This move is paralleled by the desire of archaeologists drawing on new materialism to develop alternative ways of thinking about meaning without resorting to representation (see, for example, Jones and Alberti 2013; Harris 2016a).
5 For accounts that draw on both Peirce and theories of materiality see, for example, Boivin 2008; Jones 2007; Malafouris 2013: chapter 5.
6 Saussure 1986.
7 Preucel 2006: 22–5.
8 Saussure 1986.
9 Pinney 2005.
10 See many more interesting examples of this phenomenon at http://www.eleceng.adelaide. edu.au/Personal/dabbott/animal.html.
11 Bauer 2002, 2013; Cipolla 2008, 2013b; Crossland 2009, 2013, 2014; Jones 2007; Keane 2006; Knappett 2005; Lele 2006; Liebmann 2008; Preucel and Bauer 2001; Preucel 2006; Watts 2008.
12 Preucel 2006.
13 For further reading on this topic, see Daniel 1984; Keane 1997; Parmentier 1994; Peirce Edition Project 1998.
14 Preucel and Bauer 2001.
15 Peirce 1998 [1895].
16 Capitalised hereafter to denote specific reference to Peirce's concepts.
17 Bauer 2013: 13–18; Parmentier 1994.
18 Peirce 1998 [1895].
19 Menard 2001.
20 E.g., Peirce Edition Project 1998.
21 Peirce 1998 [1894].
22 Peirce 1998 [1895].
23 Peirce 1998 [1903a].
24 Peirce 1998 [1894], 1998 [1895].
25 Technically speaking, this discussion is out of sequence. Peirce referred to icons and 'Firsts', indexes as 'Seconds' and symbols as 'Thirds'. We chose to begin this part of the discussion with symbols or Thirds because we already provided information on cultural convention and arbitrary sign relations in our discussion of Saussure's work.
26 Peirce referred to this as a First.
27 Peirce referred to this as a Second.
28 Peirce 1998 [1894].
29 Bauer 2013: 14.
30 Bauer 2013.
31 Parmentier 1994: 4–5.
32 Remember the Interpretant in this case is not the golfer on their own; it is the entire scene (i.e., the golfer, the way the ball is hit, the landscape, etc.).
33 Bauer 2013.
34 Bauer 2013; see also Bauer 2006.
35 Bauer 2013: 4.
36 Bauer 2013: 22.
37 Crossland 2013.
38 Crossland 2014.

39 Crossland 2013: 84.
40 Crossland 2013: 84; see also Comaroff and Comaroff 1991.
41 Crossland 2013: 87.
42 Crossland 2013: 91–2.
43 Crossland 2013: 96–9.
44 Crossland 2013: 98–9.
45 Keane 2005.

8
FINDING SYMMETRY
Actor-Network-Theory and new materialism

Introduction: do guns kill people or do people kill people?

If someone gets shot, who or what is to blame? The person who pulled the trigger, or the gun in their hand (Figure 8.1)? Should our response as a society be to increase the punishment for the gunman, to make prison sentences longer or to put them to death? Or should we try instead to reduce the number of weapons on the street, to ban people from owning guns? These questions remain critical in political debates across the world, and especially in the United States. If we see people as solely to blame, then changing the material world (for example, their access to guns) won't prevent them from killing people and we would be unfairly punishing those good citizens who use their guns appropriately. If we see guns as the major issue, then the only way to reduce gun fatalities is to reduce the number of firearms in circulation and prevent people from gaining access to them. Depending on what country you live in, and where you stand on the political spectrum, you may have passionate views on this argument one way or the other.

For the sociologist Bruno Latour, however, the debate misses a simple but critical point: it is people *with* guns that kill people.[1] Neither the gun nor the person alone could act in the same way they do when joined together. From this starting point, Latour has constructed an approach to the world that aims to radically challenge how we normally think, to undermine the differences between people and things, and culture and nature, and to approach the world in what he sees as a more 'symmetrical' manner.[2] For Latour, the key element is not the person or the gun, but rather the relationships they are caught up in, or their *network*. The whole world for Latour is made up of these networks, which include multiple different actors, some of which are human and some of which are not. This emphasis on actors and networks is where these ideas get their name, 'Actor-Network-Theory' or *ANT*. As we will see, this goes beyond previous attempts to work out how structure and

FIGURE 8.1 Who is the guilty party? Drawing by K-Fai Steele

agency are caught up in a recursive relationship (as we saw with practice theory in Chapter 3) and indeed other attempts to share agency with objects (as we saw with Alfred Gell's work in Chapter 5). Instead this new symmetrical approach seeks to rethink the way in which people and things work together. Since the start of the current millennium, some archaeologists have become increasingly drawn to Latour's work, some even using it to declare a new 'symmetrical archaeology', complete with its own manifesto.[3] Their battle cry, 'Things are Us!',[4] captures the way in which they hope to open up a new way of approaching archaeology as a discipline, and goes beyond the claims that people make things and things make people that defined the approaches to materiality we saw in Chapter 6. Not only do symmetrical archaeologists see themselves as finally ridding the discipline of those pesky dualisms we have encountered throughout this book, they also aim to reincorporate elements of archaeology that are normally opposed to one other, including 'science' and 'theory'.

Alongside such symmetrical approaches we can identify a similar and related set of theories that have sought to re-examine the material world, and to reinvigor- ate it in new ways. Although these don't really have a single unifying slogan or approach, we can broadly term them 'new materialist', as they tend to draw on a related set of philosophies that come under this term.[5] New materialism,[6] like symmetrical archaeology, wants to think about how people and things are not two very different kinds of entities (that we might term subjects and objects), but rather they emerge together, a bit like the guns and people above. New materialism in particular has taken a great deal of interest in what it terms the 'vibrancy of matter', or the way in which matter itself can be thought of as 'alive' in one sense, and contributing to the world in all kinds of ways.[7] New materialists differ from symmetrical archaeologists both in their terminology (the former prefer terms like meshwork or assemblage to ones like network) but also in more substantive ways, as we will see.[8] However, the two share a number of similarities including a desire to place 'science' and 'theory' on a level playing field, rather than separating them into different camps. Indeed the division between them can be slightly arbitrary as many scholars draw on elements of thinking from both of these approaches to develop new lines of enquiry.[9] Critically, both approaches would see themselves as having turned away from the divisions that separated processual and postprocessual archaeology (Chapter 2).

In this chapter we will look at these new approaches to the past. In the next section we will begin by examining Latour's work in a little more depth to consider the background of symmetrical archaeology. We then explore symmetrical archaeology itself and look in more detail at the arguments it has put forward, including a Latourian case study focusing on whaling in the Arctic in the first millennium AD. This section will also set out some of the challenges that a symmetrical approach poses to the way in which we normally think about archaeology. Next, we turn to new materialism, examining the ways in which it is both similar to but also different from symmetrical archaeology. We then consider a case study applying these approaches to the past, looking at new understandings of materials from Palaeolithic Europe. In the final section of the chapter, we reflect on these ideas together and consider the extent to which they potentially offer a significant development compared to previous approaches in archaeology.

To modernity, and beyond! The challenge of Bruno Latour

In the last 20 years Bruno Latour (Box 8.1) has emerged as one of the rarest things, a cross-disciplinary academic star, whose work is devoured in numerous disciplines: geography, anthropology, sociology, science and technology studies (a discipline he co-founded), philosophy and, of course, archaeology. Latour started his academic career as a sociologist of science, and published numerous articles and books examining how scientists go about their work.[10] What Latour became interested in was how seemingly dry and fixed scientific facts emerge from complex processes of negotiation involving the scientists themselves, their interpersonal networks at work and the institutions that fund them. So, for example, a particular archaeological site doesn't just present us with a date, e.g. 'Stonehenge was built in 2500 cal BC'. Instead, that date emerges from a network of people who excavated the site, the material they recovered, their interpretation of the archaeological sequence, the funding body that paid for a radiocarbon date, the importance of Stonehenge as a national icon in the UK which means it attracts both people and money, and so on. This 'fact' actually emerges from the work of many different entities. Latour's work at this stage can sometimes be read as an argument for the 'social construction of science'; that is, that science is not a separate way of knowing the world removed from politics, daily life and the normal concerns of human beings. Instead, science is always involved in and in part formed from those more everyday concerns (these latter issues were also noted by early postprocessual authors[11]). This implies that science does not discover absolute facts about the world, but rather helps to create them. This point is very controversial, and many people would deny it absolutely.

From the early 1990s onwards, however, Latour developed this critique in a much more significant way. A crucial publication was *We Have Never Been Modern*,[12] first published in French in 1991 and translated into English in 1993. In this book Latour expands his analysis of the history of science to suggest that modern people (that is, people living in the modern western world today and in the last 200 years or so) think about the world in a very strange way. Latour argues that we spend most of our time trying to separate things out into neat categories and trying to make sure those categories don't mix. This process is what Latour calls *purification*.[13] This purification tries to separate things into neat packages that match

---

BOX 8.1 BRUNO LATOUR

Bruno Latour is a French sociologist of science and one of the founders of Actor-Network-Theory. He is a professor at Sciences Po, Paris. His work in science and technology studies has made him one of the most famous academics in multiple disciplines. His main works include his books *Science in Action*,[14] *We Have Never Been Modern*[15] and *Reassembling the Social*.[16] The gun here relates to the classic issue of where agency lies, with the person or the gun, which Latour poses in his work.

Image by Adam Hill (own work) [CC0], via Wikimedia Commons

the kinds of Cartesian dualisms we are now familiar with, like culture and nature, mind and body, subject and object, and so on. To use an example from Chapter 1, whenever you have a conversation where you discuss whether something arose because of 'nature' or 'nurture', you're engaging in this kind of 'purification'. As we have seen, of course, the problem with these kinds of separations (as you'll know if you've ever tried to work out whether some aspect of your personality is due to nature or nurture) is that they don't actually work. Latour also identified how these separations disguise all the ways in which things that don't seem to neatly fit into either set of categories get increasingly common in the modern era. If you think back to the sprinter in Chapter 1, while we try to keep nature and culture separate by banning 'performance-enhancing drugs', in fact everything from the surgeries to repair injuries, to the food consumed, to the trainers that are worn blurs these divides. In reality, Latour argues, rather than nature and culture being separate, or object and subject being opposed, the world is a complex network of relationships defying these boundaries. In turn, if breaking up the world into nature and culture is a classically modern thing to do, but in reality we always fail to do that, then, in effect, we have never been modern.

Okay, but what does this have to do with archaeology? On one level it is another tool for rethinking dualisms, which as we have seen are under attack from all sorts of directions. What marks this out as different? Well, the crucial move Latour makes next is one that some think has real significance for archaeology. Because of Latour's work in laboratories, he has become attuned not just to the work of the scientists themselves, and their relationships with one another, but also to the various roles performed by the nonhumans that populate this world from microscopes to microbes.[17] Here we see how Latour's philosophy – his ontology – demands a place in his networks not just for human beings, but for all the nonhumans of the world as well. Thus microscopes are not just the product of a genius human mind that allowed new kinds of progress to be made, but active players in revealing new worlds that the human eye cannot see alone. When we stop saying that human *subjects* employ *objects* to look at nature – an outcome of our *cultural* world – then suddenly the way in which things and people together produce new kinds of actions and new kinds of understandings begins to become apparent. From these perspectives, the fallen tree we encountered back in Chapter 7 definitely makes a sound, whether or not any human being or living thing happens to be around to hear and interpret it.

If we escape the idea that the world is made up of nature and culture, and objects and subjects, and we start to think about the networks and relationships through which things operate, then our ideas of agency and history start to shift. Up to now, nearly all chapters in this book explored approaches that fundamentally placed human beings at the centre of things; what we referred to as anthropocentrism. From structuralism with its emphasis on meaning (Chapter 2), via agency theory where humans are always the agents (Chapter 3), even via notions of the secondary agency of objects (Chapter 5) or how humans make their worlds with things (Chapter 6), humans have been at the centre of history. However, if we don't have a notion of history based around thinking subjects deciding what to do next, acting on passive, pliant, recipient objects, then suddenly the role of material things becomes very different. Instead of simply being the markers of identity, tools for humans to conquer the environment or complex ways of symbolising meaning, material things become active participants in the world. Just as you can't shoot without a gun, so Neolithic people can't farm without axes with which to chop down trees. Even the approaches of Peirce in the last chapter required the presence of organic living creatures to interpret signs, even if these might be more than just humans. Here, instead, we move towards a genuinely non-anthropocentric approach to the past.

The role of humans and nonhumans together is what is crucial from this perspective and that is why it is described as 'symmetrical' by Latour, and by the archaeologists who have drawn explicitly on his work. It is also why these approaches are sometimes described as posthumanist.[18] This means that they developed in contrast to the humanism of Enlightenment philosophy that placed human beings (rather than God) at the centre of the universe. Agency here does not *belong* to objects. Instead, agency is a quality of a relationship, meaning that the agency of the gun–human relationship is qualitatively different to the agency of the human-without-a-gun.[19] Indeed there is no human alone or any object separate from a subject to 'possess' agency. Rather than refer to agents or actors, Latour talks about '*actants*'[20] so as to avoid any indication as to whether these are human, nonhuman or some combination of the two. As symmetrical archaeologists have pointed out, material things pre-exist our species by millions of years; they were part of the condition through which we evolved, and thus, as they say, 'humanity begins with things'.[21]

Archaeology, the discipline of things

Archaeologists became interested in Latour's work in the mid-1990s, with serious engagement starting in the early 2000s, as scholars became increasingly disenchanted with both the emphasis on language and linguistic meanings on the one hand, and the continued separation of archaeology as 'science' and archaeology as 'theory' on the other. Where traditional postprocessual archaeology, especially in its most strident 1980s forms, had declared that material things were a text to be read (Chapter 2), archaeologists in the 2000s wanted to consider things much more in their own right (as we saw in Chapter 6). Andrew Jones used Latour's work in his 2002 book *Archaeological Theory and Scientific Practice*[22] to offer a first attempt to rethink the gaps between science and theory in archaeology.[23] Inspired by Latour's work, Jones argued that archaeology was split between two ways of thinking about the past. On the one hand were scientific archaeologists, who were broadly processual in outlook, and who thought about archaeological materials as static objects that could – with the correct application of techniques – be persuaded to give up their secrets.[24] On the other hand were socially orientated and broadly postprocessual archaeologists, who were interested in questions of meaning, agency and the fluid and flexible nature of the past.[25] Going beyond who was right and who was wrong, Jones pointed out how this division itself neatly mapped on to the kinds of modernist dichotomies Latour had critiqued. On one side, what mattered was the natural, the material and the scientific; on the other, the cultural, the ideas behind it and the act of interpretation were king. Thus the whole debate around archaeological theory was never going to be able to escape these dichotomies in the form that Jones found it at the end of the last millennium. This is because it was based precisely *on* those divisions (a point we return to below), just as we saw in Chapter 2.

In parallel with these criticisms, another group of scholars developed a set of approaches drawing on the work of Latour. Beginning with a publication by Bjørnar Olsen in 2003[26] (Box 10.5 in Chapter 10), work by Olsen, Christopher Witmore (Box 8.2), Michael Shanks and Timothy Webmoor has come to be known as 'symmetrical archaeology'.[27] Although not only drawing on the work of Latour (see Chapter 10), the self-proclaimed title of the approach indicates explicitly the principal inspiration.[28] The central point of symmetrical archaeology is that for a subject so overtly concerned with material things, our discipline has traditionally spent a great deal of time trying to get beyond them. In the case of culture history, archaeologists wanted to know about the cultural or ethnic groups that made the artefacts; in the case of processual archaeology, it was the processes of material adaptation – economic or environmental – that were critical; for much of early postprocessual archaeology, it was the meanings and symbols hidden behind the artefacts that were sought after. From a perspective that embraces the philosophy of Latour, however, there is no hidden 'social' realm behind these objects because material things are the very means by which history happens; it is their relationships with human beings *and with each other* which allow us to trace histories. The gaps between people and things begin to collapse here, or, to put it another way, *things are us!*[29]

A number of critical challenges and points emerge from this new way of thinking. First, symmetrical archaeology asks us to rethink the purpose of archaeology at quite a fundamental level. No longer should we be interested primarily in people, but rather in the relationships – the network[30] or mixtures[31] – out of which our ideas of people and things emerge. This means in our archaeologies of how people discovered metallurgy, we have to think about how one kind of network – including wood, fire, charcoal, ores, clay and people – came together to reveal the existence of another form of material: metal. When metal emerged and joined with this network, it created new possibilities for action. People still play a role here, but it is very different from the one archaeologists have imagined for them in the past. People of the past are no longer alone in driving history forward and archaeologists are no longer solely interested in artefacts for what they tell us about people. It also means we need to resist explanations that place another level of meaning 'behind' or 'above' the specific networks we are exploring. When we suggest that the Roman empire collapsed because of 'economic' reasons, or farming spread because of new 'social' relations, for symmetrical archaeologists we are using the terms 'economic' or 'social' to hide[32] the actual changes we need to

BOX 8.2 CHRISTOPHER L. WITMORE

Christopher L. Witmore is Associate Professor of Classics at Texas Tech University. His work has focused on conceptualising archaeology as a discipline that can undercut traditional modernist dualisms, looking at landscapes in Greece over the long term. He is co-author of *Archaeology: The Discipline of Things*,[33] and also wrote the founding manifesto of symmetrical archaeology.[34] One of Witmore's key ideas is that time is not necessarily linear; it can return in unexpected ways. He illustrates this with a picture of Oxford Street, London (see image) which runs along the route of a Roman road.[35] In this case, we must ask: is the road Roman or modern? Past or present? Does time flow in one direction or does it come and go?

Image: https://en.wikipedia.org/wiki/Oxford_Street#/media/File:Oxford_Street_December_2006.jpeg

explain; they are not forces that operate outside of the relations between people and things, but are instead entities produced by these relations.[36]

An example can help us think this through in a little more detail. Peter Whitridge has drawn on Latour's work to examine Thule whalers of the North American Arctic in the first millennium AD.[37] The groups he examined conducted whaling through a collective enterprise led by an *umialik* – or wealthy boat captain – who sponsored, led and made the most profit from the hunt if it was successful.[38] The hunting in turn worked by gathering men into a large open skin boat used to pursue bowhead whales, harpoon them and drag them to shore. From a practice theory perspective (Chapter 3), we would think of this as an example of the agency of the *umialik* in gathering the people together and persuading them to go off hunting, one that worked through and sustained the structure of 'the hunt' and the broader community.

Whitridge, however, argues that when we take a perspective rooted in Actor-Network-Theory we can develop a very different understanding of these processes. To begin, he looks at the changing technology of harpoon heads. While this might seem like a relatively trivial detail of technical development, Whitridge demonstrates how treating the harpoon head as an *actant* within a network reveals how these changes have major consequences. If you change the number of barbs on the harpoon, you also have to change the socket and foreshaft of the harpoon, how the end is configured and a number of other seemingly minor details. In turn, this changes the surrounding equipment including the kinds of boats you use. Changing these technologies is not simple, but requires new kinds of resources (skins, wood, oil, labour, etc.). As Whitridge puts it, 'the slightest change in harpoon technology had the potential to redistribute actors on a disproportionately vast scale'.[39] Critically, none of these changes were likely intended by the designer or designers of this new harpoon head, but rather came about because of the network as a whole. Agency here was distributed across the different *actants*.

Whitridge develops this idea further to consider the general process of whaling at this time, and how this was linked not just to the hunters and hunting technology, but also to the families of people on the shore. Just as harpoons, ropes, whales and boats are physically joined together at sea, so these relations form themselves on land as the families are connected (or bound) in to the work of processing the whale. So changing whale hunting technology also affects more traditional 'social' relations as well – revealing how trying to keep the social and the material apart is very problematic. More than this, of course, the whales themselves are essential parts of these collectives, as their biology and ecology are critical to the different ways in which these hunting networks are articulated (we will return to similar arguments in Chapter 9). Rather than seeing the social as being the preserve of human beings alone, technological change as a process of adaptation or agency lying solely with the (male) hunters, Whitridge's approach offers a very different view of these hunter gatherers' lives.[40]

Symmetrical archaeologists, and those who draw on Latour more broadly, have argued strongly that archaeologists should think much more seriously about the objects we encounter. Rather than simply emphasise the role of human beings, we ought to concentrate on how we are always caught up with objects, mixed up in ways that mean that any attempt to separate the past out into different camps becomes problematic. Through this approach, symmetrical archaeologists argue that they have finally overcome (although they would prefer to say undercut[41]) the kinds of dichotomies that archaeologists have been rallying against for some time.

Drawing on these approaches, they have developed interesting investigations of how we might understand archaeological practice – the actual acts of digging – differently and how we can think about time not as something that goes in a straight line but something much more tangled.[42] They offer a quite different way, potentially, to think about archaeology. If materiality and entanglement, which we encountered in Chapter 6, begin with the notion of the co-constitution of people and things,[43] here instead people and things are the outcomes of relationships, of mixtures, rather than the starting point for investigation. Although as we will see in Chapter 10, some elements of symmetrical archaeology have been developed in a new direction by Olsen in particular. These new arguments, which we can see as 'second-wave' symmetrical archaeology, suggest in even more radical ways that archaeologists have a political, moral and ethical commitment to giving things their due,[44] and even to going beyond these relational approaches.

From symmetry to new materialism

Alongside the turn to symmetry has come another set of posthumanist approaches also interested in bringing out the role material things, and especially matter itself, have to play in our understandings of the past. If symmetrical archaeologists have stressed the relationships between people and things, those interested in new materialism have tried to delve even deeper to think in more detail about the substances that objects are made from and what these bring to the table. No longer is it about the relationships between people and their guns, but the role of metal, gunpowder, plastic, bodies and the substances that make up a body, together. These approaches embrace a wide range of influences from philosophy to the hard sciences. For example, alongside the writings of philosophers like Gilles Deleuze (Box 8.3), the work of people like the physicist Karen Barad[45] has been enormously influential.[46] This way of thinking is known as 'new materialist' to differentiate it from older materialist approaches associated with Marxism.

One of the first people to draw archaeologists' attention to the importance of this kind of approach was anthropologist Tim Ingold (Box 9.1 in Chapter 9) in a paper in 2007 that he published in *Archaeological Dialogues*.[47] In the paper, Ingold did something quite original by asking the reader of the paper to go out and get a stone, dip it into a bucket of water and leave the wet stone next to them as they read the paper. As the paper proceeds, Ingold returns to the stone from time to time and points out how it is changing. By the end of the paper it has dried out, perhaps just leaving a few damp patches. The stone feels different now; it is less shiny, and if you knock it against something, the noise it makes is different.[48] The properties of a material like stone, something that seems totally fixed and unchanging, thus turn out to vary depending on the relationships the stone is caught up in at any one time. Is it wet or dry? Is it warm or cold? The stone does not have a particular nature, but instead a particular kind of history:[49] how recently was it made wet, has it been knocked by something that makes it sharp, or eroded in a stream that makes it smooth? Ingold thus managed to show us that even something like stone – the very material we use to signify unchanging eternity – is actually variable, vibrant and transformative – in a sense, animate.

The implications of this, however, are much more significant than simply reconsidering the way in which we understand the properties of a single stone. In Ingold's piece, the properties of the stone emerge through its relationships with the world around it. These sets of relations are what Ingold would call a 'meshwork' and what many new materialists call *an assemblage*,[50] a term taken from the work of the philosopher Gilles Deleuze[51] (Box 8.3). Archaeologists have been interested in assemblages for a long time, of course; it is a term we use to describe a collection of flints, pots or metalwork from a site. For instance, 'have you studied the ceramic assemblage from the houses you excavated?' is a question an archaeologist might pose. In a sense, the term assemblage as it is being used in theoretical archaeology today has something in common with this. An assemblage is the coming together of multiple different kinds of things into what we can consider a single whole. These include materials, but also ideas, beliefs, emotions, memories, symbols and more.[52] These assemblages operate at multiple scales, from a water molecule, which is an assemblage of two hydrogen atoms and one oxygen atom, via a pot, which is an assemblage of clay, temper and heat, to a solar system, which is an assemblage of a star, planets, moons and asteroids.[53] Of course, archaeologists are interested in particular scales of assemblages, but even these vary from a single pot, to whole sites, to regional studies. Assemblages are also always in the process of '*becoming*' as Deleuze would put it. This means that they are the outcome of certain kinds of ongoing processes that involve particular kinds of histories, rather than being static and unchanging. How does using assemblage theory change how we think about archaeology?

One of the ways in which we can use assemblages is to rethink the concept of how design works. When archaeologists think about somebody making a pot, for example, we typically emphasise the way in which people have an idea of what they want the pot to look like which they then impose onto a malleable material – clay.[54] Equally when we imagine a knapper working on a flint nodule we tend to think about them having the design of what they want (e.g. the arrowhead, the scraper) in their mind before they start to work with the material. This concept of how people go about making things is known as the 'hylomorphic'[55] model, and it goes back to the Ancient Greek philosopher Aristotle.[56] In fact, if you think of the very commonplace archaeological term 'material culture', this captures the hylomorphic model precisely; it shows how an object (a piece of material culture) is made up of a combination of ideas or culture imposed onto matter.[57] However, there is good evidence that this does not really capture the way in which making takes place. To start with, it tends to emphasise the creativity of the human being at the expense of the materials. There is an obvious sceptical response here – okay, but surely it is human beings doing the designing or doing the making, and they are only *constrained* by the materials? At best, you might be willing to concede that materials can act as proxies for humans and their agency (remember our discussion of houses and architects in Chapter 5).

BOX 8.3   GILLES DELEUZE

Gilles Deleuze (1925–95) was a French philosopher. In his work he tried to develop an alternative account to the dominant traditions of western philosophy. Although his great masterpiece is his book *Difference and Repetition*,[58] he is most famous for two of the books he wrote with the psychoanalyst Felix Guattari, *Anti-Oedipus*[59] and *A Thousand Plateaus*.[60] Famously difficult to read and understand, and often dismissed as a result, Deleuze has become increasingly influential in many of the social sciences in the last 15 years, especially in geography.[61] Below is a photograph of a rhizome – the growing horizontal roots of a plant. Deleuze and Guattari use the notion of a rhizome as a way of thinking about different models of connectivity that are non-linear and yet still always becoming. Rather than a hierarchical 'tree' of knowledge, the rhizome suggests there are multiple ways of finding out about the world.

Image: https://commons.wikimedia.org/wiki/File:Bamboo_with_rhizome_1.JPG

When we think about these things in terms of assemblages, however, a different possibility emerges.[62] The philosopher Manuel DeLanda in both his lectures and written work often uses the example of the German architect Frei Otto to offer an alternative understanding of the roles of materials in design from a perspective rooted in assemblages.[63] Frei Otto was in charge of designing the Olympic stadium in Munich for the 1972 Olympic Games (Figure 8.2). He was famous for producing light tent-like structures and wanted to do the same on this occasion. In the days

FIGURE 8.2   The 1972 Olympic stadium in Munich, Germany, with the roof
co-designed by Frei Otto and soap film

*Image: by 2014_Olympiastadion_Munich_l.JPG: derivative work: Hic et nunc [CC BY-SA 3.0 (http://
creativecommons.org/licenses/by-sa/3.0)], via Wikimedia Commons*

before computer-aided design (this was the 1960s, after all) he needed a way of
calculating the roof-shape that he envisioned. In a traditional model of design we
would presume that using a combination of mathematics, drawing and his own
genius, Otto would have calculated the shapes he needed. In fact he did nothing
of the sort. Instead he employed a different and very humble material to do these
calculations: soap film. Otto knew that soap film has an interesting property. It
will form shapes of least resistance, which is why when you blow a bubble in the
bath it forms a sphere; in more Deleuzian terms, when it encounters certain forces,
it *becomes* something else. So Otto arranged a series of lollipop sticks and pieces
of string on a board in the broad shape he had in mind and lowered it through a
film of soap. The soap then calculated the shapes of the curves he needed – in this
case what mathematicians call hyperbolic paraboloids.[64] The design of the Munich
Olympic stadium thus originates not just with Frei Otto, but also with the soap
film, and indeed with the lollipop sticks and pieces of string. The design draws on
the tendencies of this particular matter to take a specific form (what a philosopher
would call its morphogenetic capacity), and thus emerges as an assemblage of the
architect and the different materials they engage with. As with Ingold's stone,
when we take materials seriously, a seemingly inert substance turns out to be much
more vibrant than we previously thought.

New materialism in archaeology

New materialist approaches are growing rapidly in archaeology. Ideas of assemblages are being explored in connection to how we think about materials, burial
practices, communities and even the very processes and practices of archaeology

itself.[65] They also offer up new ways to think about how the world is experienced; they argue that the sensorial properties of things form a critical part of the assemblages through which people live.[66] This new attention to the materials themselves also opens up new routes for reconciliation between more scientific and theoretical approaches because of the way in which scientific approaches allow us to attend to what Jane Bennett (Box 8.4) calls the *vibrancy* of matter;[67] that is, the capacities

---

BOX 8.4 JANE BENNETT

Jane Bennett is Professor of Political Science at Johns Hopkins University. Author of *Vibrant Matter: A Political Ecology of Things*,[68] Bennett pioneered a new materialist approach in political science to argue for more sustainable ways of living in the world. Here we include an image of a pylon because one of Bennett's most famous examples of how assemblages help us think about the world is her description of a 2003 electricity blackout in the US. Where we might normally think of this as something caused by human error, or mechanical failure, Bennett traces how it depended on everything from the properties of materials, to company policies, to people's actions and a particular wildfire. She showed that to understand a blackout, you had to think about the whole assemblage.

Image by Arnoldius [CC BY-SA 2.5 (http://creativecommons.org/licenses/by-sa/2.5)], via Wikimedia Commons

---

matter has to operate in certain ways, as we saw with the soap bubbles above. Paying close attention to materials, how they work, what they are like and how they change in different circumstances allows us to think about the assemblages they form with human beings in new and interesting ways. This encourages us to see how the engagement of people and materials, with the specific properties, memories and experiences that each of them bring, can lead to the emergence of new kinds of assemblages – or to the process of *becoming*.

One of the most innovative studies influenced by these approaches has come from Chantal Conneller (Box 8.5), in her book *An Archaeology of Materials*.[69] In the

---

BOX 8.5   CHANTAL CONNELLER

Chantal Conneller is Senior Lecturer in Archaeology at the University of Manchester. An expert in Palaeolithic and Mesolithic Britain, she researches the way in which we can think about hunter-gatherer societies and their relationships with materials and animals, especially through ideas of new materialism. Her publications include the book *An Archaeology of Materials*[70] and the article *Becoming Deer*.[71] The latter inspires our choice of image here – an antler frontlet from the Mesolithic site of Star Carr in Britain, with holes drilled to allow it to be worn. Conneller, who has directed excavations at this site, has used these frontlets to think about how they might have functioned to allow people to take on some of the attributes of deer, to become more like deer, through the assemblage of person and mask.

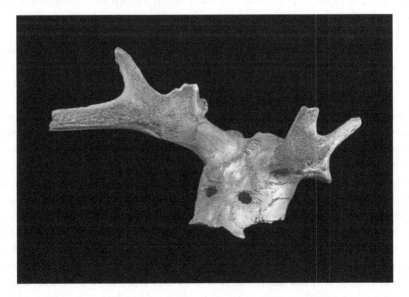

Image © the Trustees of the British Museum

book Conneller draws on new materialist approaches (as well as some of the ideas from nonwestern ontologies we will encounter in Chapter 10) to try and rethink many of the issues we have touched on here in relation to objects from Upper Palaeolithic and Mesolithic Europe. One example from her book touches on the role of materials and their relationship to form and design in particular. Conneller looks at so-called *contours découpés* (Figure 8.3), pendants usually shaped like a horse head, made from the throat bones of horses (Figure 8.4). These pendants date to the period between 14,800 and 13,000 years ago, known as the Middle Magdalenian.[72] The horse hyoid bone, Conneller points out, needs only rather minimal modification to be changed into something shaped like a horse's head, and then followed up with engravings to produce the final image. Indeed the very shape of the material suggests a horse's head, and no doubt contributes to this design. Similarly, in contemporary cave art, Conneller points out, the shapes of rock walls often lend themselves to specific depictions of animals,[73] much as you might 'see' the shape of an animal in a cloud floating above your head. In both cases we can see here how the materials involve themselves in the design.

However, Conneller's point is not that human beings are universally attuned to spotting these particular forms in certain materials. Rather, these particular qualities of both stone (in the case of cave art) and bone (in the case of the *contour découpés*) emerge in the specific assemblages of the Magdalenian. Just as you are unlikely to spot the shape of an animal you have never seen in the clouds above you, not everyone in all times and places would recognise a horse's head in the hyoid bone. It emerges in conjunction with the process of hunting and butchering horses, the tradition of animal art in the Magdalenian, and the material qualities of bone itself that allow it to be shaped. Neither a form simply hidden in the material nor an imposition from human beings, the *contours découpés* emerge as the specific outcomes of these assemblages.

Conneller then contrasts these assemblages with a different relationship between form and material in an earlier case from the Upper Palaeolithic: Aurignacian basket-shaped beads from southwest France that date to 33,000 years ago.[74] In this context people took various materials, including enormous mammoth tusks, and transformed them into beads. If the form of the horse hyoid bones bore a visual resemblance to the objects they would eventually become, no such similarity seems detectable in the case of the mammoth tusks! More than this, the complex ways in which the beads were manufactured involving the splitting of the ivory tusks into rods, in a manner that ran counter to the tendencies of this material, *seemingly* demonstrates that people paid no attention to the material properties of the tusks themselves.[75] Whatever material they made basket-shaped beads from, the same technique was used to produce the same form. Surely this has to be a case where people had an idea in their mind of what they wanted to make, and imposed this on the material? Conneller argues convincingly that this is not the case, however. In this context it is not the hardness or how easy ivory is to work that matters, but its other material properties, especially the way in which it could be polished to make it lustrous and shiny.[76] All of the materials used for Aurignacian beads,

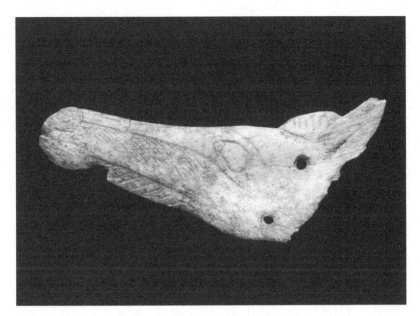

FIGURE 8.3 Magdalenian contour découpés of a horse's head from Isturitz, France

Photo © RMN-Grand Palais (musée d'Archéologie nationale) / Loïc Hamon (after Conneller 2011, figure 1.1)

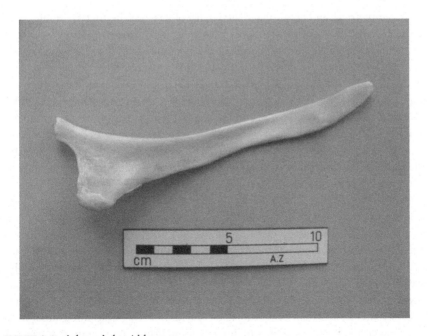

FIGURE 8.4 A horse's hyoid bone

After Conneller 2011, figure 1.2. Photo courtesy of Chantal Conneller

including talc, shell and teeth, have this same property. Critically, they are all also made to resemble each other in form. Thus, rather than people simply imposing a design located in their minds onto a substance (ivory in this case), people and other technologies came together to elicit these qualities from the material. The forms revealed in the beads were located as much in other beads as they were in the minds of the people polishing them. Once again it is the assemblage that emerges as critical to the final object and to the ways in which we – as archaeologists – understand their manufacture.

To trace assemblages from thousands of years ago, Conneller pays close attention to the materials themselves. She examines the shapes of bones, considers butchery processes and lists in detail the material properties of ivory. Most of all, she does not consider that materials are simply static things waiting for humans to come along and transform them; instead they are active players in the histories we write as archaeologists. They are animate, changing, vibrant and becoming. In different assemblages they can do different things, and rather than fixed and 'natural', they are thus just as contingent as human beings. This does not mean of course that materials can do *anything*, but they can certainly do more than we sometimes give them credit for.

Conclusions: beyond processual and postprocessual archaeologies?

Both symmetrical and new materialist archaeologies ask us to take things seriously, to consider how objects allow people to act in the world in new ways, how they make distant times present in the here and now, how their properties change and alter in the different networks and assemblages in which they find themselves. These approaches have certainly been hotly debated,[77] and there are important differences between them, which we will return to in Chapter 11. One criticism of both, often voiced in conferences but rarely in print, has been to question how different such an approach really is from the postprocessual emphasis on context. After all, didn't postprocessual archaeologists argue that it was only by attending to the context of an artefact that we could understand how it worked in the world (see Chapter 2)? The difference is twofold. First, where postprocessual archaeologists placed their emphasis on meaning, and therefore saw language as an appropriate metaphor for the archaeological record, both symmetrical and new materialist archaeologists see meaning as only one part of how objects work – indeed for some of them meaning is entirely unimportant (see below). Second, both symmetrical and new materialist archaeologists place an emphasis on the way in which things and materials themselves bring elements to the table that go beyond what human beings think, know or understand about them. They require us to pay attention to their properties and capacities, forcing us to think about how these aspects might change as part of different assemblages. This means that science, which for postprocessual archaeologists often seems to have been a poor cousin to the really meaningful acts of interpretation, takes its place as part of the central way in which archaeologists can attend to the material worlds of the past we encounter in the present.[78] In this, these fresh approaches genuinely draw on ideas that would have been familiar to at least some of the early generation of New Archaeologists.[79]

The fundamental aim of both symmetrical archaeology and new materialism then is to get away from the kinds of divides and debates that have characterised archaeological theory since its inception.[80] The dualism between immaterial ideas and material things, and culture and nature, which we saw Latour attacking at the start of the chapter, maps neatly onto the swings in archaeological theory that we described in Chapter 2; between culture historians (it's all about shared *ideas* of culture) to processualists (it's all about how we adapt *social and material* resources to the *natural* world around us) to postprocessualists (it's all about what things mean in particular *cultural* contexts). For archaeologists arguing from the perspectives we introduced in this chapter, then, the debates we have had over the last 50 years of theory have all been conducted from within a very particular and problematic understanding of the world that prevents us from really giving things and materials their due. What we need, both groups argue, is a completely different way of understanding archaeology – what we need is a new *ontology*. Ontology, as we saw in Chapter 2, means a theory of being, and it is a word used increasingly in both archaeology and anthropology to capture the ways in which these kinds of debates are attempting to generate a radically different way of thinking about the world. Both symmetrical archaeologists and new materialists are attempting to institute a '*flat ontology*'[81] in that they place humans and things on an equal footing. This does not mean that humans and things *are the same*; there are obviously important differences between a human and a cup of tea, and a human and a computer, both actual and ethical. However, there are also differences *between a cup of tea and a computer*. It is also worth emphasising that starting with a flat ontology does not mean ending in the same way – with no variations in power or authority at the end of the analysis. These approaches ask us to explore all of these differences rather than deciding beforehand that one particular difference (that between humans and everything else) is worthy of special, ontological, status. This emphasis on ontology includes not only these kinds of ideas emerging from western thinkers like Latour and Deleuze, but also from a set of perspectives trying to take the ideas of nonwestern people much more seriously than they have been previously, as we will see in Chapter 10.[82]

This approach goes a step further than the other approaches explored thus far in the book. In practice theory, the dualisms remain between structure and agency (Chapter 3). In accounts of object agency (Chapter 5), agency can be *accorded* to things but is always secondary, not the primary agency of human beings. In Chapter 6 we saw a number of different approaches to materiality that made the relationships between objects and people more complex. Nevertheless, these approaches all remained fundamentally anthropocentric in a way that is not the case for symmetrical archaeology and new materialism.[83] Even Hodder's recent theory of entanglement does not go as far in removing dualisms as these approaches do (and Hodder explicitly acknowledges this).[84] He argues that the removal of dualisms in ANT in particular means that the material qualities of things cannot be fully appreciated, and we must therefore continue to insist on a dialectic that separates humans and nonhumans.[85] Whether or not you agree with this, it certainly shows that Hodder continues to work within dualisms and to separate out humans in a way that approaches centred on Latour and Deleuze do not. In Chapter 7 we saw an account of meaning that began to move away from a concern solely with humans and symbols, but again did not go as far as the approaches we presented here.

A second criticism of symmetrical archaeology and new materialism is that a range of important factors that archaeologists, especially postprocessualists, have become interested in are ignored or downplayed in these approaches. In symmetrical archaeology in particular, questions of power, inequality, identity, gender and personhood are largely absent.[86] This is no small thing. One of the major recognitions archaeologists made in the 1980s especially was the political impact of our work, and the way in which by failing to engage with the complexities of gender roles, for example, we implicitly imposed modern preconceptions onto the past (Chapter 4). Therefore, abandoning the search for these complex past identities would seem to be a significant backwards step. In their strident criticisms of postprocessual archaeologies' explanations, have these approaches lost sight of some of the complexities of the *human* elements of the past? Potentially so. Yet there is no reason *per se* why symmetrical or new materialist approaches cannot focus on issues of power or identity, and indeed attempts have been made in this direction, particularly by those archaeologists influenced by the latter.[87] The way in which we develop our understandings of these elements of life will need to be rethought in the light of the new role we give materials in producing the worlds of the past, and thus in making, and not merely marking or symbolising, the identities of the people who lived in them.

When we go back to think about where we started the chapter, we have clearly come a long way. At the start of the chapter we asked whether we should blame the person or the gun when somebody gets shot. The answer might be that we need to blame the individual – after all, they made the decision to shoot – or that if we could only ban guns, the whole thing could have been avoided. Now we might think about it differently. It is not that the gun itself is somehow to blame, but rather that the network or assemblage has a much bigger role to play. We no longer have a dichotomy with people and their agency on one side and things and 'society' on the other that simply provide a structure for human lives. People are no longer the driving forces of history; instead they are one element of a set of relationships of swirling materials and forces that come together in the world, and allow for certain kinds of action and not others. Archaeological sites are excavated not just to understand the people who lived there but to look at the materials that were transformed there as historical actors in their own right. This does not absolve people in the past or present of responsibility for their actions, but it does ask us to think about the wider sets of processes and relations in which any specific act takes place.

We have looked at materials and objects in this chapter, but of course they are only one set of the kinds of things archaeologists write about. If we are giving more credit to their role in history and in design, what does this mean for how we think about some of the more lively members of the past? If we're willing to make objects serious players in history, surely animals and plants need to have their role expanded as well, as Ingold has emphasised.[88] How does this fit with the big stories of evolution beloved by so many archaeologists? We turn to these questions next.

Notes

1 Latour 1999: 176–80.
2 See Latour 1993, 1999, 2005.
3 Witmore 2007.
4 Webmoor and Witmore 2008.
5 See, for example, Coole and Frost 2010 or Dolphijn and van der Tuin 2012 on the philosophical backstory.
6 Some authors refer to this in the plural as new materialisms to capture the variety inherent in the approach. Here, for simplicity, we stick with the singular.
7 Bennett 2010; Ingold 2007a (for an excellent set of papers exploring some of the range of new materialist thinking in archaeology see Alberti, Jones and Pollard 2013).
8 For an analysis of some of the important differences see Garcia-Rovira 2015.
9 Indeed Witmore 2014 attempts to unite them under a single banner – see Chapter 10.
10 E.g. Latour 1987.
11 E.g. Shanks and Tilley 1987a.
12 Latour 1993.
13 Latour 1993: 10–11.
14 Latour 1987.
15 Latour 1993.
16 Latour 2005.
17 E.g. Latour 1999.
18 The term posthuman can seem to evoke a spectral figure from science fiction, something that is 'more than human'; in fact, it instead helps us to think about how the version of being human which we assume to be true, which we might term 'Man' (one that combines body with mind, has risen above nature, is somehow separate from the world, is a unique individual), never in fact existed. Thinkers like Foucault (who we met in Chapter 4) and Heidegger (who we met in Chapter 6) are sometimes called anti-humanists because they were central to the criticism of the notion of 'Man', building on the work of the German philosopher Friedrich Nietzsche (Thomas 2004). Posthumanist thinkers build on this to try and develop a more radical view on how people and things (for authors like Latour or Rosi Braidotti (2013)) or people and animals (like Donna Haraway (2008), who we will meet in the next chapter), bring each other into being.
19 Cf. Fowles 2010.
20 Latour 1999: 303, 2005: 54–5.
21 Witmore 2007: 549.
22 Jones 2002.
23 See also Boivin 2008.
24 Jones 2002: 169.
25 Jones 2002: 169.
26 Olsen 2003.
27 See Olsen et al. 2012, but also Olsen 2007, 2010; Witmore 2007, 2012; Webmoor 2007; Shanks 2007 among many others.

28 As we mention later and will discuss in more details in Chapters 10 and 11, one can divide symmetrical archaeology into a first and second wave with a clear change in emphasis between the two – here we are discussing the first wave specifically.

29 Webmoor and Witmore 2008.

30 Latour's discussion of networks has also been combined in places with more formal network analysis, which unfortunately we do not have the space to do justice to here – see Knappett 2011 for more information.

31 Witmore 2007.

32 Latour (e.g. 1999) would call this black boxing.

33 Olsen et al. 2012.

34 Witmore 2007.

35 Witmore 2007: 557.

36 Webmoor and Witmore 2008.

37 Whitridge 2004.

38 Whitridge 2004: 458.

39 Whitridge 2004: 464.

40 Attentive readers will note we have not selected an example from one of the explicitly symmetrical archaeologists. In fact, applications of 'symmetrical archaeology' to the study of the past are quite hard to find. We will return to this point in Chapter 11.

41 Webmoor and Witmore 2008.

42 See for example Witmore 2006, 2007; Olsen et al. 2012.

43 Remember the slogan? People make things and things make people.

44 Olsen 2012.

45 Barad 2003, 2007.

46 For Barad's influence in archaeology see Fowler 2013; Marshall and Alberti 2014.

47 Ingold 2007a.

48 Ingold 2007a: 15.

49 Ingold 2007a: 15.

50 The differences between the terms network, assemblage and meshwork can be a bit confusing, especially as authors use them in different ways to mean different things. For example Ingold (2015: 7) says that his meshwork differs from an assemblage because assemblages are static and deny life to things. This is precisely the opposite of how authors like Jane Bennett (2010) have used the term. Networks are sometimes seen as quite different in turn because they can imply a clear boundary between the nodes that make the network up and the relations that link them (in contrast to a meshwork or an assemblage). However, Latour's own networks are not really like this. In reality the term you use really relates to the particular set of tools you are using. So if you are following Latour you refer to networks; if you are following Ingold you use meshworks; if it's Deleuze you say assemblages.

51 See especially Deleuze and Guattari 2004.

52 For archaeological approaches that look at emotions, memory and affect in assemblages see Hamilakis 2013; Harris 2014a.

53 DeLanda 2006.

54 Conneller 2011; Ingold 2013.

55 From the Greek 'hyle' meaning matter, and 'morphe' meaning form (Ingold 2012: 432).

56 Deleuze and Guattari 2004: 450; Ingold 2012.

57 Thomas 2007.

58 Deleuze 2004.

59 Deleuze and Guattari 1983.

60 Deleuze and Guattari 2004.

61 See for example Dewsbury 2011; Thrift 2008.

62 And in archaeology see the work of Lesley McFadyen (2008, 2013).

63 E.g. DeLanda 2007.

64 DeLanda 2007: 22.

65 See for example Cobb and Croucher 2014; Fowler 2013; Harris 2014a, 2014b, 2016a, 2016b; Harrison 2011; Jones 2012; Lucas 2012; Normark 2009. A great place to start

reading about assemblages and archaeology is the special section on this subject published in Volume 27, Issue 1, of *Cambridge Archaeological Journal* from 2017, edited by Yannis Hamilakis and Andrew Jones.

66 Hamilakis 2013.
67 Bennett 2010; Harris 2014b.
68 Bennett 2010.
69 Conneller 2011.
70 Conneller 2011.
71 Conneller 2004.
72 Conneller 2011: 33.
73 Conneller 2011: 37.
74 Conneller 2011: 41.
75 Conneller 2011: 45.
76 Conneller 2011: 46.
77 Symmetrical archaeology in particular has been the subject of significant criticism, e.g. Hillerdal 2015; Lindstrøm 2015; Preucel and Mrozowski 2010; Preucel 2012; Sørensen 2013, 2016; Wallace 2011.
78 Harris 2014b.
79 E.g. Binford 1965.
80 In passing it is worth making a quick point about the difference between dualisms (especially the Cartesian dualisms we have been criticising in this book like nature and culture) and the use of different terms to explore particular processes in new materialism. If you explore assemblage theory in more depth – for example in Manuel DeLanda's (2002, 2006) work – you will find lots of terms that are contrasted with one another. For example, DeLanda, drawing on Deleuze, explores how assemblages come together (which he terms territorialisation) and break apart (which he calls deterritorialisation). (For more on the definitions of these terms see DeLanda 2006; Harris 2014b; Lucas 2012.) These terms are not dualisms, however, because they are not in opposition to one another, but rather different elements of a continuous process, and also because the same things operate at both ends of the spectrum at the same time. When something leaves one assemblage (deterritorialises) it almost always becomes part of another (territorialises). This is very different from the antithetical opposition of dualisms we have been discussing so far.
81 DeLanda 2002.
82 There is also a tension here between philosophical approaches to ontology, like those of DeLanda, Deleuze and Latour, that offer a worldwide vision for a single ontology, and the kinds of local nonwestern ontologies we will see in the next chapter. We will return to this tension in Chapter 11.
83 Ingold 2007a; although cf. Ingold 2012: 430–1 which accuses even symmetrical archaeology of latent anthropocentrism!
84 Hodder 2012: 93.
85 Hodder 2012: 94.
86 Preucel and Mrozowski 2010: 17; Preucel 2012; Harris 2016a.
87 E.g. Harris 2016a; Normark 2012.
88 Ingold 2012.

9

MULTI-SPECIES ARCHAEOLOGY

People, plants and animals

Introduction: archaeology beyond the human

Imagine the scene 12,000 years ago in south-western Anatolia, Turkey. People are erecting circles of large, T-shaped, stone pillars. This requires a huge amount of effort and lots of people gathering together, working towards a common goal. What happens when you gather lots of people in one place? You need to feed them, of course. As a result, the plants in the local area begin to be harvested more intently. Their seeds are gathered and replanted, and other people bring new seeds from their own local areas to plant them as well. As the plants grow, people preferentially begin to select certain varieties that have characteristics that suit them better – size, flavour, seasonality or otherwise. This changes the plants' biology. Slowly the plants begin to depend on people and they fall under their control. What was once a 'natural process' is now at the mercy of 'culture'. People have turned something that was once 'wild' into something that is now 'domesticated'. A few millennia later, not far away, a similar process will happen with animals as first sheep and goats, and later cattle, will begin to be contained, herded and selectively bred for particular characteristics. In these moments human beings throw off the shackles of nature and assert their mastery of the world around them. No longer hunter gatherers, these people are now farmers. The great march of civilisation has begun, resulting – inevitably – in the world we know today.

Now hopefully after what you've read so far in this book, the paragraph above already strikes you as pretty problematic. To begin, you may think it is a very short summary of some very complicated processes (it is) or that the archaeologists who write about this think in more nuanced ways than this (they do). But putting that to one side, many of the themes outlined do crop up (pun intended) in how archaeologists discuss the process of domestication.[1] Humans, for example, are seen as opposed to animals and plants, especially once they asserted their dominance over them. Here, culture – the preserve of humans – is separated from nature, the domestic from the wild and farmers from hunter gatherers. In other words, our traditional understandings of the emergence of agriculture are entirely dominated by the kinds of dualisms we have been so critical of in this book.

In the last chapter we looked at how symmetrical archaeology and new materialism have asked us to begin to think quite differently about how people and things, and materials more broadly, interact with each other. Once we start thinking about things in these new ways, we are naturally drawn into asking different kinds of questions about people, animals and plants as well. What might the process of domestication look like if instead of thinking about people as separate to plants and animals, we began to think of them as caught up in relationships, networks or assemblages? What happens if we think about plants or animals having *agency* in the manner we thought of in Chapter 5? Or concentrate on their materiality, just as we did with things in Chapter 6? The domestication of plants and animals is often treated as the most significant transformation in human history. How would our self-understanding change if this moment of domestication suddenly became as much about the lives of plants and animals as it was about people's control of them? How might this challenge the anthropocentrism that some archaeologists have grown more critical of? The issue of relationships is central to our concerns here once again (Figure 9.1).

If you think about the animals and plants in your own life, you can start to pick apart the simplistic distinctions that form the basis for how archaeologists have traditionally thought about animals and plants in the past. Think about how their needs shape yours – the fact that they demand to be taken for a walk, or need you to be home to feed them, or need watering, or wake you up by sitting on you far earlier in the morning than you would like. The key thing, as with our trowel in the cartoon below (Figure 9.1), is that we have relationships with these other beings, and just like the dog, these beings look back at us.[2] The philosopher of science Donna Haraway[3] (Box 9.2) has suggested we would be better off thinking about the other animals in our lives as companion species, rather than pets or

FIGURE 9.1   Relationships with plants and animals; both are active in the world, though the danger of being chewed by a dog may be more obvious to our trowel. Drawing by K-Fai Steele

property, and in this chapter we will consider how developments in these directions both within and outside archaeology are having an important impact.

We begin the chapter by looking at the first moves in this direction as archaeologists in the 1980s and 1990s became very interested in what animals and plants meant to people in the past – what they symbolised. We build upon these early studies by then looking at how thinkers outside archaeology have begun to develop much more critical ways of understanding and writing about animals and plants, leading to the possibility of a 'multi-species' approach to the past. Tim Ingold (who we met in the last chapter; Box 9.1) and Donna Haraway (Box 9.2) are critical thinkers in this regard. Following this, we turn to look at how archaeologists have begun to apply these ideas. This leads to an examination of the broader challenges these approaches raise, including for how archaeology engages with wider debates about evolution. This will lead us back to a discussion that touches on some of the ideas and thinkers we discussed in Chapter 7, as well as proposing that evolutionary thinking has much to offer, providing it is included in a *non-dualist* manner. We conclude by returning to the issues of domestication raised above.

Archaeology, plants and animals

Processualists, of course, were really the first group of archaeologists to take plants and animals seriously. As you'll recall, processual archaeology (see Chapter 2) was very interested in topics like economy – how people made their living and survived – and also sought to develop scientific approaches to the past. The study of plants and animals, archaeobotany and archaeozoology, soon became full-fledged sub-disciplines within archaeology. Scholars like Eric Higgs[4] led attempts to consider how different economies could be constructed around different patterns of hunting, herding, milking, gathering and harvesting. What was critical here was not what an animal meant, or whether people cared about them, but the 'hard' issues of calorific content, kill-off patterns and seasonality.

For postprocessual archaeologists, it quickly became clear that there was more to be said about animals than just how many of them there were or when and how they were slaughtered. As we saw in Chapter 2, one of the great influences on early postprocessual archaeology was structuralism, especially through the work of the anthropologist Claude Lévi-Strauss. Lévi-Strauss[5] famously said that natural species were not just 'good to eat', but also 'good to think'. Postprocessual archaeologists took this idea and ran with it, particularly in relation to animals. Suddenly the bones of animals found at archaeological sites were not simply representative of one kind of economy or another; they could indicate a whole wider set of important concerns. Animal bones became 'symbolic'. For example, looking at the Late Mesolithic hunter gatherers of Southern Scandinavia, a group known today as the Ertebølle, Christopher Tilley argued that red deer were of 'great symbolic significance'.[6] Examining the decoration of hunting points used to kill them, the use of deer teeth as decoration, the presence of antler in graves as well as their importance economically, Tilley suggested there were a whole host of metaphorical connections between people and deer. Deer offered people a 'symbolic resource' they could draw on to create 'allusions and analogies'.[7]

Although initially driven by the theoretical interests of early postprocessual archaeologists, it was not long before many zooarchaeologists themselves became interested in the social aspect of animal worlds and animal lives. Drawing on their expertise as specialists in animal bone studies, as well as an engaged reading of wider theoretical issues, authors such as Nerissa Russell[8] have sketched out the way in which these kinds of data can engage with cultural questions. For example, Russell and her colleague Kevin McGowan studied the bones of cranes from Çatalhöyük in Turkey (the same site we saw Ian Hodder discussing in Chapter 6). They discussed the recovery of the left wing of a crane from a particular deposit also containing a dog skull, a complete cattle horn core and two wild goat horn cores.[9] The wing seemed to have been deposited whole, and a close analysis of the bones revealed no evidence of butchery. The cut marks that were present seem instead to indicate that holes had been made in the wing to attach it to something. Drawing on this evidence, alongside representations of cranes at the site, Russell and McGowan argued that someone might have worn the wing during particular rituals.[10] Cranes dance, and this may have been witnessed and mimicked by people at Çatalhöyük. They suggest that because in contemporary nonwestern societies there is an association between fertility and cranes, this may mean that a similar association existed there. Cranes at the site symbolised life, whereas vultures (which often appear on the walls of the houses there) symbolised death.[11] In this example we see how a close analysis of the bones themselves can present interesting possibilities for the ways in which past people might have thought about animals.

Occasionally, archaeologists have also focused on the symbolic potential of plants, and the roles they may have played in past societies. For example, Christine Hastorf and Sissel Johannessen[12] examined the role of maize in Peru between 500 and 1500 AD and suggested that it became increasingly symbolically powerful through time. They argued that, in the Mantaro Valley of Peru, the increase in the amount of maize grown through time reflected an increase in the production of maize beer. Drawing on ethnographic and historical records, they showed how maize beer is important to indigenous communities of the region; in particular it plays a critical role at certain social events through its *symbolic* power. In turn they linked the archaeobotanical evidence for increased production, and the evidence for different processes of working the crop, to other signs of growing social inequality to argue that maize beer played a critical role in developing political power structures. This took place primarily through the way elites hosted feasts where the local community would be given the beer.[13] These acts of feasting created debt relationships that were repaid in labour, confirming the political inequalities of the period. The symbolic power of maize was critical because this transformed the nature of the debts that were incurred, making their repayment obligatory. The authors emphasise that the archaeological evidence can tell us much more than just that people were growing and using maize; in fact, when linked with other areas, it tells us about the social and political lives of people at the time.[14]

These archaeologists are among many that have done an excellent job of linking the 'hard' data of animal and plant remains to broader kinds of 'social' questions. At the same time, however, it is worth noting that for all their discussions of animals and plants, their real focus lies somewhere else . . . on human beings! So Tilley can examine red deer not only for their economic importance but also for their symbolism, or Russell and McGowan can discuss what humans believed about cranes, or Hastorf and Johannessen can set out the political and social capital maize creates, but the interest and the focus is primarily on the human. Now as archaeologists this is unsurprising; of course we are interested in humans. Yet in this approach the focus on human beings creates a gap between them and everything else in the world. What matters about cranes or maize or deer is what they *symbolise*, what they *represent*, and thus what matters is how they appear in people's heads, rather than the full role they played as living agents in past worlds. As we saw in the last chapter with material things, this gap or separation between humans on the one side and everything else on the other is not just one of degree, but rather one of kind. The difference, in other words, is *ontological*. This means that dualisms sweep back in: human versus animal or culture versus nature, with all the attendant problems we have discussed in this book. So archaeologists need to find a way of discussing humans, plants and animals that doesn't hide our interest in human beings, but equally avoids separating them off as a uniquely special entity in the world. We need a flat ontology, in other words (see Chapter 8). In a moment we will look at archaeologists who are trying to do exactly that, but beforehand it is worth outlining some of the important thinkers who have influenced this debate. This will also help us draw out how our understandings of animals and plants have remained largely anthropocentric, and how we can seek to challenge this.

Thinking about a multi-species world

In many disciplines closely related to archaeology, scholars have become increasingly interested in the roles of plants and especially animals alongside humans in creating particular kinds of society, and particular kinds of worlds. For example, in geography a number of fascinating studies have looked at the role of elephants,[15] reindeer[16] and monkeys[17] in working with humans to shape the conditions of each other's lives. Part of the motivation for these new ways of thinking has come from close studies of animal behaviour,[18] but perhaps more important has been the criticism of anthropocentrism and the dichotomy of nature and culture on which this rests. Many authors have written on these subjects but when it comes to plants and animals, two have been especially important: Tim Ingold and Donna Haraway.

BOX 9.1 TIM INGOLD

Tim Ingold is Professor of Social Anthropology at the University of Aberdeen. His work in the 1990s was especially influenced by ecological psychology and phenomenology, and was brought together in an exceptional set of essays titled *The Perception of the Environment*.[19] In more recent years he has interrogated the notions of making and the importance of lines, and has taken an approach increasingly influenced by Deleuze and Guattari (see Box 8.2). This can be found in his books *Lines*,[20] *Being Alive*[21] and *Making*.[22] Here we use a tree to represent Ingold's work as it fits the example below. This tree is one that grows in a park in Leicester. It was planted by people and is regularly tended by them – at some point it may be cut down by them. It shares relationships with humans but also many other creatures including dogs, birds and squirrels.

Photo: Oliver Harris

We encountered the work of Ingold in the previous chapter where we looked at his important paper considering the animate nature of a simple stone. He is perhaps more famous, however, for his work attacking and undermining the dichotomies of nature and culture through his anthropological analysis of the ways in which humans, animals and plants live, and the surprising similarities in the nature of their Being-in-the-world. Being-in-the-world . . . sound familiar? We encountered that turn of phrase when we looked at phenomenology in Chapter 6. Ingold's attack on dualisms between humans and nonhumans has been greatly influenced by the work of Martin Heidegger (and to a lesser extent, Maurice Merleau-Ponty) who we discussed in that chapter. This does not mean that Ingold wanders around landscapes thinking about what it would be like to be an animal. Instead he uses the ideas of Being-in-the-world, and especially Heidegger's concept of dwelling, to bridge the gap that seems to exist between humans, animals, plants and landscapes.

Ingold draws on Heidegger to discuss what he calls the 'dwelling perspective', an approach that has quite profound implications for how we think about the differences between humans and animals. There are lots of examples of this in Ingold's work, but a great one comes from his consideration of the nature of architecture. Now architecture normally is taken to be a uniquely human thing. Unlike large plant organisms like trees, which might operate as a kind of shelter for an animal, or even more formal kinds of building that animals make and inhabit, ranging from beavers' lodges to birds' nests, human architecture like a house seems different. Human architecture follows cultural patterns and deliberate choices. Unlike animals, seemingly, 'humans are the authors of their own designs'.[23]

We have already seen in the last chapter how views of human design like this one are not very satisfactory. This is because they don't take into account the role material things play in the process of building. Such views are also, as Ingold points out, clearly based on the distinction between nature and culture. They presuppose that human beings operate within the world, but also simultaneously outside of it, as somehow above nature. Instead, Ingold insists, quoting Heidegger, 'to build is in itself already to dwell'.[24] That is, to make something in the world, you have to be fully part of it, to be immersed within it. Okay, but what does this mean in practice, and what does it mean for plants and animals? Ingold asks us to consider the differences between an oak tree on the one hand and a house on the other. Which of these is architecture? Pretty obvious, you might think. The house is designed and built intentionally by people, while the tree is just 'there' naturally. But as soon as you start to think about it from a position outside of the nature versus culture dualism, these distinctions may not be as clear-cut, Ingold suggests. The tree, just like the house, is lived in by all sorts of things: a fox digs a den among the roots, an owl builds a nest in the tree, squirrels run over its branches and beetles bore into it.[25] The shape of the tree has been altered over many years by all of these things and more, the different flows of wind and weather, the places the roots can get to and so on. The form of the tree is not prefigured in its genetic structure, in other words – which in itself is historical, of course – but rather emerges through its Being-in-the-world, in the actual process of it growing and existing in a set of relationships with other beings, and we do not need to privilege the human relationships here as we saw with our fallen tree in Chapter 7. Then think about the house; it too doesn't emerge as a final and fixed thing out of nowhere, but rather as a process involving the materials it is built from, the people and animals that start to live in its nooks and crannies.[26] To keep the house standing – alive, you might say – it requires repair and treatment, just as an oak tree needs water and sunlight. It too is part of a relational 'meshwork', Ingold would argue, of people, animals, plants and materials.[27]

The difference between a tree and a house is thus not one of natural organism versus cultural design; it is not one of absolutes therefore, Ingold argues, but rather about the degree of human involvement in the process of their emergence.[28] There are trees that grow in the world with no human engagement with them, some that grow in woods tended by humans and some that are planted, shaped, trimmed and felled by people. There are different kinds of relationships going on here. Now human beings may well be more involved in the building of a house, but this does not move it entirely into a separate ontological realm. The collapse of the nature/culture dualism allows Ingold to challenge other dichoto-mies as well, such as the difference between domesticated plants and wild plants. Traditionally the former have been seen as part of culture, the latter as part of nature. Instead, Ingold argues that the difference is only one of degree – the degree of human involvement in the conditions of growth.[29] This means we do not need to search the past for the moment of domestication; instead we can trace histories of humans, plants and animals becoming increasingly caught up in rela-tions with one other – interlocking dependences and dependencies, in Hodder's[30] terms (see Chapter 6). This collapse of the difference between culture and nature also has implications for the distinction between history and evolution, a point we return to below.

Donna Haraway's work on animals has had a profound impact across the human-ities and social sciences. While her direct influence on archaeology doesn't quite match Ingold's, she stands at the forefront of a set of approaches that are becoming increasingly important, as we will see below. Haraway's work on animals focuses on what she terms companion species.[31] She means not just pets by this term (although she includes them too) but also all the animals that humans encounter, work and live with in cities, farms, parks and medical testing labs. For Haraway the traditional hard divides between humans and animals are deeply unsatisfactory. She argues strongly that the way in which humans are seen as uniquely different to all other nonhuman animals has emerged out of the same lines of thinking that would privilege particular forms of humanity (male, white, heterosexual) over others. More than this, Haraway says, we cannot hope to understand the actual complexity of the world if we start with these hard and fast 'great divides' (and here she harks back to Bruno Latour who we met in the last chapter).[32]

BOX 9.2 DONNA HARAWAY

Donna Haraway is Distinguished Professor Emerita at the University of California, Santa Cruz. Having completed a PhD in biology at Yale, her work has focused on a wide range of questions that concern science and technology studies and feminism. She made her name when she published *A Cyborg Manifesto* in 1985, which argued that the blurring of human/machine boundaries pointed the way towards resolving issues like the nature/culture dichotomy, an argument developed in *Simians, Cyborgs and Women*.[33] More recently, her work has focused on human–animal relations, both within and outside of the medical and scientific sphere, in books like *Modest Witness@Second Millennium. FemaleMan©Meets OncoMouse™: Feminism and Technoscience*[34] and *When Species Meet*.[35] Here we use a picture of the second author's companion animal to stand in for Haraway's work.

Photo: Craig Cipolla

Rather than dividing the world into prefigured neat little packages, therefore, Haraway[36] suggests we need to pay attention to the process of 'becoming with', the way in which people and animals work together to exist in the world. As she puts it, 'the partners do not precede their relating'.[37] In other words, we cannot take a single category of animal (like a cow, say) and think about it outside of all the relations it has with the world, including the farmer who owns it. Nor can we think about the farmer without also thinking about the cow (and all the animals that she works – or becomes – with). One of the consequences of this, for Haraway, is that we need to pay very close attention to animals, to what they do and what they tell us, as well as the way in which they interact with people if we want to understand their – and therefore our – histories. In particular it is these relationships that are absolutely key, making Haraway's work a great example of relational thinking.

This emphasis on relations allows Haraway to tease out the differences between traditional views of how animals exist in the world, with her emphasis on becoming with. For example, she looks at the work of the bioanthropologist Barbara Smuts.[38] During the work for her PhD, Smuts (after some adventures involving kidnaps and ransoms) studied baboons in Kenya. She had been told that in order not to disturb the baboons 'natural' behaviour she should stay as still as possible when near them and avoid engaging with them in any way. However, Smuts found that this act completely put the baboons off what they would normally be doing – they found the presence of a human acting like a rock to be quite strange (as might any of us). In fact Smuts found it was only when she started to respond appropriately, to look at and acknowledge the baboons, that they began to relax (after shooting her some dirty looks) and act normally at all. In contrast to the image of the 'objective' scientist not interfering with the experiment, it was by learning to engage with and respond to the baboons that Smuts was able to form a relationship with them and study them. Both she and the baboons had to learn together – to become with one another in Haraway's terms – to get along.

Haraway's own research follows similar lines. In examining the history of dog breeding she has shown how processes of domestication are the particular 'knots' that interweave humans, animals and other organisms together in new ways.[39] Quite different from the human-centric process we started the chapter with, this way of understanding human–animal relationships focuses on how both emerge out of a process of 'becoming with'. She also combines these histories with detailed studies of the relationships between particular dogs and particular humans, and between particular dogs and other animals – she resists any attempt to simply lump them all together, to *homogenise* them.

Haraway's work, particularly because of the way she embraces science and technology and rejects what she calls 'the foolishness' of human exceptionalism, is sometimes referred to as posthumanist, a term we encountered in Chapter 8. This might sound like the stuff of science fiction, but as we saw, it is really about taking a position that rejects the idea that human beings are at the centre of everything (a notion we might call 'humanist'). Haraway herself rejects the term posthumanism,[40] but her work is consistently associated with a wider set of approaches that do fall under this banner and are attempting to explore what this might mean for how we understand humans in the present, always caught up in the 'dance of relating'[41] with materials (as we saw in the last chapter) and nonhuman organisms we have seen here. The key point Haraway makes is that all of this does not mean going around making animals just like humans (anthropomorphising them[42]) or presuming that the differences between them are absolute (and thus ontological). Remember, we first raised this point in Chapter 1 where we elaborated on our reasons for anthropomorphising the trowel in our cartoons. We also noted that the cartoons represent an oversimplified view of our trowel, but one that we feel works as a teaching device in this setting (i.e., an introduction to contemporary archaeological theory). When you think about the cartoons, please remember that things aren't so simple. This means that we need to explore the differences (between animals, plants, humans, trowels, etc.) to engage with them, to consider how power works across them and to give these differences the weight they deserve.[43] For the purposes of this chapter, we need to think about the relations that make people and animals from the very start.

More-than-human archaeology

Ingold and Haraway, among other authors, have begun to tease out the way in which plants, humans and animals emerge together in bundles of historically situated relationships. All very well, but how have these ideas been applied archaeologically? We are still in the early days of archaeologists engaging with and trying to figure these sorts of ideas out, but already certain articles are beginning to develop ideas for how these might lead to new ways of thinking about animals and plants in the past. Here we want to look at some examples of this to show the differences that these new theoretical ideas are making.

Let's start with the ever-popular animals. A great example of how archaeologists are trying to think about animals differently comes from the work of Nick Overton and Yannis Hamilakis.[44] They have proposed that archaeologists need to develop a social zooarchaeology. This is a somewhat confusing name, as it is also the name of the approach Nerissa Russell[45] gives her work despite the considerable differences between them. A better way of thinking about Overton and Hamilakis' ideas actually comes from a term they develop within the article – zoontology.[46] Drawing on thinkers like Haraway in particular, Overton and Hamilakis are critical both of traditional zooarchaeology (animals are all about calories and economy) and more recent approaches that have concentrated on animal symbolism or their role in ritual. In both cases, as we saw above, the approaches remain anthropocentric, meaning that animals are assumed to be there purely for the *benefit of humans*.[47] They also argue that simply putting all nonhumans of this form under the category of 'animal' oversimplifies the world by lumping a variety of different organisms together. Just like Haraway, they ask us to attend to the detail of animals' lives and the detail of their relationships with human beings. Species here are caught up in what they call 'co-shaping' – exactly what Haraway calls 'becoming with'.

How does this actually work in practice? Overton and Hamilakis explore these ideas in more depth with a case from the last period of hunting and gathering in Southern Scandinavia – the same Mesolithic Ertebølle groups we saw Tilley looking at above. In particular, the authors are interested in the relationship between humans and a particular type of swan. They re-examined the site of Aggersund in Denmark, which was traditionally interpreted as a place where humans gathered in the winter months to hunt swans. Within the typical framework of the 1970s, when the site was excavated, such economic concerns were paramount. Overton and Hamilakis[48] do not deny that swans were hunted at the site, but their concern was to develop a way to think about how swans and humans *came to understand each other* through their experiences of the world. So they look in detail at what we know about swan behaviour, about the patterns of action that the swans would have undertaken and that humans would have witnessed – the mating pairs, the patterns of food consumption and acts of migration. They also stress how we need to think about the swans not simply as all the same; people may have noticed the difference in sex among the swans and would certainly have seen the different ways swans acted and looked as juveniles. Overton and Hamilakis combine this examination of swan behaviour with detailed analysis of butchery of the animals to create a complex picture of how swans and humans engaged with one another in Denmark more than 6,000 years ago. A swan's wings are critical to the dances they perform and the ways that they communicate; the removal of the feathered part of these wings by people thus takes on new importance.[49] Critically, the role of the swans and the detail of their practices and performances are as central here as the understanding and engagement of human beings.

When we think about the societies we study in the past, it is pretty easy to imagine animals playing an important role. Thinking about animal 'agency' is actually much more straightforward than thinking about the kinds of object agency we encountered in Chapter 5. After all, we can debate about whether objects can act in the world, but no one doubts that animals can, even the apparently most placid of our current domesticated companion species. But what about plants? Surely plants are pretty passive; after all, as frightened as one might be crossing a field full of cows, no one looks down at the grass shivering and wondering if it might bite them . . . . Think about how we contrast 'vegetative' with 'animate' or why we might call someone a couch potato.[50] Of course, like so many things, this just reveals our assumptions about how the world works. Plants do move, often towards the sun. Plants also affect and shape the world around them. Roots grow and undermine buildings, flowers attract insects and fruits encourage us to care for their trees and plant their seeds. As the geographers Leslie Head, Janet Aitchison and Alison Gates[51] have pointed out, the notion of the 'passive' plant depends on very traditional western perspective going back to Aristotle, and tells us almost nothing about how plants actually operate, or how they interweave with humans.

Archaeologists are beginning to explore these issues. Marijke Van der Veen,[52] for example, has explored the co-evolution of people and plants together in many different contexts, and looked at how the material properties of plants affect how they interact with the world. She points out how plants' tastes and chemical properties can change how people experience the world around them when they are consumed. The needs of plants also tie people into relationships of dependency of different kinds. Critically, however, she recognises how these properties emerge through the relationships plants have with people.[53] Sugar, for example, became a widely traded product through a complex history not only involving its flavour, but also slavery and capitalism; the associated historical connections at the time also introduced maize to Africa, sustaining a population that was then raided for further slaves to grow more sugar.[54] Many different plants have enmeshed humans in their relations with the world, and just as (some) humans have benefited from this, so have (some) plants, allowing new forms of practices, like farming, to come into existence.

Plants can also propagate in ways very different from human beings and other animals. Huw Barton and Tim Denham[55] have explored how vegetative propagation (that is, asexual reproduction where cuttings of plants can be taken and replanted elsewhere) provides alternative models for kinship relationships in Melanesia and South-East Asia (Figure 9.2). In western society we sometimes use agricultural metaphors; think of 'ploughing a furrow' or 'sowing the seeds of discontent'. In other words, our history of certain kinds of relationships with cereal plants gives us certain tools to think about the world. Using both ethnographic and archaeological evidence, Barton and Denham are able to show how the material properties of plants like taro and yams lend themselves to different practices of harvesting and movement, and thus certain kinds of relationships with people – what they term 'vegecultures'.[56] Because the plants Denham and Barton study reproduce very differently to western cereal crops, they offer people other ways of thinking about and constructing society. Alongside this, the way people move the cuttings of these plants around creates the possibility for new forms of plant hybrids to emerge. New forms of plant can thus emerge even as these plants themselves create the possibilities for different kinds of human communities – people and plants *becoming with* each other indeed.

These different approaches tie together. Using them, we can think about the wider environment, which we might term landscape. Whereas in previous traditions of thought, landscape was seen as something that formed a backdrop of economic resources to human actions (processualism), something that symbolised things to people (postprocessualism) or even something that people simply experienced (phenomenological approaches), it is now something much more active. People, plants, animals and the material of the earth itself all play their role in shaping and being shaped by each other. This is a way of thinking about the world as an ecosystem but one that does not require the concept of nature to operate. The landscape itself is understood as an ongoing product of these histories of interaction, of what Haraway calls the 'dance of relating' between all of these different elements, living or otherwise.[57]

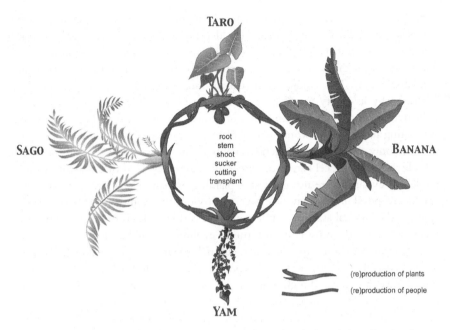

FIGURE 9.2 The mutually entangled character of social and plant (re)production in vegecultural systems

Image devised by Tim Denham following conversations with John Muke, reproduced with kind permission of Huw Barton and Tim Denham (after Barton and Denham 2011: figure 2.2)

Beyond history versus evolution?

Where does this leave evolution in all of this? There has been a long-standing interest in evolution in archaeology, particularly among those who orient to processual ways of thinking.[58] How different or similar are their approaches compared with what we described so far in this chapter? To start, we must note that evolutionary archaeology is a big and complex field that comes in many different forms. However, it often draws directly on approaches that can be traced back to the ideas of Charles Darwin and are therefore often referred to as Darwinian. If you're interested in these approaches, you can read more about them in many different places.[59] As we stressed in Chapter 1, evolutionary archaeology does not feature heavily in this book because we are tracing a particular trajectory of archaeological thought, a particular set of relations, and not trying to be encyclopaedic; it's the same reason we don't discuss important contributions in Russian or Czech archaeological theory,[60] to give two random examples. Nevertheless, in this context it is certainly worth exploring some of the overlaps that exist with evolutionary archaeology.

The first critical overlap with the approaches we have discussed in this chapter is that Darwinian approaches not only engage with plants and animals, they also avoid anthropocentrism.[61] By saying that human beings are the subject of evolution just like plants and animals, you immediately 'decentre' people.[62] The difficulty is that this leaves evolutionary archaeology in a difficult position with two options. The first possibility is that you reduce *all* human behaviour to the rules of Darwinian natural selection. This would mean that all human behaviour would need to be explained by its ability to affect reproductive success. This would be extremely reductive and quite problematic because it would *reduce* everything to a single motivating factor. How would you explain the great variety of human practices that not only diminish reproductive likelihood, but even remove it all together (of which becoming celibate is the obvious example)? Given that straightforward models of evolution are not great at explaining human behaviour, therefore, the alternative possibility is that you have to propose that somewhat different rules apply to the cultural aspects of inheritance. This is what leads to 'dual inheritance theory',[63] one of the most popular forms of evolutionary archaeology. One part of the inheritance is natural and the other, cultural. Instantly we are back in the world of dualisms, and humans are different once again.[64] As Hodder[65] argued, relationships between people, things, animals and places have lots of variables and the chance of reproductive success on which most evolutionary archaeology depends is only one of them. More recent approaches exploring the interweaving of cultural and genetic change together point towards the possibility of more productive ways forward, *if* we can discuss them without reverting back to unhelpful dualisms.[66] Similarly, approaches that recognise we cannot begin with a dualism between organism and environment, or organism and material thing, but rather see how both emerge together (because as much as the organism adapts to the environment, so it also shapes its environment) have much to offer.[67]

The other critical difference between the approaches advocated here and evolutionary archaeology is in the attitude towards relations. In his book on evolutionary archaeology, Stephen Shennan takes a look at the entangled bank with which Charles Darwin finishes off his famous *On the Origin of Species*. The bank was full of birds, insects and plants interwoven with one another. Shennan[68] bemoans the way in which archaeologists have become 'beguiled' in the complexities of their own 'entangled banks'. In other words, he suggests most archaeologists have become too parochial, and need to pull back from the specificities of the small-scale to generate more general histories.[69] The approaches we have looked at here would take a different view – it is in the very detail of these entangled relations, in the ecological account of organisms in their environment, in the *becoming with* of these different species that we would look to for our new understanding. This is the case whether we work at the small or the large scale.[70]

From the perspective of authors like Ingold or Haraway, the move we need to make is thus not to reduce history to the rules of evolution. Nor is it, of course, to ignore the biological processes that make organic life what it is. Instead we need to see how the difference between history and evolution is in itself another dichotomy we need to escape from, and that doing so will allow us to think about the co-evolution and the mutual becomings of the plants, animals and people we study.[71] In other words, we need to focus on a broader ecology that includes people, plants, animals and, indeed, materials.[72]

Biosemiotics

One further link between the approaches we have discussed in this chapter and those looked at elsewhere in the book can be developed by thinking through ideas of *biosemiotics*, which takes us back to Chapter 7. Remember semiotics? That is the study of signs, and biosemiotics is a set of approaches that apply these theories not just to human beings, but to the rest of the world as well. In Chapter 7 we looked at the way in which a three-way (or triadic) system can help us think about how meanings are generated relationally. A biosemiotic framework takes this and applies it to the world well beyond humans. For instance, Charles Sanders Peirce, who you read about in Chapter 7, wrote of the interaction between a sunflower and the sun as a semiotic process.[73] Sunflowers move throughout the course of the day; their faces follow the sun as it travels the sky from east to west. For Peirce, the movement of the sunflower *indexically* links (that is, through a spatiotemporal connection) to the movement of the sun; through this indexical relationship, a new 'interpretant' eventually emerges: a new generation of sunflowers that acts in just the same way as this generation. Biosemiotics thus also draws on evolutionary thinking in its focus on the process of reproduction and forward-moving change. However, it does so in a way that is much more compatible with the relational approaches we have been looking at in this book. Its primary focus is *life*.

John Barrett[74] draws on the work of Charles Sanders Peirce to think about how we can conceptualise the process of life in a way that does not radically separate human beings from plants, animals and other organisms. Barrett[75] argues that Peirce's scheme emphasises the relations that an organism has with its environment. Neither the organism nor a particular process – like evolution – can exist outside of the specific and particular relationships through which life takes place.[76] Within this account, for Barrett, 'humanness' becomes something that is situated and relational (much as it is for Haraway and other thinkers we might call posthumanist). The aim of archaeology, therefore, should be primarily aimed at explaining the emergence of these different kinds of humanity.

One interesting point of emphasis that emerges from these perspectives marks a critical difference between the kinds of relational approaches we saw in the last chapter and the biosemiotics that Barrett employs. It is the distinction between organic life and the rest of the material world. In the last chapter we saw how new materialists see material things as 'vibrant' or as living in one sense. Jane Bennett,[77] one of the leading figures in this field, argues explicitly that she wants to break down the boundaries between organic and inorganic matter. In contrast, Barrett argues we must impose a firm division, you might say construct a dualism, between living and non-living things. An organism, he says, is 'directed towards its self-affirmation and renewal', unlike non-living things.[78] Is this true? Does there need to be a hard and fast dualism between living and non-living things? Or is there a way we can attend to what Deleuze and Guattari call 'a life proper to matter'?[79]

There are certainly archaeologists who view this dualism as an unhelpfully hard line to draw in that it insists that there is an ontological distinction between you and the clothes you wear, between a bird and its nest and so on. In Chapter 11 we will return to this point as it relates to our individual views on theory. For now, we will mainly point the way to other archaeologists who wrestle with this question. For instance, Lambros Malafouris[80] has recently put forward a compelling argument that to understand the emergence and evolution of human intelligence, you have to think about how people learn to think through and with material things. For him the boundaries of the human stretch out into and include the material world. There can be no hard and fast division here between what is 'organic' and what is 'inorganic'. This is not to suggest there aren't any differences between living and non-living things, but that these distinctions no more deserve to be made ontological than that between an amoeba and an elephant or between a grain of sand and a skyscraper.

Conclusions: back to domestication

We started this chapter with a traditional story of domestication; as people incorporated plants and animals within their worlds, they became part of culture, rather than solely 'natural'. In contrast to this view, we have looked at some of the approaches to plants and animals that do not see them solely as resources (economic or symbolic) for people in the past (and archaeologists in the present) to draw upon. Instead we have begun to think about what it might mean to see humans, plants and animals as caught up in a process of becoming with one another. We also explored what it might mean to think about these collectives as the focus of our efforts, rather than taking a fixed idea of humans as the starting point and then turning to work out what they did with the world around them. What would this mean for domestication?

To begin, we cannot talk about humans domesticating plants and animals – that implies that this is something that active subjects in the world (people) do to passive and unresisting objects (animals and plants). In other words, this automatically brings in dualisms (culture/nature and subject/object). So instead we have to approach this as a process that entwines plants, animals and people together. This allows us to see how animals changed through the process of domestication but so did people, not only in terms of their society, but also in their physiology and their genetics, such as the (relatively) recent ability to digest milk in adulthood.[81] These changes also involved ways of living and material things as well, and indeed also transformed landscapes in turn. As people became dependent on crops, they cleared areas for them. This can create issues with erosion changing water runoff patterns, leading to flooding, requiring people to move the locations of settlements and forcing new relationships with plants and animals as they do so. Here, then, whole landscapes emerge as interconnected suites of relationships, as ecologies, linking earth, water, weather, people, plants and animals together. Domestication here is an evolutionary process as much as a historical one, and one in which we cannot divide different changes into two opposed camps.

In this chapter we have looked at how archaeologists are beginning to grant plants and animals a different role in our accounts of the past, and the relational theories they have used to do this. In one sense we could think about plants and animals as examples of groups of 'Others' we normally give a secondary place to in our accounts of the past. In the next chapter we turn to the voices of a nonwestern people to see how these too can add to our accounts, both in relation to colonialism but also as a force for the construction of theory itself. We also turn to some recent calls to employ the 'postcolonial' critique to things themselves, and with that the first arguments that relational thinking may not be all it's cracked up to be.

Notes

1 E.g. Clutton-Brock 1994.
2 Cf. Derrida 2002.
3 Haraway 2003.
4 Higgs 1975.
5 Lévi-Strauss 1964: 89.
6 Tilley 1996: 62.
7 Tilley 1996: 64.
8 Russell 2011.
9 Russell and McGowan 2003: 446.
10 Russell and McGowan 2003: 451.
11 Russell and McGowan 2003: 452.
12 Hastorf and Johannessen 1993.
13 Hastorf and Johannessen 1993: 130.
14 Hastorf and Johannessen 1993: 132.
15 Lorimer 2010.
16 Lorimer 2006.
17 Fuentes 2007.
18 Smuts 2001.
19 Ingold 2000.
20 Ingold 2007b.
21 Ingold 2011.
22 Ingold 2013.
23 Ingold 2000: 175.
24 Ingold 2000: 186.
25 Ingold 2000: 187.
26 Ingold 2000: 187.
27 Ingold 2013.
28 Ingold 2000: 187.
29 Ingold 2000: 186.
30 Hodder 2012.
31 Haraway 2003.
32 Haraway 2008: 9.
33 Haraway 1991.
34 Haraway 1997.
35 Haraway 2008.
36 Haraway 2008: 17.

37 Haraway 2008: 17.
38 Smuts 2001; Haraway 2008: 23–7.
39 Haraway 2008: 218.
40 Haraway 2008: 19.
41 Haraway 2008: 25.
42 Perhaps as we did with our trowel back in Chapter 1?
43 Haraway 2008: 15.
44 Overton and Hamilakis 2013.
45 Russell 2011.
46 Overton and Hamilakis 2013; see Wolfe 2003.
47 Overton and Hamilakis 2013: 114, original emphasis.
48 Overton and Hamilakis 2013: 122.
49 Overton and Hamilakis 2013: 134; there are similarities in the emphasis on animal behaviour with the work of Russell and McGowan 2003 we saw earlier, but the focus here is not solely on human perception of that behaviour.
50 Head, Atchison and Gates 2012.
51 Head, Atchison and Gates 2012.
52 Van der Veen 2014.
53 Van der Veen 2014: 802.
54 Van der Veen 2014: 807.
55 Barton and Denham 2011.
56 Barton and Denham 2011.
57 For a good example of these approaches, which also incorporates ideas from geography and from philosophers of space like Henri Lefebvre, see the recent work by Adrian Chadwick (2016a, 2016b). For an example in historical archaeology, see Stephen Mrozowski's (2006) *The Archaeology of Class in Urban America*.
58 On evolutionary archaeology see Lyman and O'Brien 1998; Shennan 2002, 2008, 2012; for an introduction to the related approach of human behavioural ecology see Bird and O'Connell 2012.
59 Cochrane and Gardner 2011; Hodder 2012; Johnson 2010; Shennan 2002, 2008.
60 E.g. Klejn 2013; Neustupný 1998.
61 Shennan 2002.
62 As both Hodder (2012: 239) and Johnson (2011: 321) have pointed out.
63 Boyd and Richerson 1985
64 Malafouris 2013: 39; although Shennan (2012: 17) acknowledges that a hard divide between nature and culture is unhelpful, the maintenance of a clear boundary between the two remains explicit in his work.
65 Hodder 2012: 147.
66 Laland, Odling-Smee and Myles 2010.
67 Boivin 2008: 187; Lewontin 2000; Malafouris 2013.
68 Shennan 2002: 271.
69 Cf. Johnson 2011: 308–9.
70 We return to the question of scale in Chapter 11.
71 Ingold 2000.
72 Ingold 2012.
73 Peirce 1958–65, volume 2, paragraph 274.
74 Barrett 2014.
75 Barrett 2014: 70.
76 Barrett 2014: 71.
77 Bennett 2010.
78 Barrett 2014: 70.
79 Deleuze and Guattari 2004: 454; cf. Ingold 2012.
80 Malafouris 2013.
81 Boivin 2008; Itan et al. 2009.

10

'OTHERS'

Postcolonialism, the ontological turn and colonised things

Introduction: from stones of Others to stones as Others

Figure 10.1 shows a 'nontraditional' perspective of how an archaeology trowel interacts with a stone. We mentioned in Chapter 1 how people understand – and interact with – stone in different ways, so why not have a stone socialise with one of our trowels? Do you remember the examples we gave at the start of the book? Delving a bit further into the different perspectives on stone introduced there, we might learn how in certain Native American contexts, stones can converse with humans.[1] Contrasting this notion is our Scottish archaeology example, where an unmodified stone was considered 'dead weight'. Things are interactive and knowledgeable in one situation, but unsociable, unthinking and inert in the other. How can this be? And, more importantly, who is correct? Is it the people who speak with stones or the people who see stone as a stubborn and inconvenient impediment to their excavations? Can stones speak or not? Are there social bonds between trowels and stones at archaeological sites, or not? Hopefully you recognise that these are trick questions. As we have demonstrated, questions are most dangerous when they only offer two options: right or wrong, alive or dead, speaking or mute. Does this pattern ring a bell? Yes, of course! Behind these questions lurks a familiar set of characters: the dualisms we targeted in the last nine chapters.

In this chapter we explore how ideas associated with the *postcolonial critique*, the *ontological turn* and the *turn towards things* have impacted archaeological theory in the new millennium, particularly the pesky dualisms associated with our question above. These three themes are unified in their concern over *the Other*. Keep in mind that each group of scholars defines Others in a variety of ways. Others are indigenous people living under the oppression of colonialism. Others are

FIGURE 10.1 Stone socialising with trowel. Drawing by K–Fai Steele

'nonwestern' people with beliefs, practices and things perhaps very different from the ones in your life. Others are the people of the past, which, we have been told, is a 'foreign country'.[2] Others are any human 'subjects' described and interpreted by western scholars. And here is the most radical proposition discussed in this chapter: Others can be nonhumans too, not only the plants and animals we saw in the last chapter, but objects as well. As Severin Fowles[3] has pointed out, the language of postcolonial studies, normally reserved for thinking about disenfranchised people, has recently been explicitly drawn on to think about things too.

So what do all of these things have in common? Western scholars prize each of these Others for what they take from them: a sense of what they (the western scholars) are *not*. At a time when anthropology focused on the study of nonwestern cultures, Clyde Kluckhohn[4] famously characterised the discipline as a 'mirror for man'. Anthropology in the mid-twentieth century focused on the 'primitive' and the 'exotic'. Anthropologists explored the world to study nonwestern groups. Shamanistic practices in the Amazon, kinship relations among Native American tribes and patterns of gift exchange in remote islands of the Pacific were the bread and butter of the discipline. Kluckhohn suggested that anthropologists use their observations of these 'Others' to help solve problems of the modern, western world. For our purposes, then, the main criterion for 'Otherness' is a belief that the observed person, society or thing exhibits *absolute and radical difference* from the observer. A critical term here is *alterity*, which refers to this kind of radical difference. The recognition of this alterity is an important ingredient in the observer's self-understanding. The west constructs itself in terms of what it is *not*. Ironically, it does so by comparing itself in relation to Others, which it classifies in terms of what they lack (usually western characteristics). The thinkers discussed below promise to help end this circular reasoning.

In the next section, we explore the postcolonial critique. There we introduce a range of scholarship that challenges the basic premises of how westerners study and relate to nonwestern peoples. We learn about the dangers of colonial representation. For instance, in recognising absolute and radical difference between their own society and the nonwestern societies they observe and interpret, scholars often generalise and simplify. Painting with a broad brush in these situations results in a world fashioned after a coin: one side western, the opposite side *not*. This is the same framework that anthropologist Eric Wolf[5] critiqued as 'Europe and the people without history'. We spend a good deal of energy thinking about the problem of representing foreign culture and people in this way. This concerns *what* we represent in our archaeological interpretations (i.e., a vision of the past) and how we can improve these through the elimination of western assumptions. However, we also consider how we actually represent the past, by briefly recognising a new and ever-growing literature on forms of archaeological practice that involve indigenous people as the archaeologists or as part of archaeological teams. Think of the speaking stone. We will explore how western scholars represent this 'foreign' interaction (that is, between a person and a stone). This involves challenging western European perspectives as the only way to see – and be in – the world. However, postcolonialism also concerns a practical set of problems related to colonial inequality and how some approaches to studying Others justify colonialism.

Following on from this, we consider a bold new move that urges us to consider the possibility of *multiple worlds*. Here, you will have to be patient and open to experiment. A return to our trusty stones will help us explain. With one set of approaches to the questions posed above, we might ask: *why and how do some people have a fundamentally different understanding of the stone than, say, western scholars?* How is it that two people can look at the same stone and see two different things: on the one hand, a speaking stone and on the other, an inert chunk of minerals. Cloaked within this type of question is always an assumption that there exists a right way to see the world and a whole variety of different (wrong) ways to see the world. We can translate this into a set of questions more appropriate for archaeologists. For example, why and how was stone symbolic for group X in the past? How can we see this symbolism in archaeological patterns? Why do some cultures think that things and animals possess what westerners see as fundamentally human qualities or vice versa? This is what we might refer to as the original study of *animism*, a process by which select humans, things and animals can take on one another's properties. For instance, shamans in some indigenous societies believe they have the ability to become jaguars.

With a new set of approaches, inspired by what is known as the 'ontological turn', we might ask *in what type of worlds do stones speak or people transform into jaguars?* Does this sound similar to the question raised in the previous paragraph? If yes, then take a quick break and compare these two questions. How are they different? The first assumes that the world out there (the stone in this instance) is the same for each interpreter. In this sense, the first set of questions concerns worldviews, or ways of knowing (*epistemologies*). It just so happens that each interpreter has different ways of knowing the world 'out there'. In short, one world plus two worldviews or epistemologies interpreting it in different ways. The second makes no such assumption about the singularity of the world. It approaches the problem in terms of *two different worlds*: one in which stones speak like people and another where they do not. What is the nature of this radically different world? If humans *can* (and do not simply *believe* they can) occasionally transform into jaguars there, what is the rest of that world like? This set of questions is what we refer to as the *new animism*. We witness a shift here from questions focused on worldviews or knowledge construction (epistemologies) to questions concerning being and becoming in the world (ontologies).

The later parts of the chapter push us even further. Building on the spirit of symmetrical and new materialist approaches discussed in Chapter 8, we consider what it means to think of nonhuman things as Others. Have people colonised things? Is the current status of things similar to the status of colonised subjects discussed by postcolonial theorists? You likely agree that people often assume that nonhumans, especially non-living things, are very different from humans. Yet, throughout this book, we have presented a series of challenges to this basic assumption. Things have agency (Chapter 5). Things make people (Chapters 6, 7). Things are us (Chapter 8)! These new propositions challenge western understandings of non-living matter and artefacts. So, if it is true, as argued above, that we build our self-understandings in terms of what *we are not*, then these claims of object agency, object personhood and person–thing admixture seem to suggest that we don't truly understand what people are! In other words, if qualities that are often assumed to be the domain of humans and humans alone (e.g., agency) are now extended to nonhumans, we may need to rethink what it means to be human altogether. All of these notions are part of the larger 'posthuman' critique in the new millennium. In the final section of the chapter, we return to our stones to briefly compare our three approaches to these Others.

Postcolonial theory: understanding and representing Others in a shared world

---

BOX 10.1   CHRIS GOSDEN

Chris Gosden is Chair of European Archaeology at the University of Oxford. His 2001 chapter, 'Post-Colonial Archaeology: Issues of Culture, Identity, and Knowledge',[6] is one of the earliest archaeological forays into postcolonial theory. He is author of numerous influential books in archaeology, including *Archaeology and Colonialism: Culture Contact from 5000 BC to the Present*.[7] In it, he explores the notion of 'terra nullius', meaning 'no man's land', a classification used by colonists to justify taking indigenous land. Gosden[8] discusses this idea as it relates to the painting shown here by Albert Eckhout. The painting contrasts an indigenous woman and child – nude and 'natural' – in the foreground against an ordered, colonial landscape in the background.

Nationalmuseet [Public domain or CC BY-SA 3.0 (http://creativecommons.org/licenses/by-sa/3.0)], via Wikimedia Commons

We start, however, with one of the most critical areas of thought in the wider academic world: postcolonial theory. One of the first archaeological engagements with postcolonial theory came in 2001 in a chapter by Chris Gosden (Box 10.1). Since then, there has been a dramatic rise of postcolonial[9] archaeologies. This movement represents yet another example of archaeologists importing theory from other disciplines.[10] In this case, the influence comes largely from the field of literary criticism. Postcolonial scholarship usually consists of nonwestern critics examining western ways of knowing (epistemologies). These thinkers focus specifically on how western observers – including scholars – produce information related to 'Others'. Remember that in this section of the chapter, these Others are people who have been (or remain!) colonised. In this sense, Others are often 'nonwestern', indigenous and/or living in Third World countries. Postcolonial authors often refer to Others as *subaltern* groups. This simply means a group who is represented as *inferior and different*, a theme that relates directly the central concern found in nearly all postcolonial literature: relationships between coloniser and colonised.

BOX 10.2   EDWARD W. SAID

Edward W. Said (1935–2003) was Professor of English, History and Comparative Literature at Columbia University. He is best known for his book, *Orientalism*,[11] a critical analysis of western representations of Middle Eastern cultures. This is a mural from Palestine – where Said grew up – honouring him and his work.

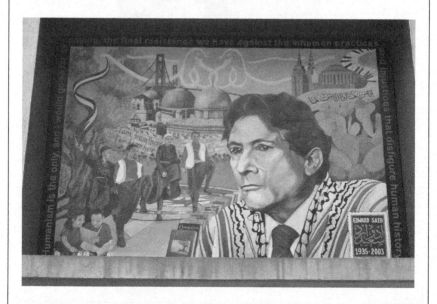

By Briantrejo (own work) [GFDL (http://www.gnu.org/copyleft/fdl.html) or CC BY-SA 3.0]

On this most basic level, the postcolonial critique asks how western observers misunderstand and distort the cultures and colonial experiences of these Others while at the same time framing Others as inherently inferior (to the west).[12] Throughout the history of colonialism, colonists have justified their imperialist activities with a common excuse: the colonised group was inferior. In this sense, misrepresenting Others in such a way is a means of justifying colonialism.

The most influential postcolonial thinkers are Edward Said (Box 10.2), Gayati Chakrovorty Spivak (Box 10.3) and Homi Bhabha (Box 10.4). Said[13] offered a sharp critique of western representations of the people and cultures of the 'Orient', or Middle East. For him, 'Orientalism' is a form of *essentialism* that misrepresents Middle Eastern cultures. Essentialism assumes that all members of a group possess key characteristics and values. These characteristics and values are unchanging and *essential* to the group. In Chapters 1 and 2 we saw how archaeologists have often been essentialist in assuming that certain elements of modern human life (for example, dualisms, binary concepts of gender and so on) are essential to all people in all times and places. In that context essentialism ran at a large scale and helped to disguise difference between groups. Here we can see how essentialism is used to portray Others in direct opposition to the 'west' (and the same as all other Others), and thus is used in a different (but equally problematic) way. For instance, European colonists of North America insisted that many of the indigenous groups who they encountered and colonised did not have the ability to 'improve' their own lands and maximise its fruitfulness. As the story goes, it was therefore part of the colonists' 'natural right' and responsibility to take over and improve. In this case, colonists represented indigenous groups as unsophisticated, passive and lazy (the opposite of how European colonists saw themselves!). Here we encounter an important set of dualisms that postcolonial critics challenge. Western observers often insisted that the Others they observed were essentially the opposite of western colonial cultures. On the one hand, these Others were static (meaning they didn't invent new things and change), technologically inferior and socially simple. On the other hand, westerners often framed their own cultures as dynamic, technologically advanced and socially complex (see Box 10.1).

Archaeologist Severin Fowles[14] recently pointed out how western understandings of nonwestern pasts are based on a common 'thing': absence. Whether they are missing metallurgy, agriculture, political leadership or secular understandings of the world, nonwestern groups are often characterised by what they lack rather than what they possess. Fowles argues that these absences have a 'thingly' nature in that they are treated as *real* characteristics that all societies need to fill to evolve or improve. Remember the circular reasoning discussed in the introduction to this chapter? As Fowles and Heupel[15] warn, we must remember that '[p]rimitivity is an ideological creation of civilisation; civilisation is not an evolutionary product of primitivity'. This critique points to certain assumptions in the western world about social and cultural evolution. But more importantly for our purposes, this focus on absence helps us to see the deep-seated need of western academics to find simple oppositions – in this case, artificial gaps in nonwestern societies – between themselves and the foreign groups who they study.

Gayati Chakrovorty Spivak[16] famously asked, '*Can the subaltern speak?*' This key question relates back to the forms of essentialism critiqued by thinkers like Said. Spivak wondered if it was possible for scholars to move beyond the dualisms just introduced and give voice to subaltern groups of the past who are primarily represented through historical accounts of elite westerners. Of most importance for our purposes, Spivak asked if historians should simply avoid representing the pasts of Others. Spivak concluded that the subaltern *cannot* speak through elite western representations (historical texts) because in those forms of representation, the subaltern experiences of colonialism, colonial inequality and indigenous culture in general are always filtered and coloured by western sensibilities. However, Spivak did not simply condemn all studies of subaltern peoples and history. In fact, she pointed out that what is often most important about colonial or subaltern pasts derived from western historical records is exactly what cannot be said, what is missing.[17] Perhaps for archaeologists, the most important message from Spivak's work is that the archaeological interpreter is the voice that speaks for the material remains. As Matthew Liebmann[18] asked, 'is archaeology merely an exercise in ventriloquism, throwing our own voices into the mouths of the people in the past?' This question reminds us that it is the archaeologist's responsibility to maintain critical attention to just how the past emerges through them and how they situate the past from their particular perspectives in the present.

The final postcolonial thinker to explore is Homi Bhabha. The most important aspect of his work for archaeologists is his critical consideration of cultural hybridity and ambivalence.[19] Remember the colonial dualisms introduced above? Bhabha's work demonstrates that these dualisms are false. His work challenges these simple oppositions between coloniser and colonised. Rather than simply cataloguing the mixing of different cultural traditions in colonial situations, Bhabha's work considers how old (traditional) and new (foreign) practices and materials are redefined and often confused in the process of colonialism. This is the *ambivalence* of the process of cultural hybridity. Most important, however, are the ways in which cultural hybridity offers subaltern groups a means of negotiating and resisting colonial power structures. For instance, Barbara Voss[20] provides excellent examples of what might be classified as 'cultural hybridity' between a number of different ethnic groups involved

---

BOX 10.3   GAYATRI CHAKRAVORTY SPIVAK

Gayatri Chakravorty Spivak is Professor of English and Comparative Literature at Columbia University. She is a founding member of the Institute for Comparative Literature and Society. A central figure in postcolonial theory, Spivak is best known for her critical essay, 'Can the Subaltern Speak?'.[21]

Can the subaltern speak?

in Spain's colonisation of California. Voss shows the creation of a new ethnic identity ('Californio') that combined different elements of a variety of cultural practices and materials. Most importantly for us, Voss shows how this new combination of cultural practices allowed 'Californios' to resist the Spanish system of racial classification. In spite of excellent examples such as Voss' work, many archaeologists tend to focus on categorising things as hybrid without much attention to the power structures and agency that might have characterised those instances of cultural admixture. Archaeologist Stephen Silliman[22] makes a similar set of observations, challenging archaeologists using the notion of hybridity to push their interpretations past the point of simply finding evidence for 'Frankensteins' or 'mules' and placing their examples of hybridity into better critical context (in the spirit of postcolonialism). For example, archaeological studies of hybridity rarely consider what happens next (after hybridity) or if and how hybridity ends. Silliman argues that without addressing these critical questions about the diachronic contexts of hybridity (as discussed in Chapter 3, related directly to the complicated relationship between cultural continuity and change), the term has limited use in contemporary archaeology.

BOX 10.4 HOMI K. BHABHA

Homi K. Bhabha is Professor of English and American Literature and Language and Director of the Humanities Center at Harvard University. He introduced a number of central concepts used widely in postcolonial studies, including cultural hybridity and ambivalence.[23] This photo shows Bhabha's alma mater, the University of Mumbai.

By Appaiah (Flickr) [CC BY-SA 2.0 (http://creativecommons.org/licenses/by-sa/2.0)], via Wikimedia Commons)

It is useful to reiterate that postcolonial thinkers are largely concerned with issues of knowledge production, or epistemology and how it affects the world. Remember that the postcolonial critique originates from the field of literary criticism. Postcolonial thinkers focus on colonial representations. However, the second way that the postcolonial critique has transformed archaeology moves beyond epistemology in some ways. This second transformation relates to indigenous individuals and communities who are beginning to practise their own forms of archaeology. This is evident in the massive amount of archaeological literature concerning tribal archaeology, indigenous archaeology and various forms of community-based archaeology. In many ways, this parallels the postcolonial critique in that it involves members of colonised or formerly colonised groups becoming part of these processes of archaeological interpretation and representation.[24] Here, we begin to witness archaeologies built within indigenous ontologies or between indigenous and western worlds. New forms of collaborative-indigenous archaeology lead to hybridised archaeological practices such as ritually cleansing field equipment or performing ceremony as part of routine archaeological activities.[25] This movement in archaeology is part of a growing concern in the discipline over its broader social impacts beyond academia. Robert Preucel and Stephen Mrozowski[26] refer to this as a 'new pragmatism' in archaeological practice. For our purposes, pragmatism asks how archaeologists can use their work to improve the world that lies beyond the ivory tower. Or this could entail indigenous people and/or indigenous archaeologists using archaeology to improve their worlds. As highlighted in our discussion of the postcolonial critique, archaeologists are beginning to ask critical questions about the relationship between their research and colonialism. By turning a critical eye to their work and building new connections to indigenous communities, these archaeologists are attempting to 'decolonise' the discipline.[27]

New animism and Other worlds

Alongside the postcolonial critique, anthropologists and archaeologists are also beginning to ask radically new questions about nonwestern understandings of the world.[28] While it is true that the subaltern groups discussed in the previous section *might* understand the world in different ways than western observers, we are not necessarily discussing colonialism and its related power imbalances here. Instead we focus on the intellectual – rather than pragmatic – challenges of trying to use nonwestern perspectives in archaeological theory. In some ways this matches up with the initial spirit of the postcolonial critique. We are trying to incorporate other ways of seeing the world to help diversify and challenge our western views.

You might have noticed that we used the plural, world*s*, in the subheading above. Why would we do such a thing? The general idea is that we are trying to move beyond the limitations of a western perspective that sees *one world* best explained through scientific inquiry. Western science tells us that the world 'out there' is knowable and predictable through scientific laws and methodologies.[29]

At times we encounter people who believe in phenomena that completely contradict these laws and methodologies. So when the shaman tells us that she can transform into a jaguar, we don't actually believe her. 'She must be mistaken', we think. Perhaps she has fooled herself into thinking that she turns into a jaguar because her people venerate the jaguar for its hunting prowess. Maybe she chemically alters herself and hallucinates the transformation. Or perhaps both of these options explain her 'mistaken' belief about our shared world. In any case, we do our best to explain her (wrong) understanding of the world from our own perspective. In this section, we introduce a new set of approaches to studying phenomena such as people transforming into jaguars. Instead of trying to explain these radically different beliefs and practices in terms of how they work in *our world*, we ask if we can use knowledge of these beliefs and practices to better understand the workings of *their world*. This means we must be open to exploring *multiple worlds*.

As already indicated, in some of these Other worlds, boundaries between persons, animals and 'inanimate' things are often quite permeable. The question remains as to whether such boundaries are permeable *regardless of human understanding* or *because of a specific human cultural perspective*. This distinction relates directly to the different disciplinary uses of the term *ontology* pointed out briefly in Chapter 2.[30] A philosophical approach might use the term to refer to a single model of how the world works regardless of human understanding (the former option above) while an anthropological approach might seek out specific human or cultural understandings of the world and how it works (the latter option above). In the spirit of anthropology, western observers have used the term 'animism' to lump together a wide variety of nonwestern human–environmental relationships, often discussed as part of 'primitive religious beliefs'.[31] María Nieves Zedeño explains that animism is part of a worldview that recognises a life force or soul in things. Animism is 'an object's capacity for becoming a person and behaving like one'.[32] Severin Fowles[33] recently challenged the roots of anthropological classifications of nonwestern religions by revealing how our modern notions of religion dictate how we 'see' religion in almost any context, past or present. In this general spirit, we must question the fundamentals of our worlds, such as the distinctions between categories that we see as completely obvious. What are the connections between science and belief or social relations and religion? We must probe deeply into these relationships to try and avoid mapping our own sensibilities and classifications onto people of the past.

In some cases, archaeologists approach this type of problem in a more 'traditional' anthropological manner. For instance, Zedeño sees the return to animism as an invitation to incorporate nonwestern ontologies into archaeological interpretations (à la the postcolonial critique). In this case, Zedeño argues that we need to fit these ontologies – in the anthropological sense – into our epistemology (as archaeologists). She is particularly interested in taxonomies of artefacts. She notes that in western epistemologies animacy is 'an absolute and constant state – a foundation of dualist, or Cartesian, thinking. Therefore, it cannot be transferred from one class of natural object to another'.[34] She provides examples of how Native American understandings of animacy might help to modify and improve western archaeological taxonomies. For instance, she identifies certain 'index objects' that – in Native American worlds – have the power to animate the other objects around them. Although Zedeño certainly paints with a broad brush, perhaps even essentialising Native American communities from across the North American continent, her work strives to incorporate Native American ontologies into archaeological theory, hybridising our epistemologies if not our ontologies. Similarly, Timothy Pauketat[35] has developed the Native American idea of 'bundling' to examine how we can better understand both intimate practices and the process of long-term change in North America.

For some archaeologists, the return to animism is even more radical than the model proposed by Zedeño or Pauketat. This 'new' animism is part of a bigger change in archaeology and anthropology: the 'ontological turn'.[36] Ontology is a state of being, how one relates to – or regards – the world. As archaeologist Benjamin Alberti[37] puts it, ontology is 'a theory and experience of what exists'. Here the 'turn' involves asking a new set of questions when we encounter 'Other' cultures of the past and present. Do you remember how postprocessual archaeology focused our attention on social relations and symbols (Chapter 2)? Built into the questions and research interests that postprocessual archaeology celebrated in the 1980s and 1990s was an assumption that we (the archaeologists) share the *same world* that the people of the past inhabited. This doesn't mean that archaeologists assumed that Neanderthals had mobile phones, took 'selfies' and had 'western' sensibilities and interests. However, it does assume that, in the time of the Neanderthals, some of the same general forces that govern our world existed. Even though Neanderthals had different (or perhaps no) understandings of some of the governing forces of their world – say, natural selection or germ theories of disease – these worldly powers still shaped their lives.[38] These forces were at play in the worlds of all past peoples. The ontological turn asks us to ignore *our interpretations of why people had different (mistaken) views of the world* (e.g. people turning into jaguars or linking illness to witchcraft). Instead, we must start anew, asking: if people turn into jaguars in that world, if witches cause illness in that world or if stones can speak in that world, what type of world is it?

A good example of this comes from the work of anthropologist Martin Holbraad.[39] He works with Cuban diviners (*babalawos*), and is particularly interested in the powder, *ache*, that they use in their divining. This powder, the diviners say, is power. Powder is power. Now the initial reaction to this is to presume that this is a kind of symbolism, that powder means power, or stands for power or represents power, or that the locals *believe* it is power.[40] How would our approach change, though, if we did not do this, if we did not presume that the diviners are mistaken, but that powder actually *is* power? Taking this claim seriously allows Holbraad to think about the kinds of assumptions we tend to begin our investigation with, like the idea that a thing and the concept it represents will be separate and linked by language or some other means. Taking the *babalawos'* argument seriously means having to challenge *our* thing/concept dichotomy and to consider the possibility of a world where powder is power, where these things are the same as one another. This offers up a moment of radical difference – alterity – between our world and the world of Cuban diviners; and points the way to a different ontology. The potential for multiple ontologies, and thus perhaps for multiple worlds, has led many different scholars in anthropology to explore these questions. The founding figure of these kinds of investigations, Eduardo Viveiros de Castro,[41] explored what the world of Amazonian peoples must be like if we are to understand how a shaman can turn into a jaguar. He developed the term 'Amerindian perspectivism' to attempt to understand a world in which nature rather than culture is variable.[42] On a grander scale, Philippe Descola[43] has tried to group together different ontologies into a four-fold scheme that shows how they vary across the world. All very well, but how can we use our new knowledge of that Other world as archaeological theory?

Alberti provides a good example of this type of experimentation. His research on La Candelaria 'body-pots' from northwest Argentina[44] demonstrates what it might mean for archaeologists to reach for 'worlds otherwise'.[45] The pots in question date to the first millennium AD and come in a variety of 'biomorphic' shapes. This simply means that the pots were made to resemble parts of humans and other animals (Figure 10.2). They appear to mix ceramics with what Alberti sees as very different entities, including humans, birds and other animals. Some pots appear almost identical to one another, only differing in the human shapes they resemble, otherwise known as *anthropomorphic* qualities.[46] When examining singular pots, Alberti developed expectations for what other body-pots would look like, but expectations were rarely met. Where he expected to find a human face on a pot,

FIGURE 10.2 Body-pots discussed by Benjamin Alberti

Photographs by Benjamin Alberti, reproduced with permission. From Alberti and Marshall 2009

the pot was faceless. Where he expected to find human arms or legs on pots, he found mysterious bulges. Based on these observations, he argued that body-pots 'not only force a comparison with [human or animal] bodies; they also deliberately stage the absence of specific bodily features'.[47] He also noted that the physical form of the body-pots suggests that they were made hastily – resulting in sloppy workmanship – or simply left unfinished.[48]

A conventional archaeological approach to these pots might ask: what did they mean or represent for the La Candelaria people? Those archaeologists sympathetic to the ontological turn might condemn such an approach for its bifurcation, or division, between immaterial meanings and the hard, material substrate to which they tie. Alberti[49] discusses this as a 'hylomorphic approach' to artefacts (see Chapter 8), where archaeologists assume that humans actively inscribe form – in this case the shape of body-pots – onto passive matter. As we saw in Chapter 8, things are not so simple.

We could offer similar critiques of meaning and symbolism. Think back to Chapter 7, where we discussed structuralist approaches to semiotics that characterise signs as composed of two parts: 'signifier' (in this case, a body-pot) and that which is 'signified' (in this case, the riddle which conventional archaeology might try to solve: what does it mean?). As we discussed above, this type of approach tends to mask the assumption that a western scientific perspective is the only right way to see the world. From this stance, western science tells us that human-animal hybrids do not exist in nature. Therefore, the only possible explanation for the existence of body-pots must be cultural convention, right (Chapter 7)? In other words, the group who made and used body-pots had a culture that combined animals and humans in its symbology, misrepresenting nature. Alberti and Yvonne Marshall note that such a 'representationalist' approach 'assumes that the thing as sign vehicle reveals a story or set of cultural beliefs inscribed in it and read off it'.[50] So, what did the body-pots stand for? Why did the 'body-pot culture' believe that humans could sometimes take on the characteristics of animals?[51] This is, of course, the spirit of the original study of animism!

Can you think of any other possible approach to these body-pots? At the heart of this question lies a much bigger question that we have already addressed: what is *new* about the 'new animism'? Remember our discussion of *multiple* worlds? Alberti and Marshall[52] urge us to move beyond epistemological questions of right and wrong (regarding nature and humans' abilities to take on animal forms) to ask about the world in which body-pots exist as a single entity rather than a symbol. This is the crucial move from one world to two or more worlds. It is a move that takes western science off its pedestal and asks: what am I (the western observer) missing? What don't I understand about the observed group's (or thing's) world? We must push further to discover the 'ontological logic' that such pots embody.[53] Alberti and Marshall argue that body-pots, taken from this perspective, suggest two related possibilities: first, 'that matter and physical form were considered inherently unstable', and second, 'that the pots can be understood as inserting a difference and therefore bringing into local determinacy a potential belonging to indeterminate (or indifferent) but dynamic background matter'.[54] In other words, the authors suggest that in this 'Other world', things were constantly transforming. Perhaps the body-pots froze material in certain configurations to prevent it from continuing to transform. These things stopped bodies/pots from taking on new forms. The reason Alberti and Marshall refer to these as body-pots is precisely because the difference between a body and a pot may not be clear in this ontology. Remember how for Cuban diviners powder was power? Here Alberti and Marshall argue there is an ontology where pots are bodies – not representations of bodies, not symbols of bodies, but *actual* bodies.

Now these ideas are complex and interesting but can also be quite troubling.[55] Several scholars have raised concerns about the turn to these kinds of alternative or multiple ontologies, and even Holbraad has slightly rowed back from the claim of multiple worlds.[56] Severin Fowles,[57] for example, has argued that claims to multiple worlds undermine many political issues in the present where western and nonwestern groups are precisely arguing over the same world. On the ground, claims to 'worlds otherwise' do little to help the Amazonian tribe resisting the actions of a logging company. Other scholars have suggested that any group of people is likely to have access themselves to multiple ontologies that they switch between.[58] Some of these will overlap with those shared by other groups and others will not. Nonetheless, these ontological critiques are having a noticeable impact on many disciplines[59] including archaeology, and offer very provocative tools to think with. As Bruno Latour (who we met in Chapter 8) has asked, are these kinds of approaches simply another way of looking at the world, or something that explodes our assumptions?[60] They have certainly influenced him in his recent attempts to provide a much more complicated anthropological account of the western world today.[61] We will touch on these issues again in the next chapter.

In defence of things

> Archaeologists should unite in a defence of things, a defence of those subaltern members of the collective that have been silenced and 'othered' by the imperialist social and humanist discourses.
>
> *Bjørnar Olsen*[62]

Similar to those archaeologists taking influence from postcolonialism and the ontological turn, some of the archaeologists working under the banner of 'symmetrical archaeology' (Chapter 8) express concern for Others. However, the shared postcolonial rhetoric,[63] seen in the above quotation, is where the similarities between postcolonialism and this brand of posthumanism end. For this section of the chapter, the Others we focus on are 'things', defined broadly.[64] So, following this logic, rather than freeing people from the tyranny of colonialism, it is things themselves that require our assistance.[65] A leader in this movement is Bjørnar Olsen (Box 10.5),[66] who sees the turn towards things as nothing short of a radical transformation (a revolution!) in archaeological theory. Thinkers in this camp often use similar terminology to archaeologists who study colonialism or work with indigenous communities who still suffer from deep-seated colonial inequalities. Frustrated with the symbolic and social archaeologies of the postprocessual era, Olsen[67] urges archaeologists to let things have their own say. Instead of reducing things to the 'stuff' through which people expressed themselves and their social relations, he argues for a need to seriously engage with the 'otherness of things'.[68] This means approaching things 'as things' in their own right rather than as inert and static vehicles for human expression and use. We must develop a 'respect for what things are in their own being', says Olsen.[69] He asks, 'What things could more resolutely and effectively oppose the humanising and interpretive exploitation [of things]

BOX 10.5   BJØRNAR OLSEN

Bjørnar Olsen is Professor of Archaeology at the University of Tromsø in Norway. He is a leader in symmetrical archaeology and author of numerous influential articles and books, including *In Defense of Things*[70] and *Archaeology: The Discipline of Things*[71] (co-authored with Michael Shanks, Timothy Webmoor and Christopher Witmore). Much of his recent work focuses on the archaeology of ruins, such as the remains of this farm in Skíðadalur, Iceland.

By Árni Hjartarson (own work) [CC BY-SA 3.0 (http://creativecommons.org/licenses/ by-sa/3.0)], via Wikimedia Commons

than smashed pots, slag lumps, flint debris, caulking resins, burnt bones . . . storage rooms, and labs?'[72] Although it is safe to classify Olsen's arguments as 'posthuman' in their orientation, this does not mean that he and other like-minded archaeologists are less interested in people.[73] As we saw in Chapter 8, they want to work towards an archaeology that starts with a flat ontology – humans and things on an equal footing. That is the definition of the symmetry in symmetrical archaeology, after all. If things are colonised Others in need of liberation through our turn back to them, how are we to let these new subalterns speak?

Olsen's thought, and increasingly that of Christopher Witmore,[74] represents a clear development of the symmetrical approaches set out in Chapter 8. Bruno Latour directly inspired the early phases of symmetrical archaeology. Relations were at the heart of this, and so Witmore, in his manifesto published in 2007, declared that symmetrical archaeology 'begins with mixtures',[75] and that the '"principle of symmetry" begins with the proposition: humans and non-humans should not be regarded as ontologically distinct, as detached and separated entities, *a priori*'.[76] The relations here are critical, and we can think of this as 'first-wave' symmetrical archaeology.

However, Olsen[77] and Witmore[78] now seek to go beyond a fully relational account, and are critical of the early reliance on relations that symmetrical archaeology demonstrated.[79] In this sense they represent a clear difference from the other approaches we have explored in this book so far. Since the engagement with practice theory (Chapter 3), archaeologists have become increasingly interested in theories of relations, drawing on a variety of different approaches, whether it was Haraway's study of relations with animals (Chapter 9), DeLanda's description of how soap and architects design together (Chapter 8) or Strathern's ideas of relational personhood (Chapter 4). In contrast Olsen urges us to attend to the 'individual qualities of things'.[80] Things, he argues, whether a boat or an axe, have qualities to them that are primary, and stand prior to the relations they enter into.[81] Instead of thinking of things as the outcome of relations, which was the aim of thinkers like Ingold for example, we should instead, Olsen[82] insists, recognise that things are what relations emerge out of. This in effect argues that things have a form of 'essence', a position very different from the others we have encountered so far. Although still labelled by Olsen and Witmore as symmetrical archaeology, this now clearly defines a 'second wave' of thinking under the same banner.[83]

Where does this rejection of relations come from? If Latour was the primary influence on the early phases of symmetrical archaeology, he has been replaced in these later accounts by a different figure – the philosopher Graham Harman.[84] Harman is one of the leading lights in 'speculative realism' (a particular philosophical school of thought), and has developed an approach he calls Object-Orientated Ontology that – as the name suggests – focuses on objects.[85] Although Harman draws extensively on Latour, his primary influence comes from his particular reading of Heidegger, the German phenomenological philosopher we met in Chapter 6.

Harman argues that things can never be exhausted by their relations; they always keep something in reserve that we can never fully access. To explain this he builds on Heidegger's example of a hammer that we encountered earlier. Heidegger, as we saw, contrasted the hammer when it is ready-to-hand – that is, when you are using it without thinking about it – and when it is present-at-hand – that is, when you hit your thumb with it and accuse the hammer of all manner of ungodly sins. In this latter case your attention is focused on the hammer; in the former case the hammer fades into the background, just one part of the 'equipmental totality' (see Chapter 6). Harman argues that neither of these can exhaust all the elements of the hammer, however. The hammer always exceeds our understanding of it because it has qualities that we do not attend to either in practice (ready-to-hand) or theory (present-at-hand). Thus an object, he insists, is always more than the relations it has with the world;[86] all objects have an essence and a reality of their own, and can interact with each other without the need for a mediating human being.[87]

These approaches are the first attempt by archaeologists to turn away from relational approaches to the past towards something else, and can be seen as a wider attempt to reconfigure archaeology away from the study of the past towards being a 'discipline of things'.[88] We might question, though, whether we can ever really cut off an object from *all* of its relations, or whether it is helpful to see one set of qualities as more primary than any other. The kinds of new materialism inspired by Gilles Deleuze[89] and assemblage theory we saw in Chapter 8, for example, would stress that everything is always caught up in the process of becoming, and thus any attempt to cut an object off from the world will be artificial, what Ingold would call an inversion.[90] Other archaeologists have suggested we can tack between positions that embrace an object's reality and its connections with the wider world without rejecting a relational approach.[91] We will discuss some of the wider implications of this attempt to move past relations in our final chapter.

Conclusions: different approaches to 'Others'

In this chapter, we presented three different ways to investigate and perhaps critique the interaction between trowel and stone depicted in Figure 10.1. First, the postcolonial critique asks how this view of indigenous perspectives on the world – in this case, one where stones and trowels speak – might distort reality and justify colonialism. By emphasising the 'mistaken' and 'backwards' nature of beliefs in animate stones (and trowels, for that matter), perhaps we also justify the maintenance of colonial inequality in the name of western reason. The postcolonial critique asks us to scrutinise our research for the possibility of new forms of colonialism (neo-colonialism). Also in the postcolonial spirit, indigenous interpreters (from a group where stones speak) might use their own knowledge to conduct their own forms of archaeology, where they will correct 'traditional' western misunderstandings and biases. Next, the ontological turn urges us to accept the 'foreign fact'. In this case, we might ask how our understandings of stones or people change in this new world where stones act like people. Finally, the turn towards things asks us to start with the stone instead of 'colonising' it as an inert symbol used by humans. What if we begin our analysis by simply addressing the stone, perhaps asking questions about the dynamic substance of stone (Chapter 8)? What do we miss when we treat stones and humans as opposites? Or, taking influence from speculative real- ist philosophers like Graham Harman, might we ask how trowels always exceed what people know of them, and retain their very own essence? These approaches represent discussions taking place at the cutting edge of archaeological theory as we write this book, and they pose very big questions for the discipline. What would an archaeology that really embraced alternative ontologies look like? If we decolonise things and study them for their own sake in the present, where does that leave the narratives we want to write about the past? For now, we leave you with these questions, but will return to some of the bigger themes related to them in the next and final chapter.

Notes

1 Deloria 1973.
2 Lowenthal 1985.
3 Fowles 2016.
4 Kluckhohn 1949.
5 Wolf 1982.
6 Gosden 2001.
7 Gosden 2004.
8 Gosden 2004: 25–30.
9 It is important to point out a common misunderstanding of the term 'postcolonialism'. The 'post' in the name does not necessarily imply a critique that came about *after* colonialism ended, since postcolonial thinkers argue that colonialism has no clear end; the inequalities that came with colonialism still persist in many 'former' colonies (see Liebmann 2008: 3–4; Silliman 2005). Instead of referring to a time period, these theorists used the term 'postcolonial' to critique western, Eurocentric sensibilities that creep into representations of Others.
10 Gosden 2001; Lydon and Rizvi 2010; Liebmann and Rizvi 2008; Silliman 2015; van Dommelen 2002.
11 See Cipolla 2013b; Cipolla and Hayes 2015.
12 Said 1978.
13 Said 1978.
14 Fowles 2010.
15 Fowles and Heupel 2013.
16 Spivak 1988.
17 Liebmann 2008.
18 Liebmann 2008: 9.
19 Bhabha 1994.
20 Voss 2008a.
21 Spivak 1988.
22 Silliman 2015.
23 Bhaba 1994.
24 Atalay 2012; Bruchac et al. 2010; Colwell-Chanthaphonh and Ferguson 2008; Preucel and Cipolla 2008; Watkins 2000.
25 Cipolla and Quinn 2016.
26 Preucel and Mrozowski 2010.

27 Cipolla and Quinn 2016; González-Ruibal 2010; La Salle 2010; Rizvi 2015.

28 Alberti and Bray 2009; Alberti et al. 2011; Henare, Holbraad and Wastell 2007; Viveiros de Castro 2004.

29 These scientific laws and methodologies, like many epistemologies, are the frameworks through which most western societies judge whether interpretations about the world out there are *either* right *or* wrong.

30 See Chapter 2, note 42.

31 Zedeño 2009: 408.

32 Zedeño 2009: 408.

33 Fowles 2013.

34 Zedeño 2009: 409.

35 Pauketat 2013a, 2013b.

36 Henare, Holbraad and Wastell 2007; Paleček and Risjord 2012.

37 Alberti 2014: 107.

38 In this sense, we might argue for a perspective that recognises multiple ontologies that co-exist, overlap or operate at different scales. Here we can recognise a 'metaontology' of natural selection and germs as important players in the world of Neanderthals while still recognising *their* ontology, *their* world, which did not likely include conceptual space for these forces.

39 Holbraad 2007, 2010, 2012a, 2012b.

40 Holbraad 2012a: 17.

41 Viveiros de Castro 1998.

42 Viveiros de Castro's (1998) argument is very difficult to grasp. As we have seen in this book, the standard western view is that nature is a stable substance on top of which culture can be added – so all human beings have the same 'nature' – what we differ in is our culture. This idea lies behind the commonplace notion of multiculturalism. For Amerindian groups, Viveiros de Castro suggests, the reverse is true – instead of a fixed nature and variable culture, it is nature that can change while culture remains the same. Whether you are a jaguar, a tapir, a fish or a human you all have the same culture, but the physical world is liable to change. The material world is unstable here, whereas culture is fixed for all the different animals; they all drink manioc beer, live in houses and so on, but they appear differently to different creatures. This means when a jaguar sees another jaguar they do not see a furry spotted cat, they see a human being. But when they look at a human being they see a tapir – a prey animal they might hunt. When a tapir sees a tapir they see (you guessed it) a human being, but when they see a human, something that hunts them, they see a jaguar. Very powerful humans (like shamans) and very powerful animals are able to change their perspective and thus see the world as other animals do – and thus change their physical bodies. This all sounds pretty fanciful, doesn't it? It completely clashes with how we think about the world. The key question that Viveiros de Castro is asking us to think about, though, is what the world must be like for these kinds of perspectives to make sense, and how we have to challenge our understandings to see the world in this way.

43 Descola 2013; see also Sahlins 2014 for a more sceptical reading of the differences between these ontologies.

44 Alberti 2014; Alberti and Marshall 2009.

45 Alberti et al. 2011.

46 Alberti 2014: 113.

47 Alberti 2014: 113, our parenthetical; cf. Bailey 2005.

48 Alberti 2014: 112.

49 Alberti 2014.

50 Alberti and Marshall 2009: 351.

51 See papers in Brown and Walker 2008.

52 Alberti and Marshall 2009.

53 Alberti and Marshall 2009: 351.
54 Alberti and Marshall 2009: 352.
55 Bessire and Bond 2014; Todd 2016; Weismantel 2015.
56 In Alberti et al. 2011: 902.
57 In Alberti et al. 2011: 907.
58 E.g. Harris and Robb 2012.
59 Jensen 2016.
60 Latour 2009.
61 Latour 2013.
62 Olsen 2003: 100.
63 As pointed out by Fowles 2016.
64 Witmore 2014.
65 Things, Ewa Domańska (2006: 183) says, are trapped in a 'paradigm of paternalism'.
66 Olsen 2003, 2007, 2010, 2012.
67 Olsen 2012: 13.
68 Olsen 2012: 21.
69 Olsen 2012: 23.
70 Olsen 2010.
71 Olsen et al. 2012.
72 Olsen 2012: 21, our parenthetical.
73 Olsen 2012: 29.
74 E.g. Olsen and Witmore 2015. In a recent paper Witmore (2015) argues that new materialism is defined by these particular sets of approaches. This, however, does not really acknowledge that most new materialist approaches (both inside archaeology and without) do not embrace the notion of an object's essence, or indeed the idea that objects rather than processes are where archaeology should begin. There are clear links between the developed version of symmetrical archaeology and new materialism, but they are not one and the same thing (*contra* Witmore 2014). Indeed, as Irene Garcia-Rovira (2015) has perceptively pointed out, approaches orientated towards new materialism are far more interested in explaining process and historical change than their symmetrical counterparts (Chapter 11).
75 Witmore 2007: 549.
76 Witmore 2007: 546.
77 Olsen 2010, 2012.
78 Witmore 2015.
79 Olsen and Witmore 2015: 190.
80 Olsen 2010: 156.
81 Olsen 2012: 23.
82 Olsen 2010: 157.
83 Indeed this even includes a separation of symmetrical archaeology from the 'principle of symmetry' (Olsen and Witmore 2015: 193) that Witmore began his 2007 manifesto with. It is certainly a little confusing, as Tim Fløhr Sørensen (2016: 121) has noted, to call something 'symmetrical archaeology' yet to move away from the 'principle of symmetry'.
84 See Harman 2009, 2011 among many publications, and for an engagement with archaeologists directly see Harman 2016.
85 On the potential relationship between archaeology and speculative realism see Edgeworth 2016; Normark 2014.
86 In contrast he sees approaches that focus on the relations from which objects emerge (like Haraway) as 'undermining' and those who focus on the relations between different objects, including people (like Latour), as 'overmining' (Harman 2011).
87 Something that Hodder's (2012) concept of entanglement also allows for; indeed, Harman (2016: 39) approvingly notes this in a recent paper.

88 Witmore 2015: 203.
89 Deleuze famously said that 'relations are external to their terms' (Deleuze and Parnet 2007: 41) which might be taken to imply that the terms (which includes objects for Deleuze) are somehow bounded and cut off from these relations. However, the order Deleuze uses is critical here – the relations are external to their terms not necessarily vice versa, and all terms are emergent assemblages for Deleuze; that is, the temporary outcome of sets of relationships. While assemblages have relations of exteriority (so they can form relations with other assemblages without changing themselves), this does not mean that they are not relational themselves.
90 Ingold 2011.
91 Fowler and Harris 2015.

11

ON BREAKING WALLS AND BUILDING RELATIONS

A conclusion

Introduction

How do books end? Just like a good essay, a book should finish with a clear and concise conclusion. But theory has no conclusion, no end point, no moment of completion. Theory, like Donna Haraway's dogs (Chapter 9), is always in the process of 'becoming with' us as archaeologists. Writing a book on contemporary archaeological thought means that even as we draft this text, new ideas are emerging and being discussed, and the role of theory in archaeology debated;[1] indeed, the present moment feels as lively as it ever has.[2]

In this book we have tried to capture some of the story of this ongoing vitality and vibrancy. Now that you've made it through ten chapters, you're all too familiar with the main villains and heroes in our narrative. The role of our antagonists is, of course, played by intellectual dualisms, while the protagonists are a series of proposed relational solutions. We have traced the growth of our heroes and the challenge they pose to dualisms through ideas of practice, identity, object agency, materiality, semiotics and symmetry, among others. Although relations recently came under fire by some branches of 'second-wave' symmetrical archaeology (Chapter 10), these ideas have nonetheless played a crucial role in developing approaches in archaeological theory in the current millennium.

One way of thinking about the dualisms explored throughout this book is as unfriendly neighbours. It's not that they don't like each other, it's that they haven't had the opportunity to interact; they can't start a conversation with one another or compare their worlds. At times, the walls between them seem insurmountable. The poet Robert Frost famously wrote, 'good fences make good neighbours', but most of the archaeological thinkers highlighted in this book disagree. The wall must come down, they say, or at the very least we need a good ladder so we can see over the top and link the two sides together. In each chapter we explored different attempts to build ladders and to disassemble and remove the walls, freeing up our various sets of neighbours to see one another for the first time, maybe shake hands and eventually learn of some common ground between them.

These various intellectual demolition projects go about their business in the general spirit of Bruno Latour's critique of *purification*. As you'll recall from Chapter 8, Latour's attack on dualisms is a core inspiration for the initial version of symmetrical archaeology. As we noted, one of Latour's most well-known books is *We Have Never Been Modern*.[3] In it, he argued for a strange condition in the modern western world: we insist that certain things are completely separate from one another (e.g. nature and culture, or nonhumans and humans). The same goes for what we might colloquially think of as different 'spheres' in our world; economics, religion, science, politics and social relations are typically thought of as distinctive and separate in the modern west.[4] Latour argued convincingly that this is a fiction of modernity.[5] Modernity asks us to subscribe to this notion of purification, and more than this even: to actively police it. Here everything has its separate place, disconnected from the rest of the world; we feel comfortable allowing our neighbours to go on living separate lives. But while the wall between neighbours, between culture and nature or mind and body, might seem secure, in reality underneath all sorts of connections are growing, just in the manner that despite your best efforts, tree roots dig underneath the fences between neighbouring houses, denying these allegedly impermeable barriers. Indeed, as Latour argued, the more we insist on purification, the less we come to grips with the actual conditions of our world, where everything is mixed up in complex networks and where the separation between our gardens or even between our neighbours is imagined and projected. This opposition underlies the struggles we have with issues like that faced by our sprinter back in Chapter 1.

In this general spirit of anti-dualism, a number of different thinkers have cracked their knuckles and set to work building ladders or dismantling the walls separating various sets of unfriendly neighbours. In Chapter 3, we saw how Giddens constructed a ladder linking structure and agency together, offering to introduce the two neighbours so they could realise how they depend on each other and bring each other into being. Despite the ladder, though, the wall itself remained in place. In Chapter 5, in contrast, we learned of Alfred Gell's approach to these issues. For him, the problem was that humans lived on one side of the wall, while nonhumans occupied the other. Gell and his followers provided a means of taking down the wall, brick by brick. He did this with his notions of distributed personhood (via Strathern) and different types of agency (primary/secondary). However, soon after Gell took his gloves off, knocked the dust from his boots and went home to celebrate a job well done, we realised that he had inadvertently built a similar wall from the discarded bricks and mortar of the one he had just spent so much energy dismantling. Although humans had left some of their land on the other side of the wall, along with a part of their agency, they had kept most of it for themselves – objects, in the aftermath of Gell's theories, remained only secondary agents.

FIGURE 11.1   Building walls by accident. Drawing by K-Fai Steele

As we noted throughout the book, things are stubborn and obdurate. This means that when you disassemble a wall, you have to come up with a plan for disposing of the rubble. Otherwise you end up rebuilding in the background what you take apart in the foreground (Figure 11.1). In this sense, the neighbours are just as unfriendly as ever; the wall separating their garden simply moved a few metres one way or the other. They still can't see one another, offer a greeting or start that overdue conversation. We encountered similar scenarios throughout the book. As soon as a new group of archaeologists emerges with solutions for how to make our neighbours friendly, it seems that another group points to a new wall built up from the spoil heap.

Towards the end of the book (starting with Chapter 8), we introduced the latest group of archaeologists to declare all such walls defunct through a series of approaches associated with posthumanism. As you'll recall, Latour convinced us that the modernist ideology of purification masked mixtures and continuities. Using his ideas, among others, these archaeologists demonstrate the error of purification (and just how deeply engrained it is in our ways of thinking and doing). These approaches, in different ways, do seem to offer something more radical. Does this mean that the wall is finally disposed of? Do the dualisms that have beset archaeology lie vanquished in the dust? Or are other issues hiding around the corner? Have the neighbours realised they're not as different as they once thought? Or maybe in certain cases not different at all? Does this really amount to a paradigm shift?

A new paradigm?

Let's step back and put these developments into further context. Assume for a moment that the posthuman[6] approaches we have been discussing in the last part of the book did become widely embraced in the way in which processual and postprocessual archaeology have been. Would this amount to a new paradigm for archaeology? At the start of this book, in line with some other recent takes,[7] we suggested that the transitions from culture history to processual archaeology, and from processual to postprocessual, did not amount to paradigm shifts. This was because all of these approaches implicitly continued to draw on the previous ones (whether that's typology, carbon dating or whatever), and because they all operated within a single ontology – one that based itself on the binary oppositions we know as dualisms. It is certainly the case that the new approaches we discussed in Chapters 8, 9 and 10 open up access to different ontologies – but nonetheless we would still suggest this is not a paradigm shift for two reasons. First of all, archaeologists will continue to use older approaches.[8] We will mention fieldwork and science in a moment, but (with apologies for spoilers) it seems very unlikely that new materialism – for example – will revolutionise the process of excavation; that is, *how we actually dig*. Equally, it may allow us to understand how and why typologies work in new ways, and even restore to them a sense of ontological integrity,[9] but it is very unlikely to lead to the complete demise of typologies altogether. The second reason is that the very notion of a paradigm shift depends upon a dualist vision of change. This relies on ideas about 'before' and 'after', and assumptions that within each period things are fundamentally static rather than in a process of ongoing transformation. In other words, you have to think there was a static thing called processualism, followed by postprocessualism in turn, for a paradigm shift now between postprocessualism and posthumanism. This is not to deny that there are moments where changes gather speed, or where older ideas are reworked in especially dramatic ways; it is simply to suggest that even when this happens it does not amount to a paradigm shift.

So beyond the difference it makes to theory and the ways in which we write about the past, how else might posthumanism affect us as archaeologists? The first area that it helps us to rethink is the relationship between science and theory. In the great arguments between processual and postprocessual archaeologists, it looked as if science and theory, or the scientific and the humanistic elements of archaeology, were on different sides of an unbridgeable gulf.[10] Although the fury of those arguments has subsided today, the differences remain in place, with differing rules being applied to each side of the divide and both (in their own way) privileging human beings (whether the scientist in the present or the person in the past).[11] If you look at the kinds of ideas we have examined in Chapters 8 and 9 in particular, you can see how they do not neatly fall into this divide, however. Haraway has a PhD in biology, Deleuze drew on complexity theory, DeLanda uses chemistry and geology as well as philosophy, and Barad is trained as a physicist. These authors reveal that the dualism between science and theory is just as problematic as any other; it is equally reductionist to declare that any involvement of science in interpreting human action is wrong as it is to declare that science operates outside of the networks of relations that enmesh us all. Thus posthumanism, with its flat ontology, puts science and philosophy back into the same world; rather than one focusing on 'reality' and the other on 'human experience',[12] the wall between these two seems to have been dismantled. Science gives us important tools to attend to the vibrancy of matter, as does philosophy, and neither can be understood without the other.

The second area in which posthumanism is beginning to make an impact is on how we understand and think about fieldwork. This does not mean that these approaches will change what it is we do in a hugely significant way – remember these new ideas do not depend on notions of revolution and the complete disregard of everything we did before. In contrast, these new ideas are helping us to understand things differently. Authors like Thomas Yarrow[13] and Matt Edgeworth[14] have studied how archaeologists produce their sites as much as 'discover' them, and how in so doing we produce ourselves as archaeologists.[15] Edgeworth,[16] for example, has revealed how the acts of excavation rely on abilities to listen and attend to the vibrancy of the things we dig, to 'follow' a cut. Similarly, symmetrical archaeologists have thought about how sites are produced not just by people but by the tools we use for digging and recording, from the mattock to the planning frame.[17] Understanding what we do differently allows us to think about how we should record the past to capture some of this emerging quality. Most fundamentally of all, Gavin Lucas[18] has drawn on assemblage theory to think about the nature of the archaeological record, and the ontological status of both the sites we excavate and the archives of finds and information this produces.

The final area we can identify where these new approaches can help us think about archaeology differently is the issue of scale. The scale at which archaeologists operate has been a big bone of contention in debates about theory for many years. Many archaeologists (especially those coming from a processual background) have argued that the great strength of archaeology is its access to the 'big scale', to 'deep time', and the idea that we can study long-term processes in a way that other disciplines, at least those interested in human beings, cannot. In contrast, postprocessual archaeologists tended to look at the small scale,[19] arguing the big scale was generalising and essentialist, and suppressed the important differences in identity and history that mattered to people in the past.[20] Although the scale varied, both sides clearly thought there was one particular level at which archaeologists should operate – another dualism! Some archaeologists have long challenged this attempt to make archaeology work at a particular scale, especially those who have drawn on the historical analysis of Fernand Braudel,[21] and the ideas of *time perspectivism* that archaeologists like Geoff Bailey[22] developed from this. These approaches think about different scales but can sometimes slip back into privileging the long term, and rarely think about the relationship between those different scales.

In contrast, the development of the ontological turn has added new ways of thinking that archaeologists can draw upon to work at multiple scales and to appreciate the relationships between them. A great example of this comes from Timothy Pauketat, whose work we briefly mentioned in Chapter 10.[23] Pauketat draws on the Native American concept of the bundle to think about the archaeology of North America at a variety of different scales, from individual objects to the development of landscapes and changing celestial movements.[24] Here we can see how Pauketat gives ontological weight to a Native concept, and how this opens up a new way of conceptualising and engaging with the archaeology he studies from the very smallest moments of intimacy to the long-term processes of change. The way in which bundles work at multiple scales has much in common with the ideas of assemblage that we saw in Chapter 8; these ideas are largely compatible with one another.

A dialogue between authors

Up until this point we have tried to present different theories from a position of sympathy. Indeed, this isn't forced; we *are* sympathetic to the approaches we have outlined in this book, to a greater or lesser extent. This relative neutrality has to some degree meant that we've not always expressed precisely what we think individually, what our distinctive opinions are and precisely where (or why) they might differ. Theory, however, lives and thrives in these alternatives, in the cut and thrust of the gaps between positions and the differences they make to the past. In this segment of the chapter we celebrate these differences by exploring some of the arguments we think are most critical in archaeological theory at the moment, and returning to some of the current debates we introduced in previous chapters. To do so we will for the only time in this book write separately from one another, to distinguish between our voices and opinions. This also requires a slight change in the way we write about our respective concerns. Compared to the rest of the book, you may find the writing in the dialogue that follows to be slightly more complicated. This is because, rather than just describing contemporary theory as we do in nearly the entire book, here we step back and bring these ideas into critical dialogue with the challenges we face as professional archaeologists working in very different contexts. Our dialogue centres around the critical issue of whether the approaches outlined in this book can really eliminate the wall between dualisms, or have merely transposed it somewhere else. The final segment of the chapter brings our voices together again and goes back to the standard writing style of the rest of the book. Together, we provide further thoughts on the future of archaeological theory and the relations we must continue to build.

CNC

Ollie, posthumanists claim to have finally allowed the unfriendly neighbours subject/object, nature/culture and human/nonhuman to start socialising. I wonder if – as with other solutions to dualism outlined in this book – the old bricks and mortar from each of the massive walls separating these dualisms have been recycled and are now bracing another old barrier, the one between academia and the rest of the world. Following thinkers like Robert Preucel and Stephen Mrozowski,[25] I want to ask about the pragmatic impacts of archaeology. In other words, I want to ask about the differences that archaeology makes in the broader world in which our 'ivory towers' sit. Moreover, I want to know more about how the call for a pragmatic archaeology relates to the posthuman movement, if at all.

Severin Fowles[26] recently offered an answer to this question, arguing that posthumanism tends to preclude any engagement with a broader 'human political project' because such approaches would be seen from posthumanist perspectives as 'anthropocentric imperialism'. Similarly, Robert Preucel[27] offered a pragmatic critique of symmetrical archaeology, asking 'what exactly is symmetrical archaeology good for?' He argued that symmetrical archaeology overlooks the specificity of power structures. While symmetrical archaeology might frame power as emerging out of networks, he sees power as existing before networks and thus constituting their assemblage. In reaction to critiques such as these, Olsen and Witmore[28] recently made the point that symmetrical archaeology has been demonised for 'lacking sincere ethical concerns and even, by allegedly dehumanising people, for turning humans into things in an effort to legitimise dubious political doctrines'.[29]

Perhaps Olsen and Witmore are correct in their reading of critiques of their work,[30] but the point they highlight is not my central concern with posthumanism (and symmetrical archaeology, more specifically). Symmetrical archaeology emphasises the starting point of analysis; it asks us to eliminate any assumed ontological differences before the analysis begins so as to avoid projecting our modernist sensibilities onto archaeological assemblages and the past. This focus relates to Olsen and Witmore's endorsement of 'naivety' in archaeological approaches.[31] I am not so concerned with the types of starting point that Olsen and Witmore endorse. In other words, I don't think that a 'symmetrical' (or flat) start to our work dehumanises people in and of itself.

I do, however, have major concerns over the way in which thinkers like Olsen compare the human 'colonisation' of things to the actual colonisation of people. This might not dehumanise, in the sense of the accusation that Olsen and Witmore read in critiques of symmetrical archaeology, but it certainly degrades colonised and formerly colonised communities by framing the horrors they endured as somehow similar to the intellectual problem of 'colonised' things. As discussed in Chapter 10, Olsen adopts a rhetoric that draws close parallels between subaltern things and subaltern people. According to him, the time has come to give things their due as more than *vehicles for human use and meaning*. Like postcolonial attempts to decolonise western perspectives and representations of nonwestern and colonised groups, he calls for the liberation of his new subaltern, nonhumans! For those of us working with actual colonised people, Olsen's neo–postcolonial rhetoric seems intractable. In spite of certain labels that you might sling my way ('representationalist', 'anthropocentric', 'keeper of dualisms'!), I still see the representations we create as archaeologists and the practical effects they have on other people as absolutely crucial. The words we choose are important. This means that if we are going to have a posthuman approach to the past, it must be one that is slightly more selective in its rhetoric. For me, colonised people are much more important than colonised things, and the colonised things argument only resonates in the ivory towers mentioned above. This particular rhetoric also strengthens the wall between academics and many indigenous communities; it has no purchase at the metaphorical table where collaboration and partnership take place. We must remember that this table often sits squarely on grounds taken from indigenous people, in violent acts meant to dehumanise them. On those grounds, anthropocentrism and intellectual dualisms aren't so much a problem as they are for certain academics these days! There, people have other issues to deal with and these issues often relate directly to settler colonialism and its legacies. Olsen and Witmore also note 'that assessing the world by ethical principles that restrict us to human fraternity, however well-meaning, is disquieting'.[32] This begs the question: disquieting for whom? I can't help but conclude that this sentiment only applies to a small segment of society, most of which spend their time in ivory towers. What do you think of my reservations over posthumanism?

OJTH

Craig, first of all, I am absolutely going to refer to you from now on as 'keeper of dualisms'! More seriously, though, I can quite see where some of your concerns come from. I definitely agree that we need to think about the words we use, the consequences these have for people in the present and the way in which these can construct new walls. However, I want to challenge the way in which you switch between terms like posthumanist and symmetrical archaeology. Are these terms synonymous? I don't think so. There are important differences, especially between the kinds of new materialism we saw in the second half of Chapters 8 and 9 and the second wave of symmetrical archaeology in particular. The reason I want to emphasise this is because it is not the first time I have seen someone lump together these different approaches.[33]

As we mentioned earlier, and saw in Chapter 8, symmetrical archaeology grew out of an interest archaeologists had begun to have with the work of Latour. Latour is a fascinating and sometimes almost paradoxical figure, whose work can be interpreted in differing ways.[34] Drawing on aspects of his thinking, first-wave symmetrical archaeologists engaged with the way in which relations are central to how we understand the world. They focused on nonhumans and materials, and their important role in how the past came into existence and persisted into the present. New materialist approaches, drawing on thinkers like Deleuze, Bennett, Barad and Haraway, are also interested in relations and materials. Both approaches are thus examples of *relational* ontologies, and are also both committed to challenging what philosophers call 'correlationism', the idea that the most important relationship is that between people and the world around them.[35] The flat ontologies that both of these approaches propose mean that humans take up their place as one kind of entity among many others, rather than being on one side of a divide from everything else, and therefore taking up 50 per cent of the ontological space, as Graham Harman puts it.[36] Even approaches like materiality and entanglement, which we saw in Chapter 6, still start from this fundamental axis, this fundamental dualism.[37]

However, new materialists combine this engagement with materials and the challenge to correlationism with an emphasis on process[38] – on the movement of time and the way in which particular gatherings of people and materials come together, sustain themselves and break apart. This emphasis on process and becoming is one of the critical differences between symmetrical archaeology and new materialism, and it has, as Irene Garcia Rovira argues,[39] important implications because it means archaeologists influenced by these latter approaches can remain engaged with some fairly traditional archaeological questions. New materialists are interested in exploring the similarities and differences, for example, between different periods of the past in a way in which symmetrical archaeologists have not yet done. They can remain interested in questions of identity, gender or meaning as, again, symmetrical archaeologists are not. Indeed, new materialists both within and without archaeology explicitly seek to keep a focus on these things.[40] There is a reason why our case study on symmetrical archaeology from Chapter 8 does not come from one of the main proponents of this approach, but instead from another archaeologist employing Latour's ideas.

With second-wave symmetrical archaeology these issues have become more pronounced. Christopher Witmore has proposed that archaeology become a new discipline – pragmatology – one in which different kinds of questions are posed and answered.[41] Similarly, Olsen's powerful book on objects, *In Defense of Things*,[42] does not engage with any case studies that are archaeological in the traditional sense – indeed he explicitly resists this.[43] Instead he shows us a series of photos of ruins. Again there is nothing wrong with this per se, but it is unlikely to convince an archaeologist like yourself, working with Native American people, that this approach has much to offer you. The rejection of relations, process and history is critical here – only the object in its present moment matters, in contrast to a new materialist approach that revels in the history of relations. Second-wave symmetrical archaeology is not a relational ontology, unlike its first-wave cousin or new materialism. These differences are important because they show us how posthumanist approaches are not all the same; they have different strengths and weaknesses.

CNC

I certainly see your point about differentiating between types of posthumanism and different waves of thinking within each camp. In spite of the critiques I began with and in light of your comments, I wonder about Fowles' statement from above. I am inclined to ask more about the possibilities for a posthuman pragmatic archaeology. Jane Bennett's[44] important work on the vibrancy of matter embraced new materialism while still working towards a pragmatic goal (convincing us to live in more sustainable ways). For instance, in pointing to the dynamic and dangerous qualities of landfill, could we not use her work to change the world and convince others to adjust their habits of waste disposal? My new work on the vibrancy of stone in New England tests these waters, asking if an approach inspired by new materialism can be used as part of a larger pragmatic archaeology when it comes to contested heritage. In recognising stone's vibrancy and the ways in which it acts on various groups in New England, including powwows (shamans), farmers, archaeologists and other types of earth diggers, we reduce some of the tensions between different cultural-conventional readings of stone and its history (usually Native American versus Euro-American). This might be 'disquieting' for Olsen and

Witmore (and other second-wave symmetrical archaeologists) because it certainly privileges humans. What are your thoughts on the relationship between politics and these new directions in theory?

OJTH

I think there are two implications for the kinds of political issues you mention. First, new materialism *can* embrace the kinds of concerns you discuss because it does not attempt to engage in the study of things by themselves, cut off from their relations. Nor, indeed, does it make a linguistic equivalence between colonised people and things. Second, it allows us to think about the politics of studying the past, and indeed the role of politics in the past, because it does not stop us from considering the role of gender, identity or personhood in the manner that more 'object-orientated' approaches would have us do. This matters to me, because although I do not work with people living in the aftermath of colonial worlds directly, I still see the aim of archaeology as necessarily political. Thus it matters that we write pasts that engage with the complexity of identities that existed because this allows us to challenge claims in the present that certain ways of living are 'normal', 'natural' or 'universal'. It should come as no surprise that many of the most famous academics associated with new materialism outside of archaeology are explicitly feminist thinkers, committed to political transformation in the present.[45]

This also raises another point, however. Archaeology is always situated in specific contexts, and this means that the same concerns will not always apply everywhere. In the areas I work in I also want to find ways to *challenge* what the wider public thinks about the past. So if it puzzles, or confuses, or even offends a member of the (European) public volunteering on my dig that I am concerned to give materials, animals and plants an active role in explaining history, I think that might be a good thing.[46] Therefore in certain contexts (not necessarily colonial ones) making claims that challenge public assumptions about the power of things can be appropriate. I don't mean, though, that you should feel the same way – the point is that in different kinds of political and colonial situations the wall between academics and the rest has different kinds of implication.

So while I agree that talk of colonised things can be problematic when dealing with the aftermath of human colonialism, this does not mean we need to reject these new approaches entirely. Instead, a new materialist approach can build an understanding of the past that rejects Cartesian dualisms and still attends to politics. I also think we have to embrace approaches to the past that are themselves situated in relation to the contexts where we work and the questions we want to ask. Does this address your concerns, Craig?

CNC

It certainly helps. However, I also have some related anxieties over the ontological turn or the new animism (Chapter 10). I certainly support the general spirit of this movement, which seeks to take indigenous ontologies seriously and treat them as much more than just flawed worldviews. This turn targets its wrecking ball on two of our biggest walls: those separating material/immaterial and nature/culture. Can we find any resurrected barriers lurking in the shadows here? My concern is that the new impediment in this case is the same wall that postcolonial theorists have already made much progress in taking down. I fear that certain ontological approaches are unintentionally strengthening the barrier between western/nonwestern, modern/indigenous, past/present and of course colonist/colonised.[47] These neighbours were just making eye contact thanks to postcolonialism, only to be blocked from each other once again by efforts to understand 'worlds otherwise'.

On a basic level, I have concerns over current 'ontological' efforts to make indigenous ontology into archaeological theory. This is clearly because I practise archaeology with indigenous people. I can assure you that they have been making indigenous ontology into archaeological theory ever since they became archaeologists! This means, of course, that I am not required in such a project.[48] If we want to incorporate indigenous ontologies into our discipline (which, I agree, would be an excellent addition), we should try harder to get more indigenous people practising archaeology rather than inspiring more western academics to appropriate indigenous ontologies and filter them through their western lenses.[49] This ties in to a much bigger postcolonial concern over the representations that we (as archaeologists) produce.

There is a clear contrast between the postcolonial spirit and the ontological turn. On the one hand, thinkers like Edward Said told us to use caution when approaching western representations of subaltern (colonised) peoples, as they tend to simply reiterate an inverse image of how westerners see themselves. Homi Bhabha's important work shows that the categories of colonised and colonist were in fact quite blurry in colonial contexts (rather than unfriendly neighbours living separate lives on their respective sides of an impenetrable wall). This is because cultures became hybridised and worlds became shared. An important aspect of shared colonial worlds is, of course, the ways in which colonial populations sought to exploit indigenous communities and maintain certain forms of inequality through the representations they produced. Of course, indigenous populations also actively resisted colonialism, maintained traditions and strategically navigated colonial politics. All of these important processes took place not only in *indigenous worlds* or *European worlds*, but also in *shared colonial worlds*. These crucial mixtures and interconnections in the present and the past make new approaches to ontologies such as Ben Alberti's work on body-pots[50] that we saw in Chapter 10, both alone and with Yvonne Marshall, difficult to adapt in my particular area of archaeology. In some senses, this new animism seems to unintentionally replicate some of the representational patterns that Said critiqued: taking the one instance or moment of radical alterity and embellishing it to create an Other world envisioned by a western academic. It seems like Orientalism in a new guise.

I think this tension results from the different approaches to ontology mentioned in Chapter 10. While a philosopher might use the term ontology to refer to a *singular world and its workings* (regardless of human understandings), an anthropologist would use it to refer to multiple *different ways of being human in the world*.[51] It seems that some new animist archaeologists and anthropologists combine these approaches, to some degree, in their search for multiple worlds. In my opinion, this combined approach – associated with the notion of many different worlds – loses sight of the researcher's perspective in the present. Ironically, as some scholars take this approach and look past the importance of their own cultural perspective in the interpretative process, they of course still use their western scholarly sensibilities to essentialise past people and culture, as just mentioned.

OJTH

I definitely agree with you about the dangers of creating an absolute distinction between the ontologies of other people, and dominant western ones. That was one of the reasons why John Robb and I have argued that we need to think about how multiple ontologies exist in any particular context.[52] What do we mean by this? Let's think about the anthropological example Holbraad develops that we looked at in Chapter 10 where the red powder Cuban diviners use *was* power. Remember in Holbraad's argument this wasn't representational, metaphorical or symbolic.[53] The powder didn't mean power, show power or stand for power; *it was power*. This is a point of radical difference, of alterity, that helps Holbraad build up an alternative ontology. This ontology is undoubtedly central to diviners' lives, but what happens when those diviners are out and about engaging with other people, tourists perhaps, in present-day Cuba? There they encounter and indeed live in all sorts of ontological situations that western people recognise and share. This is not to deny the reality of an ontology where powder is power, but rather to argue that it is one ontology among many.

What this means is we may also need to think about scales of ontology and how they co-exist within one another. As you mentioned, philosophers have written about ontology in terms of overarching theories about how the world works; we might refer to these as 'meta' ontologies.[54] In effect Cartesian dualisms, new materialism or animism all offer competing metaontologies, starting points from which to work. Within this we can then develop differing ontological distinctions, such as between the different dualisms in Cartesian thought when western people distinguish between two modes of having a body, one in which they are generic biological organisms and another where they are the seat of a unique individual identity. These two understandings, which have significant ontological distinctions, co-exist within a broader ontology that legitimates the existence of dualisms in the first place.[55]

CNC

I completely agree with your points. I certainly don't think that this means we must abandon these approaches completely. In the case of my own work, I do feel that we must seriously rethink this project and bring the different scales of ontology into closer dialogue with postcolonialism. This fits nicely within the bigger question of pragmatism that I raised above. We must ask what our quest for 'worlds otherwise' is good for. Is it only good for the ivory tower, adding to its thick walls, or does it have a broader, pragmatic impact? To address these questions, I suggest we turn our attention to collaborative indigenous fieldwork. Such projects represent multiple ontologies and shared worlds[56] and touch upon many of the issues highlighted in your work with John Robb.[57] Perhaps it is through these shared worlds and hybrid practices that we can better understand indigenous histories, including shared colonial histories. For instance, in our field project at Mohegan,[58] we practise archaeology in a world where stones *can* speak, but only do so occasionally and for the proper interlocutor.

OJTH

I do think, though, that opening up issues of difference and alterity is really important for allowing the radical difference of the past to speak to us in the present.[59] I admire the way in which by granting indigenous theory the status of ontology (rather than mistaken epistemology) new animists have managed to achieve this. It is very important that we discuss both western and nonwestern 'philosophies' in equally ontological terms. When Latour[60] asks if the new animism is a 'type' of thinking, another set of ways of approaching the world or a 'bomb' that blows up our assumptions, he is pointing to the fact that these approaches can certainly help us undermine some important barriers.[61] Nonetheless I do have concerns, particularly with applying these kind of approaches wholesale to different contexts. Where I work, in prehistoric Europe, with no indigenous community or collaborators to draw upon, there is no reason to think that animism, per se, has any role to play in the pasts I investigate.[62] It has already proved popular to apply these ideas there, and I find this a little problematic as rather than making the ontologies of the past more varied, it can reduce their complexity. Can we get at ontological difference in the region where I work without these kinds of comparative approaches? One thing I find very striking is that the new animism shares many connections and relations with new materialism. A key thinker for the founder of the new animism, Eduardo Viveiros de Castro, is Gilles Deleuze[63] – who we met in Chapter 8. Marshall and Alberti, who use Viveiros de Castro's work, also draw a great deal on new materialist feminist physicist Karen Barad.[64] What underlies this is the critical issue of *difference* that thinkers in both the new animism and new materialism aim to engage with.

In the context where I work, I am better off, I would argue, drawing on new materialist approaches that offer much the same in terms of conclusions, but are not part of colonial legacy in the same way. Ethnographic analogies clearly offer us outstanding inspiration when trying to think about the ways in which the past may have been different;[65] as we saw in Chapter 4 with the topic of personhood, they have opened up whole new fields of enquiry.[66] However, once that space has been opened up, whether in regard to ontological difference or identity, we may need other tools, like new materialism, to explore them. What is critical, for me, is that whatever our theoretical inspirations, we think through difference both within and between contexts, and how this can open up the possibility for multiple ontologies, rather than insisting that one particular way of Being exists.[67]

In effect I would argue that new materialism forms a useful metaontology that allows us to get at these local differences, at ontologies that operate at different scales. There are certainly tensions here – hard-line ontologists would see new materialism as just another modern imposition on to the past. Equally you might ask whether new materialism would mean that in our writings all past people everywhere would end up thinking about the past in terms of assemblages, becoming, rhizomes or whatever other fashionable philosophical buzzword you want to find. But for me we have to start somewhere, and what we need is to start from a position that attends to the differences we encounter explicitly. I think we can start from new materialism and still access worlds and ways of thinking where these things are conceptualised differently, just like I would argue that new materialism does a better job of explaining the modern world than dualist approaches do. Thus we can construct alternative worldviews, ideologies and belief systems from this perspective, and reflect on how these have ontological implications, by situating them within a broader framework that embraces relations, becoming and the role of materials.

CNC

All of the ideas explored here form part of a bigger reaction to postprocessual archaeology. It seems that the posthuman and anti-purification spirit outlined throughout this book recently inspired a new work song. As we watch various walls torn down, we now hear workers' steadfast chant, 'after interpretation'. In 2012, Bjørnar Olsen[68] used this phrase as a centre point of an article published in *Current Swedish Archaeology* where he suggested that the general posthuman[69] spirit of contemporary archaeology might constitute a gradual archaeological revolution in line with the processual and postprocessual 'revolutions' in our discipline's past (see Chapter 2). The next year, Benjamin Alberti, Andrew Meirion Jones and Joshua Pollard[70] published their edited volume, *Archaeology After Interpretation: Returning Materials to Archaeological Theory*. This new mantra of 'after interpretation' is all part of the reaction against early postprocessual fixations on human meaning and symbolism, hence the subtitle of Alberti et al.'s volume. As Jones and Alberti[71] put it in the first chapter of the volume:

> How can we understand belief, image, memory, society, and other apparent abstractions without resorting to the representationalist gambit of an interpreting subject/culture quite distinct from the world she/he interprets, but also without resorting to the opposite side of the same coin, the natural scientists' steadfast belief in a correlative theory of truth?

'After interpretation' reminds us that things are more than just vehicles for conventional or symbolic human meanings. Things are capable of much more than working for people and standing for arbitrary meanings. Our new work song also reminds us that interpretation – and agency in general – is not limited to people in the past (under study) and researchers in the present (interpreting their interpretations). As we have seen time and time again in this book, things (and their relations) are not so simple or inert as postprocessual emphases on symbolism and meaning suggested.

Within this general call for an archaeology 'after' interpretation, there is a strong anti-'representationalist' sentiment. We need to ask new questions about the past that go beyond our earlier interest in 'standing for' relationships, as discussed in Chapter 7. In other words, we need to look at things as more than 'meaning' something else for humans. For instance, as we discussed earlier in the book, red ochre is often encountered in human burials. 'After interpretation' might ask us to extend the questions beyond how red might arbitrarily *symbolise* or *stand for* life or death; it asks us to focus our attention on the ochre itself. This entails taking its material condition and its vibrancy (Chapter 8) seriously rather than only focusing on how humans in the past might have used it to communicate and read arbitrary (conventional) meanings. Clearly there are grounds here to incorporate a Peircian semiotic approach (Chapter 7) as what you referred to above as a metaontology. This perspective looks at much more than 'standing for' relations. Unfortunately, these connections are rarely explored in the literature critiquing representation and interpretation.

For me, this insistence on moving beyond representation, and perhaps away from semiotics in general, is slightly troubling. Much like the ideology of purification that masks the complicated status of our world, the ideology of anti-representationalism only tangles us further in semiotic chains that we refuse to recognise and come to grips with. For example, in Chapter 10 we discussed Alberti and Marshall's innovative approach to body-pots.[72] As our readers will recall, Alberti and Marshall didn't ask why certain pots represent bodies. Instead, they sought to understand a radically different world in which 'body-pots' were a single (seamless) entity rather than vehicles transporting human symbolism (the 'material' that represents/communicates the 'immaterial'). Here we are led to believe that Alberti and Marshall's novel approach allows body-pots to *speak for themselves*. This approach relates to philosophical uses of ontology mentioned in Chapter 10 that seek out the world's workings beyond the realm of human understanding. In other words, there is a suggestion that this orientation to body-pots is more materially mediated (rather than culturally mediated). Following Henare, Holbraad and Wastell in their use of the term 'radical essentialism',[73] which attempts to 'get around the conventional separation of a thing and its meaning', Alberti and Marshall try to approach things as the researcher encounters them (in their material state).[74] This approach opposes the notion of quickly focusing in on what those things might have stood for in past symbolic conventions.

Alberti and Marshall's archaeological example overlooks the fact that they are deeply engaged in semiotic mediations that they write off as natural or just 'out there' in the world. For instance, we must ask how Alberti and Marshall know that body-pots resemble bodies or pots. Our readers will likely remember what type of sign mode Peirce would think of in this case: icons, or signs where the sign and object are connected by physical resemblance to one another *for an interpreter*. It is the last clause of this sentence that is most important here. Icons are not purely 'natural', or just 'out there' in the world; they are understood in relation to specific cultural frameworks for specific interpreters. This means that icons are not universal (and are culturally mediated to some degree!). We demonstrated this in Chapter 7 with our discussion of the bee droning. We explored how different language speakers around the world reproduced the 'natural' sound of a bee droning in very different ways. The same bee heard by different language speakers makes different sounds. The same goes for the notion of a pot, a body or a body-pot. The more we insist that this approach to body-pots is somehow outside of semiotic mediation and our own cultural conventions, the more we ignore our semiotic conditions as interpreters. Going back to the quotation from Alberti and Jones above, we have to understand the interpreting culture or subject as part of the world that they interpret. This is also true for Alberti and Marshall's recognition of body-pots.

OJTH

OK, there are a number of ways in which I want to respond to the important issues you raise. First, we absolutely need to think critically about our role as archaeologists in the production of the past, as Chris Fowler has done recently from a new materialist perspective.[75] Indeed, I actually think we can go further along the line of critique you have set out. One of the implications of the idea that 'things can speak for themselves' is the notion that new animist approaches have escaped any overarching theoretical approach. In other words, the material things we study can suggest their own interpretation without the archaeologist bringing ideas, or theories, to the party. Alberti, drawing on Holbraad,[76] argues that the new animism frees things from theoretical baggage.[77] Holbraad, in turn, suggests that we empty things of their 'analytical connotations', rendering them 'pure'.[78] This claim is, I think, very problematic, as it suggests the ability of the analyst to step outside of their assumptions, to take a position that is very close to the idealised objective scientist of positivist philosophy and processual archaeology (that we now know was anything but). This position, as Severin Fowles has brilliantly argued, repeats the modernist arguments that these thinkers are actually trying to overcome.[79] In fact, where I find Marshall and Alberti's work most convincing is when they draw, not on the new animism, but instead on Barad.[80] It is her emphasis on the way in which difference emerges among specific sets of relations that provides them with the best opportunity to offer an alternative ontology for archaeology, and a fully relational account of the phenomena they are interested in.[81] It is in these moments where they are able to really show how an ontological approach can make a difference. This is precisely because Barad, in ways that can be related to other thinkers like Braidotti, DeLanda, Deleuze and Bennett, creates the possibility for tracing how difference – at an ontological level – comes into the world. And it is through that overarching and committed work in tracing the emergence of difference that new pasts can come into being. This is not things speaking free of theoretical baggage, but rather a set of theories allowing us to attend to the differences that things and people make in the past and in the present.

This leads us to the second issue you raised: that approaches associated with the move to 'after interpretation' or posthumanism go too far in their rejection of representation, and that we need to include Peircian semiotics to restore a sense of meaning to the past. I agree with this – but only up to a point. Again, we probably need to differentiate between some of the different positions that fall under the 'after interpretation' banner. To start with I would argue, as I did above, that symmetrical archaeology certainly goes too far in its rejection of meaning, symbolism and identity. In contrast to this, new materialist approaches include precisely these issues within their assemblages. Where second-wave symmetrical archaeologists would insist we study things stripped of their connections to humans so as not to be anthropocentric, new materialists revel in the relations that things have with people – and with each other. Such relations inevitably include language, meaning and so on. To give one example, the Crown Jewels clearly have a different kind of authority and power than they would otherwise have because of the meanings that emerge out of their relationships with human beings. Nothing in new materialism denies this. Rather than simply being anti- or non-representational, then, what new materialists seek is to be *more-than-representational*.[82] That is to make room for representation but not to split the world in half, where 50 per cent is representation and 50 per cent is represented – this is the kind of correlationist approach I mentioned above. They would also seek to avoid splitting it three ways in the manner of Peirce, where it's 33 per cent Interpretant, 33 per cent Sign and 33 per cent Object. All of this simplifies the complex assemblages that new materialists seek to understand. The danger with relying *solely* on any form of semiotics is that it has no tools for describing relations that are not semiotic. A punch to the face isn't a symbol, an icon or an index – it's a punch to the face.

CNC

First off, I am not suggesting that archaeology 'after interpretation' must be abandoned. In fact, I agree with the general sentiment of the critique. But we must look carefully at some of these arguments and search for rebuilt walls. No longer do they separate material/immaterial and humans/nonhumans, but they do divide nature and culture in ways that 'after interpretation' purports to critique. As with the examples of human perception and replication of bee droning or archaeological identification of some objects as 'pots' or 'body-pots', nature and culture are entangled in complex knots. If we are discussing and writing about them, then things are not simply speaking for themselves; our voice (and our respective cultural repertoires) also plays a part in these assemblages. For me, we can challenge the integrity of this new wall by connecting the call for archaeology 'after interpretation' with

Peircian semiotics. Peirce's triadic approach allows us to understand the continuities between nature and culture that some 'anti-representationalist' approaches reinforce. Yet, as you'll recall from Chapters 7 and 9, the Peircian semiotic maintains its own wall: the ontological barrier between living and non-living. Having noted this, there are many interesting connections where we can build a semiotic archaeology 'after interpretation'. For instance, both camps use terms such as 'mediation' and 'translation', which sit in contrast to purification.

OJTH

When I started working on this book I have to say that I was not enamoured at all of Peircian semiotics, which seemed to me to sustain, rather than help challenge, the ongoing representationalist bias in archaeology that had come out of postprocessual archaeology. Working with you has shown me there is more to it, though. What 'relational' approaches need – including the assemblage-based ones I find most appealing – are new ways of describing and talking about different kinds of relations. Otherwise we simply reduce the past to banal statements about relations. 'What caused x to happen? It's the relations, stupid!' This is part of the reason why new materialist approaches have not dealt well with power or politics. Peircian semiotics, at least as they are employed in archaeology, are useful because they offer three terms for describing particular sorts of relations – something Deleuze and Guattari realised.[83] Representational forms of relatedness are real and we need to include them so that we do not rebuild our great wall between meaning and the world, as you warn us we might. Those three relational terms – icon, index and symbol – are only three, however, of the many concepts archaeologists will need to develop to be able to write about the past in non-anthropocentric, non-dualist ways that still embrace meaning, identity, complexity and difference. That said, I still object to the split between living and non-living that these kinds of semiotics impose. It's not that there aren't differences between organic and inorganic matter (there are), but the attempt to make these divisions ontological, and thereby not just a difference but a dualism, is something I don't agree with.

CNC

I agree with you on most of these points. You are not the only one to read Peirce in this way. He was a prolific writer and – like many of the thinkers covered in this book – the complexity of his writing coupled with his love of neologisms make his work a challenge to read and bring into meaningful dialogue with archaeology. Having noted these challenges, I still find Peircian theory a bit more nuanced than you suggest above. Chapter 7 only offers an introduction to Peirce, so further exploration is due for us (in our respective writings) and for our brave readers. I think of Peirce almost in the inverse of what you describe above. In other words, I don't think of the limitations of his three parts of the sign or his three sign modes, but rather see semiotic mediation as irreducible below triadic relations (or below the number three). We were not able to explore all of Peirce's triadic relations in this book, but those two triads are only basic starting points meant to contrast his work with structural semiotics. In fact, Peirce declared that there were a total of 59,049 potential sign classes.[84] However, more important than this is the label 'semiotics' that we often stick to Peirce's writings. Perhaps it is time to just think of it as Peircian philosophy rather than Peircian semiotics. As Chris Watts[85] recently pointed out, the limitations of the semiotic label become obvious when we delve into any of Peirce's writings. Peirce was primarily interested in being and becoming in the world (similar to the phenomenological approaches outlined in Chapter 6). For instance, his grand notion of synechism aligns interestingly with some of your points about the new materialism. Synechism focuses on continuities. He wrote:[86]

> Materialism is the doctrine that matter is everything, idealism the doctrine that ideas are everything, dualism the philosophy which splits everything in two. In like manner, I have proposed to make synechism mean the tendency to regard everything as continuous.

According to this theory, as time passes, the world becomes more and more connected (including humans, nonhumans and combinations thereof) through all sorts of semiotic mediation, defined broadly. This resembles your points on the new materialist focus on the movement of time and the ways in which things and people are gathered together and so on, no?

This brief dialogue also reminds me of a crucial point that bears repeating here. While it is absolutely essential that archaeologists and students of archaeology try to fully understand each philosopher or theorist that we draw upon (whether it is Peirce, Deleuze, etc.), this doesn't mean we must wholly adopt their ideas.[87] In fact, just by bringing theories from outside of our discipline into it, we transform them in interesting ways.[88] This process of translation and hybridisation certainly deserves more attention than it has received. Olsen and Witmore[89] reminded us of the dynamism inherent in this process when they recently made the point that symmetrical archaeology should not be confused with Latour's notion of symmetry. The two are closely related, but they are not exactly the same. This is because, as archaeologists, we have built new connections between the theories of our discipline and the theory we import from other disciplines. I explored this idea of theoretical translation with Robert Preucel[90] in our consideration of archaeological uses and translations of postcolonial theory. All of this is to say that theory is in a constant state of becoming and we need not abandon all the older ways of thinking when we encounter new directions of thought. That was the whole point of Chapter 2 and its quick look at the history of theory in our discipline.

OJTH

On this we definitely agree!

Conclusions: together again

So where is archaeological theory as we write and where might it go? We are not at a moment of paradigm shift, as we have seen. Nonetheless, we are perhaps seeing a broadening in the range of archaeological theory and the development of significant new ways of thinking. This broadening is important – we can't reject the foundations of our subject, nor should we stop asking questions about what actually happened in the past, how people were different or what things meant to them. These new approaches should, most of all, be about opening up new questions to ask, at different scales and in different ways, new potentials for thinking about difference and new ways of conceptualising what it is we do as archaeologists. In addition to this, we still need pragmatic archaeology that makes a difference in the world, along with intellectually sophisticated problem solving!

Each of the issues discussed in this chapter attest to the fact that dualisms are difficult to break. Just as important, however, is the call to understand the continuities that might exist between certain 'dualist' approaches and posthumanism, which focuses on eradicating dualisms. Craig has discussed the possibility of a pragmatic archaeology that takes influence from posthumanism but does not fully escape dualisms. We have also thought about a postcolonial approach to the new animism. Here, too, certain dualities potentially persist. Craig is also keen on a semiotic archaeology 'after' interpretation. This is yet another case where a 'soft' stance on dualisms is maintained, keeping a Peircian-inspired framework that separates living/non-living but also solves certain problems inherent in this new movement. Ollie, by contrast, believes that a new materialist approach can provide a foundation for a non-dualist approach to the past that still embraces meaning, identity and even symbolism by finding a new way of talking about and describing the relations from which the world, both past and present, is constituted. For him we need to make room for meaning, politics and identity, but in a way that does not start or end with Cartesian dualisms, because any return to them binds us back into the struggles of previous archaeological generations.

As these debates make clear, the problems archaeologists face when trying to think about the past are not about to disappear. This is not a puzzle that will one day be solved as a closed and completed solution that can be applied across contexts to let a fixed and finalised past emerge into the present. What allows us to tell stories, as archaeologists, is the fact that we keep trying to ask new questions and rephrase old ones. We develop differing techniques and ways of thinking, dig new sites and work with new people. All of these make the past come alive differently, and allow us to create new kinds of evidence and new kinds of understandings. At the heart of what we do are the theoretical approaches that make us think differently, and that can help us travel into worlds close by and far away, and see them anew. It is something of the vibrancy of these ways of thinking that have become part of archaeology over recent years that we have explored in this book. We can't wait to find out what happens next.

Notes

1 E.g. Lucas 2015.
2 Contra Bintliff 2011.
3 Latour 1993.
4 See also Fowles 2013 for how this impacts our understandings of the past.
5 Modernity means both the modern era in which we live, but more importantly the broad shared understandings we have within this, closely caught up with the kind of Cartesian dualist approaches we have critiqued in this book, along with capitalism, ideas of the modern nation state and so on (for a definition of modernity see Thomas 2004: 2–4).
6 With all the caveats we noted below about treating this as a single united approach.
7 E.g. Thomas 2015b.
8 Indeed it is quite problematic to suggest we could ever wipe the slate clean (Thomas 2004: 233).
9 Fowler 2013.
10 Jones 2002.
11 Harris 2014b.
12 Which is a compromise that dates back to the work of the philosopher Emmanuel Kant in the eighteenth century.
13 Yarrow 2003, 2008.
14 Edgeworth 2012.
15 Cf. Cobb et al. 2012.
16 Although Edgeworth would argue that he is inspired by the practice of archaeology rather than external theorists, it is hard to read his work and conclude that it is not consistent with a position one would term new materialist – as he indeed acknowledges (2012: 91).
17 Witmore 2007: 552.
18 Lucas 2012.
19 Although with some notable exceptions (e.g. Hodder 1990).
20 See Robb and Pauketat 2013.
21 Braudel 1972.
22 Bailey 2007.
23 Pauketat 2013a, 2013b. Another good example of large-scale work with a materialist sensibility is Robb 2013.
24 Pauketat 2013a, 2013b.
25 Preucel and Mrozowski 2010.
26 Fowles 2016: 22.
27 Preucel 2012.
28 Olsen and Witmore 2015: 192.
29 See also Sørensen 2013.
30 Particularly Sørensen's (2013) critique.
31 Olsen and Witmore 2015: 192.
32 Olsen and Witmore 2015: 192.
33 E.g. Johannsen 2015; Witmore 2014.
34 See Fowler and Harris 2015.
35 Meillassoux 2008; cf. Edgeworth 2016; Thomas 2015a: 1291. Whether these different approaches succeed or fail to reject correlationism, or reflect strong or weak versions of it, is a matter of ongoing debate (e.g. Harman 2016; Normark 2014).
36 Harman 2016: 31.
37 Most archaeological approaches are correlationist, including things like the innovative Material Engagement Theory of Lambros Malafouris (2013), which we have only had space to cite in passing in this book.
38 Cf. Gosden and Malafouris 2015.

39 Garcia-Rovira 2015.
40 E.g. Dolphijn and van der Tuin 2012; Harris 2016a.
41 Witmore 2012.
42 Olsen 2010.
43 Cf. Preucel 2012.
44 Bennett 2010.
45 E.g. Karen Barad (2007), Rosi Braidotti (2013) and Clare Colebrook (2014).
46 For one thing it challenges the dearly held notion that Thomas (2004: 53) identifies that humans alone are the 'subjects of history'.
47 Zoe Todd (2016) and Lucas Bessire and David Bond (2014) have recently provided sharp critiques of Viveiros de Castro's perspectivism and the ontological turn in general. Similarly, Mary Weismantel (2015) has explored how these approaches can be ahistorical, and overly abstract, but can be developed to still create new and useful understandings of the past. Both Blaser (2014) and Hage (2012) disagree and argue that the ontological turn creates the possibility of much more radical politics.
48 Cipolla and Quinn 2016: 130.
49 See Todd's (2016) recent critique of the colonial undertones of certain new approaches to ontologies.
50 Alberti and Marshall 2009; Alberti 2013; Marshall and Alberti 2014.
51 Graeber 2015; Heywood 2012.
52 Harris and Robb 2012.
53 Holbraad 2007.
54 Heywood 2012.
55 Robb and Harris 2013; for a recent analysis of the many ontological modalities of the western world see Latour 2013.
56 Cipolla and Quinn 2016.
57 Harris and Robb 2012.
58 Cipolla and Quinn 2016.
59 Cf. Thomas 2004: 241.
60 Latour 2009.
61 For a positive take on the political possibilities of the ontological turn see Blaser 2014; Hage 2012.
62 And as with any analogy, there is the risk this can create a kind of equivalence between people in the present and 'our' past that allows them to be perceived as somehow 'backward' or 'primitive'.
63 Viveiros de Castro 2010, 2015.
64 Marshall and Alberti 2014.
65 Thomas 2004: 241; Whittle 2003: xvi.
66 Fowler 2004.
67 Interestingly this argument is paralleled in Bruno Latour's (2013) recent analysis of western society (or the moderns, as he refers to the people who live there) called *An Enquiry into Modes of Existence*.
68 Olsen 2012.
69 Olsen actually uses the phrase 'new materialism' but his argument aligns more closely with symmetrical approaches. This is why I chose the phrase 'posthumanism' here despite the dangers of lumping together symmetrical and new materialist approaches.
70 Alberti, Jones and Pollard 2013.
71 Jones and Alberti 2013: 16.
72 Alberti 2013; Alberti and Marshall 2009; Marshall and Alberti 2014.
73 Henare, Holbraad and Wastell 2007: 2.
74 Alberti and Marshall 2009: 350.
75 Fowler 2013.
76 E.g. Holbraad 2007, 2012a.
77 E.g. Alberti in Alberti et al. 2011: 901.

78 Holbraad 2012a: 24.
79 'Modernity squared' as he puts it (Fowles in Alberti et al. 2011: 907).
80 Marshall and Alberti 2014.
81 In this case bodies and Maori chevron amulets.
82 Cf. Anderson and Harrison 2010.
83 Deleuze and Guattari 2004: 586 n41.
84 Peirce 1958–65, volume 8, paragraph 343.
85 Watts 2008.
86 Peirce 1998[1893]: 1.
87 Wallace 2011: 16.
88 Thomas 2015b.
89 Olsen and Witmore 2015.
90 Preucel and Cipolla 2008.

REFERENCES

Agbe-Davies, A. S. 2015. *Tobacco, Pipes, and Race in Colonial Virginia: Little Tubes of Mighty Power*. Walnut Creek, CA: Left Coast Press.

Alberti, B. 2013. Archaeology and Ontologies of Scale: The Case of Miniaturisation in First-Millennium Northwest Argentina. In *Archaeology after Interpretation: Returning Materials to Archaeological Theory*, edited by B. Alberti, A. M. Jones and J. Pollard. Walnut Creek, CA: Left Coast Press, 43–58.

Alberti, B. 2014. Designing Body-Pots in the Formative La Candelaria Culture, Northwest Argentina. In *Making and Growing: Anthropological Studies of Organisms and Artefacts*, edited by E. Hallam and T. Ingold. London: Ashgate, 107–25.

Alberti, B., and T. L. Bray. 2009. Introduction: Animating Archaeology: of Subject, Objects and Alternative Ontologies. *Cambridge Archaeology Journal* 19:337–43.

Alberti, B., S. Fowles, M. Holbraad, Y. Marshall, and C. Witmore. 2011. 'Worlds Otherwise': Archaeology, Anthropology, and Ontological Difference. *Current Anthropology* 52: 896–912.

Alberti, B., A. M. Jones, and J. Pollard, eds. 2013. *Archaeology after Interpretation: Returning Materials to Archaeological Theory*. Walnut Creek, CA: Left Coast Press.

Alberti, B., and Y. Marshall. 2009. Animating Archaeology: Local Theories and Conceptually Open-ended Methodologies. *Cambridge Archaeology Journal* 19:344–56.

Anderson, B., and P. Harrison. 2010. The Promise of Non-Representational Theories. In *Taking-Place: Non-Representational Theories and Geography*, edited by B. Anderson and P. Harrison. London: Ashgate, 1–34.

Appadurai, A. ed. 1986a. *The Social Life of Things: Commodities in Cultural Perspective*. Cambridge: Cambridge University Press.

Appadurai, A. 1986b. Introduction: Commodities and the Politics of Value. In *The Social Life of Things: Commodities in Cultural Perspective*, edited by A. Appadurai. Cambridge: Cambridge University Press, 3–63.

Atalay, S. 2012. *Community-Based Archaeology: Research with, by, and for Indigenous and Local Communities*. Berkeley, CA: University of California Press.

Bailey, D. 2005. *Prehistoric Figurines: Representation and Corporeality in the Neolithic*. London: Routledge.

Bailey, G. 2007. Time Perspectives, Palimpsests and the Archaeology of Time. *Journal of Anthropological Archaeology* 26:198–223.

Barad, K. 2003. Posthuman Performativity: Towards an Understanding of How Matter Comes to Matter. *Signs: Journal of Women in Culture and Society* 28:801–31.

Barad, K. 2007. *Meeting the Universe Halfway: Quantum Physics and the Entanglement of Matter and Meaning*. Durham, NC: Duke University Press.

Barrett, J. C. 1994. *Fragments from Antiquity: An Archaeology of Social Life in Britain, 2900–1200 BC*. Oxford: Blackwell.

Barrett, J. C. 2001. Agency, the Duality of Structure, and the Problem of the Archaeological Record. In *Archaeological Theory Today*, edited by I. Hodder. Cambridge: Polity, 141–64.

Barrett, J. C. 2014. The Material Constitution of Humanness. *Archaeological Dialogues* 21: 65–74.

Barrett, J. C., R. Bradley, and M. Green. 1991. *Landscape, Monuments and Society: The Prehistory of Cranborne Chase*. Cambridge: Cambridge University Press.

Barrett, J. C., and K. J. Fewster 1998. Stonehenge: Is the Medium the Message? *Antiquity* 72:847–52.

Barton, H., and T. Denham. 2011. Prehistoric Vegeculture and Social Life in Island Southeast Asia. In *Why Cultivate? Anthropological and Archaeological Approaches to Foraging-Farming Transitions in Southeast Asia*, edited by G. Barker and M. Janowski. Cambridge: McDonald Institute Monographs, 17–25.

Battaglia, D. 1990. *On the Bones of the Serpent: Person, Memory and Mortality in Sabarl Society*. Chicago, IL: Chicago University Press.

Bauer, A. 2002. Is What You See All You Get? Recognizing Meaning in Archaeology. *Journal of Social Archaeology* 2:37–53.

Bauer, A. 2013. Objects and Their Glassy Essence: Semiotics of Self in the Early Bronze Age Black Sea. *Signs in Society* 1:1–31.

Bennett, J. 2010. *Vibrant Matter: A Political Ecology of Things*. London: Duke University Press.

Bessire, L., and D. Bond. 2014. Ontological Anthropology and the Defferal of Critique. *American Ethnologist* 41:440–56.

Bhabha, H. K. 1994. *The Location of Culture*. New York: Routledge.

Binford, L. 1962. Archaeology as Anthropology. *American Antiquity* 28: 217–25.

Binford, L. 1965. Archaeological Systematics and the Study of Culture Process. *American Antiquity* 31:425–41.

Binford, L. 1968. Some Comments on Historical Versus Processual Archaeology. *Southwestern Journal of Anthropology* 24:267–75.

Binford, L. 1972. *An Archaeological Perspective*. London: Seminar Press.

Binford, L. 1983. *In Pursuit of the Past: Decoding the Archaeological Record*. London: Thames and Hudson.

Bintliff, J. 1991. Post-Modernism, Rhetoric and Scholasticism at Tag: The Current State of British Archaeological Theory. *Antiquity* 65:274–8.

Bintliff, J. 2011. The Death of Archaeological Theory? In *The Death of Archaeological Theory?*, edited by J. Bintliff and M. Pearce. Oxford: Oxbow, 7–22.

Bird, D. W., and J. F. O'Connell. 2012. Human Behavioural Ecology. In *Archaeological Theory Today*, edited by I. Hodder. Cambridge: Polity, 37–61.

Blaser, M. 2014. Ontology and Indigeneity: On the Political Ontology of Heterogeneous Assemblages. *Cultural Geographies* 21:49–58.

Boas, F. 1911. *The Mind of Primitive Man*. New York: Macmillan.

Boivin, N. 2008. *Material Cultures, Material Minds: The Impact of Things on Human Thought, Society, and Evolution*. Cambridge: Cambridge University Press.

Bolin, A. 1996. Traversing Gender: Cultural Context and Gender Practices. In *Gender Reversals and Gender Cultures*, edited by S. Petra Ramet. London: Routledge, 22–51.

Borić, D. 2005. Deconstructing Essentialisms: Unsettling Frontiers of the Mesolithic-Neolithic Balkans. In *(Un)Settling the Neolithic*, edited by D. Bailey, A. Whittle and V. Cummings. Oxford: Oxbow, 16–31.

Bourdieu, P. 1977. *Outline of a Theory of Practice*. Cambridge: Cambridge University Press.

Bourdieu, P. 1990. *The Logic of Practice*. Stanford, CA: Stanford University Press.

Boyd, R., and P. J. Richerson 1985. *Culture and the Evolutionary Process*. Chicago, IL: Chicago University Press.

Braidotti, R. 2013. *The Posthuman*. London: Polity.

Braudel, F. 1972. *The Mediterranean and the Mediterranean World in the Age of Phillip II*. London: Collins.

Brittain, M., and O. J. T. Harris 2010. Enchaining Arguments and Fragmenting Assumptions: Reconsidering the Fragmentation Debate in Archaeology. *World Archaeology* 42:581–94.

Brown, L. A., and W. H. Walker. 2008. Prologue: Archaeology, Animism and Non-Human Agents. *Journal of Archaeological Method and Theory* 15:297–9.

Bruchac, M. M., S. Hart, and H. M. Wobst, eds. 2010. *Indigenous Archaeologies: A Reader in Decolonization*. Walnut Creek, CA: Left Coast Press.

Brück, J. 1998. In the Footsteps of the Ancestors: A Review of Tilley's 'A Phenomenology of Landscape: Places, Paths and Monuments'. *Archaeological Review from Cambridge* 15: 23–36.

Brück, J. 2005. Experiencing the Past? The Development of a Phenomenological Archaeology in British Prehistory. *Archaeological Dialogues* 12:45–72.

Brück, J. 2006. Death, Exchange and Reproduction in the British Bronze Age. *European Journal of Archaeology* 9:73–101.

Brück, J. 2009. Women, Death and Social Change in the British Bronze Age. *Norwegian Archaeological Review* 42:1–23.

Butler, J. 1990. *Gender Trouble: Feminism and the Subversion of Identity*. London: Routledge.

Butler, J. 1993. *Bodies That Matter: On the Discursive Limits of Sex*. London: Routledge.

Carrithers, M., M. Candea, K. Sykes, M. Holbraad, and S. Venkatesan. 2010. Ontology is Just Another Word for Culture: Motion Tabled at the 2008 Meeting of the Group for Debates in Anthropological Theory, University of Manchester. *Critique of Anthropology* 30:152–200.

Casella, E. C. 2000. 'Doing Trade': A Sexual Economy of Nineteenth-Century Australian Female Convict Prisons. *World Archaeology* 32:209–21.

de Certeau, M. 1984. *The Practice of Everyday Life*. Berkeley: University of California Press.

Chadwick, A. 2016a. 'The Stubborn Light of Things'. Landscape, Relational Agency, and Linear Earthworks in Later Prehistoric Britain. *European Journal of Archaeology* 19: 245–78.

Chadwick, A. 2016b. Foot-fall and Hoof-hit: Agencies, Materialities, and Identities; and Later Prehistoric and Romano-British Trackways. *Cambridge Archaeological Journal* 26: 93–120.

Chapman, J. 2000. *Fragmentation in Archaeology: People, Places and Broken Objects in the Prehistory of South-Eastern Europe*. London: Routledge.

Chapman, J., and B. Gaydarska. 2007. *Parts and Wholes: Fragmentation in a Prehistoric Context*. Oxford: Oxbow.

Childe, V. G. 1936. *Man Makes Himself*. London: Watts.

Childe, V. G. 1942. *What Happened in History*. London: Penguin.

Childe, V. G. 1957 [1925]. *The Dawn of European Civilisation*. London: Routledge and Kegan Paul.

Cipolla, C. N. 2008. Signs of Identity, Signs of Memory. *Archaeological Dialogues* 15: 196–215.

Cipolla, C. N. 2013a. *Becoming Brothertown: Native American Ethnogenesis and Endurance in the Modern World.* Tucson: University of Arizona Press.

Cipolla, C. N. 2013b. Native American Historical Archaeology and the Trope of Authenticity. *Historical Archaeology* 47:12–22.

Cipolla, C. N., ed. 2017. *Foreign Objects: Rethinking Indigenous Consumption in American Archaeology.* Tucson: University of Arizona Press.

Cipolla, C. N., and J. Quinn. 2016. Field School Archaeology the Mohegan Way: Reflections on Twenty Years of Community-Based Research and Teaching. *Journal of Community Archaeology and Heritage* 3:118–34.

Cipolla, C. N., and K. H. Hayes, eds. 2015. *Rethinking Colonialism: Comparative Archaeological Approaches.* Gainesville, FL: University Press of Florida.

Clark, J. G. D. 1952. *Prehistoric Europe: The Economic Basis.* London: Methuen.

Clarke, D. L. 1968. *Analytical Archaeology.* London: Methuen.

Clarke, D. L. 1973. Archaeology: The Loss of Innocence. *Antiquity* 47:6–18.

Clutton-Brock. 1994. The Unnatural World: Behavioural Aspects of Humans and Animals in the Process of Domestication. In *Animals and Human Society: Changing Perspectives,* edited by A. Manning and J. A. Serpell. London: Routledge, 23–35.

Cobb, H., and K. Croucher. 2014. Assembling Archaeological Pedagogy. A Theoretical Framework for Valuing Pedagogy in Archaeological Interpretation and Practice. *Archaeological Dialogues* 21:197–216.

Cobb, H., O. J. T. Harris, C. Jones, and P. Richardson. 2012. Reconsidering Fieldwork, an Introduction: Confronting Tensions in Fieldwork and Theory. In *Reconsidering Archaeological Fieldwork: Exploring on-Site Relationships between Theory and Practice,* edited by H. Cobb, O. J. T. Harris, C. Jones and P. Richardson. New York: Springer, 1–14.

Cochrane, E. E., and A. Gardner, eds. 2011. *Evolutionary and Interpretive Archaeologies: A Dialogue.* Walnut Creek, CA: Left Coast Press.

Colebrook, C. 2014. *Sex after Life: Essays on Extinction, Vol 2.* Ann Arbor, MI: Open Humanities Press.

Colwell-Chanthaphonh, C., and T. J. Ferguson. 2008. *Collaboration in Archaeological Practice: Engaging Descendant Communities.* Walnut Creek, CA: AltaMira.

Comaroff, J., and J. L. Comaroff. 1991. *Of Revelation and Revolution, Vol. 1: Christianity, Colonialism, and Consciousness in South Africa.* Chicago, IL: University of Chicago Press.

Conkey, M., and J. Spector. 1984. Archaeology and the Study of Gender. In *Advances in Archaeological Method and Theory,* edited by M. Schiffer. New York: Academic Press, 1–38.

Conneller, C. 2004. Becoming Deer: Corporeal Transformations at Star Carr. *Archaeological Dialogues* 11:37–56.

Conneller, C. 2011. *An Archaeology of Materials: Substantial Transformations in Early Prehistoric Europe.* London: Routledge.

Coole, D., and S. Frost. 2010. Introducing the New Materialisms. In *New Materialisms: Ontology, Agency and Politics,* edited by D. Coole and S. Frost. Durham, NC: Duke University Press, 1–43.

Crossland, Z. 2009. Of Clues and Signs: The Dead Body and Its Evidential Traces. *American Anthropologist* 111:69–80.

Crossland, Z. 2013. Signs of Mission: Material Semiosis and Nineteenth-Century Tswana Architecture. *Signs and Society* 1:79–113.

Crossland, Z. 2014. *Ancestral Encounters in Highland Madagascar: Material Signs and Traces of the Dead.* Cambridge: Cambridge University Press.

Cummings, V. 2002. Experiencing Texture and Transformation in the British Neolithic. *Oxford Journal of Archaeology* 21:249–61.

Cummings, V. 2009. *A View from the West: The Neolithic of the Irish Sea Zone*. Oxford: Oxbow.

Daniel, E. V. 1984. *Fluid Signs: Being a Person the Tamil Way*. Berkeley, CA: University of California Press.

Deetz, J. 1967. *Invitation to Archaeology*. New York: Doubleday.

Deetz, J. 1977. *In Small Things Forgotten: The Archaeology of Early American Life*. New York: Anchor.

DeLanda, M. 2002. *Intensive Science and Virtual Philosophy*. London: Continuum.

DeLanda, M. 2006. *A New Philosophy of Society: Assemblage Theory and Social Complexity*. London: Continuum.

DeLanda, M. 2007. Material Elegance. *Architectural Design* 77:18–23.

Deleuze, G. 2004. *Difference and Repetition*. London: Bloomsbury.

Deleuze, G., and F. Guattari. 1983. *Anti-Oedipus: Capitalism and Schizophrenia*. Minneapolis: University of Minnesota Press.

Deleuze, G., and F. Guattari. 2004. *A Thousand Plateaus: Capitalism and Schizophrenia*. London: Continuum.

Deleuze, G., and C. Parnet. 2007. *Dialogues II*. New York: Columbia University Press.

Deloria Jr., V. 1973. *God is Red: A Native View of Religion*. New York: Putnam.

Derrida, J. 2002. The Animal That Therefore I Am (More to Follow). *Critical Inquiry* 28:369–418.

Descola, P. 2013. *Beyond Nature and Culture*. Chicago, IL: University of Chicago Press.

Dewsbury, J.-D. 2011. The Deleuze-Guattarian Assemblage: Plastic Habits. *Area* 43:148–53.

Dobres, M. A., and J. Robb. 2000. *Agency in Archaeology*. London: Routledge.

Dolphijn, R., and I. van der Tuin, eds. 2012. *New Materialism: Interviews and Cartographies*. Ann Arbor, MI: Open Humanities Press.

Domańska, E. 2006. The Return to Things. *Archaeologia Polona* 44:171–85.

Earle, T. 1997. *How Chiefs Come to Power: The Political Economy in Prehistory*. Stanford, CA: Stanford University Press.

Edgeworth, M. 2012. Follow the Cut, Follow the Rhythm, Follow the Material. *Norwegian Archaeological Review* 45:76–92.

Edgeworth, M. 2016. Grounded Objects: Archaeology and Speculative Realism. *Archaeological Dialogues* 23:93–113.

Fisher, G., and D. D. Loren. 2003. Introduction: Embodying Identity in Archaeology. *Cambridge Archaeology Journal* 13:225–30.

Fitzpatrick, A. P. 2011. *The Amesbury Archer and the Boscombe Bowmen: Bell Beakers Burials at Boscombe Down, Amesbury, Wiltshire*. Salisbury, UK: Wessex Archaeology.

Flannery, K. 1967. Culture History vs Culture Process: A Debate in American Archaeology. *Scientific American* 217:119–24.

Fleisher, J., and N. Norman, eds. 2016. *The Archaeology of Anxiety: The Materiality of Anxiousness, Worry, and Fear*. New York: Springer.

Fleming, A. 2005. Megaliths and Post-Modernism: The Case of Wales. *Antiquity* 79:921–32.

Fleming, A. 2006. Post-processual Landscape Archaeology: A Critique. *Cambridge Archaeological Journal* 16:267–80.

Fowler, C. 2001. Personhood and Social Relations in the British Neolithic with a Case Study from the Isle of Man. *Journal of Material Culture* 6:137–63.

Fowler, C. 2004a. *The Archaeology of Personhood: An Anthropological Approach*. London: Routledge.

Fowler, C. 2004b. In Touch with the Past? Monuments, Bodies and the Sacred in the Manx Neolithic and Beyond. In *The Neolithic of the Irish Sea: Materiality and Traditions of Practice*, edited by C. Fowler and V. Cummings. Oxford: Oxbow, 91–102.

Fowler, C. 2008. Fractal Bodies in the Past and Present. In *Past Bodies: Body-Centred Research in Archaeology*, edited by D. Borić and J. E. Robb. Oxford: Oxbow, 47–57.

Fowler, C. 2010. From Identity and Material Culture to Personhood and Materiality. In *The Oxford Handbook of Material Culture Studies*, edited by H. D. and M. C. Beaudry. Oxford: Oxford University Press, 352–85.

Fowler, C. 2013. *The Emergent Past: A Relational Realist Archaeology of Early Bronze Age Mortuary Practices*. Oxford: Oxford University Press.

Fowler, C. 2016. Relational Personhood Revisited. *Cambridge Archaeological Journal* 26: 397–412.

Fowler, C., and O. J. T. Harris 2015. Enduring Relations: Exploring a Paradox of New Materialism. *Journal of Material Culture* 20:127–48.

Fowles, S. 2010. People Without Things. In *An Anthropology of Absence: Materializations of Transcendence and Loss*, edited by M. Bille, F. Hastrup and T. Floher Sørensen, New York: Springer, 23–41.

Fowles, S. 2013. *An Archaeology of Doings: Secularism and the Study of Pueblo Religion*. Santa Fe, NM: School for Advanced Research.

Fowles, S. 2016. The Perfect Subject (Postcolonial Object Studies). *Journal of Material Culture* 21:9–27.

Fowles, S., and K. Heupel 2013. Absence. In *The Oxford Handbook of the Archaeology of the Contemporary World*, edited by P. G. Brown, R. Harrison and A. Piccini. Oxford: Oxford University Press, 178–91.

Fuentes, A. 2007. Monkey and Human Interconnections: The Wild, the Captive, and the in-Between. In *Where the Wild Things Are Now: Domestication Reconsidered*, edited by R. Cassidy. Oxford: Berg, 123–45.

Garcia-Rovira, I. 2015. What About Us? On Archaeological Objects or the Objects of Archaeology. *Current Swedish Archaeology* 23:85–108.

Gell, A. 1992. The Enchantment of Technology and the Technology of Enchantment. In *Anthropology, Art, and Aesthetics*, edited by J. Coote and A. Shelton. Oxford: Oxford University Press, 40–67.

Gell, A. 1998. *Art and Agency: An Anthropological Theory*. Oxford: Oxford University Press.

Gero, J. 1985. Socio-Politics of Archaeology and the Woman-at-Home Ideology. *American Antiquity* 50:342–50.

Gero, J. 2000. Troubled Travels in Agency and Feminism. In *Agency in Archaeology*, edited by M.-A. Dobres and J. E. Robb. London: Routledge, 34–9.

Gero, J., and M. Conkey, eds. 1991. *Engendering Archaeology: Women and Prehistory*. Oxford: Blackwell.

Giddens, A. 1979. *Central Problems in Social Theory: Action, Structure, and Contradiction in Social Analysis*. Berkeley: University of California Press.

Giddens, A. 1984. *The Constitution of Society: Outline of a Theory of Structuration*. Berkeley: University of California Press.

Gilchrist, R. 1999. *Gender and Archaeology: Contesting the Past*. London: Routledge.

Gillespie, S. D. 2001. Personhood, Agency, and Mortuary Ritual: A Case Study from the Ancient Maya. *Journal of Anthropological Archaeology* 20:73–112.

González-Ruibal, A. 2010. Colonialism and European Archaeology. In *Handbook of Postcolonial Archaeology*, edited by J. Lydon and U. Rizvi. Walnut Creek, CA: Left Coast Press, 37–47.

Gosden, C. 2001. Postcolonial Archaeology: Issues of Culture, Identity, and Knowledge. In *Archaeological Theory Today*, edited by I. Hodder. Cambridge: Polity, 241–61.

Gosden, C. 2004. *Archaeology and Colonialism: Culture Contact from 5000 BC to the Present*. Cambridge: Cambridge University Press.

Gosden, C. 2005. What Do Objects Want? *Journal of Archaeological Method and Theory* 12: 193–211.

Gosden, C., and L. Malafouris. 2015. Process Archaeology (P-Arch). *World Archaeology* 47:701–17.

Gosden, C., and Y. Marshall. 1999. The Cultural Biography of Objects. *World Archaeology* 31:169–78.

Graeber, D. 2015. Radical Alterity is Just Another Way of Saying 'Reality'. *Hau: Journal of Ethnographic Theory* 5:1–41.

Grémaux, R. 1996. Woman Becomes Man in the Balkans. In *Beyond Sexual Dimorphism in Culture and History*, edited by G. Herdt. New York: Zone Books, 241–81.

Hage, G. 2012. Critical Anthropological Thought and the Radical Political Imaginary Today. *Critiques of Anthropology* 32:285–308.

Hallowell, A. I. 1960. Ojibwa Ontology, Behaviour and World View. In *Culture in History: Essays in Honor of Paul Radin*, edited by S. Diamond. New York: Columbia University Press, 19–52.

Halperin, D. 1996. *Saint Foucault: Towards a Gay Hagiography*. Oxford: Oxford University Press.

Hamilakis, Y. 2012. From Ontology to Ontogeny: A New, Undisciplined Discipline. *Current Swedish Archaeology* 20:47–55.

Hamilakis, Y. 2013. *Archaeology and the Senses: Human Experience, Memory and Affect*. Cambridge: Cambridge University Press.

Haraway, D. 1991. *Symians, Cyborgs and Women: The Re-Invention of Nature*. London: Free Association Press.

Haraway, D. 1997. *Modest_Witness@Second_Millennium. Femaleman_Meets_Oncomouse: Feminism and Technoscience*. London: Routledge.

Haraway, D. 2003. *The Companion Species Manifesto: Dogs, People, and Significant Otherness*. Chicago, IL: Chicago University Press.

Haraway, D. 2008. *When Species Meet*. London: University of Minnesota Press.

Harman, G. 2009. *Prince of Networks: Bruno Latour and Metaphysics*. Melbourne: re.press.

Harman. G. 2011. *The Quadruple Object*. Winchester, UK: Zero Books.

Harman, G. 2016. On Behalf of Form: The View from Archaeology and Architecture. In *Elements of Architecture: Assembling Archaeology, Atmosphere and the Performance of Building Spaces*, edited by M. Bille and T. F. Sørensen. London: Routledge, 30–46.

Harris. O. J. T. 2009. Making Places Matter in Early Neolithic Dorset. *Oxford Journal of Archaeology* 28:111–23.

Harris, O. J. T. 2010. Emotional and Mnemonic Geographies at Hambledon Hill: Texturing Neolithic Places with Bodies and Bones. *Cambridge Archaeology Journal* 20:357–71.

Harris, O. J. T. 2014a. (Re)Assembling Communities. *Journal of Archaeological Method and Theory* 21:76–97.

Harris, O. J. T. 2014b. Revealing Our Vibrant Past: Science, Materiality and the Neolithic. In *Early Farmers: The View from Archaeology and Science*, edited by A. Whittle and P. Bickle. Oxford: Proceedings of the British Academy, 327–45.

Harris, O. J. T. 2016a. Becoming Post-Human: Identity and the Ontological Turn. In *Creating Material Worlds: Theorising Identity in Archaeology*, edited by E. Pierce, A. Russell, A. Maldonado and L. Cambell. Oxford: Oxbow, 17–37.

Harris, O. J. T. 2016b. Affective Architecture in Ardnamurchan: Assemblages at Three Scales. In *Elements of Architecture: Assembling Archaeology, Atmosphere and the Performance of Building Space*, edited by M. Bille and T. F. Sørensen. London: Routledge, 195–212.

Harris, O. J. T., and J. Robb. 2012. Multiple Ontologies and the Problem of the Body in History. *American Anthropologist* 114:668–79.

Harris, O. J. T., and T. F. Sørensen. 2010. Rethinking Emotion and Material Culture. *Archaeological Dialogues* 17:145–63.

Harrison, R. 2006. An Artefact of Colonial Desire? Kimberley Points and the Technologies of Enchantment. *Current Anthropology* 47:63–88.

Harrison, R. 2011. Surface Assemblages: Towards an Archaeology in and of the Present. *Archaeological Dialogues* 18:141–61.

Hastorf, C. A., and S. Johannessen. 1993. Pre-Hispanic Political Change and the Role of Maize in the Central Andes of Peru. *American Anthropologist* 95:115–38.

Hayes, K. H. 2011. Occulting the Past: Conceptualizing Forgetting in the History and Archaeology of Sylvester Manor. *Archaeological Dialogues* 18:197–221.

Hayes, K. H. 2013. *Slavery Before Race: Europeans, Africans and Indians at Long Island's Sylvester Manor Plantaion, 1651–1884*. New York: New York University Press.

Head, L., J. Atchison, and A. Gates 2012. *Ingrained: A Human Bio-Geography of Wheat*. London: Routledge.

Hegel, G. W. F. 1977. *The Phenomenology of Spirit*. Oxford: Oxford University Press.

Henare, A., M. Holbraad, and S. Wastell 2007. Introduction: Thinking Through Things. In *Thinking Through Things: Theorising Artefacts Ethnographically*, edited by A. Henare, M. Holbraad and S. Wastell. London: Routledge, 1–31.

Heywood, P. 2012. Anthropology and What There Is: Reflections on 'Ontology'. *Cambridge Anthropology* 31:143–51.

Hicks, D., and M. C. Beaudry, eds. 2010. *Oxford Handbook of Material Culture Studies*. Oxford: Oxford University Press.

Higgs, E. S. 1975. *Palaeoeconomy*. Cambridge: Cambridge University Press.

Hillerdal, C. 2015. Empirical Tensions in the Materialities of Time. In *Debating Archaeological Empiricism: The Ambiguity of the Material Evidence*, edited by C. Hillerdal and J. Siapkas. London: Routledge, 144–59.

Hodder, I. 1982a. Theoretical Archaeology: A Reactionary View. In *Symbolic and Structural Archaeology*, edited by I. Hodder. Cambridge: Cambridge University Press, 1–16.

Hodder, I., ed. 1982b. *Symbolic and Structural Archaeology*. Cambridge: Cambridge University Press.

Hodder, I. 1986. *Reading the Past*. Cambridge: Cambridge University Press.

Hodder, I. 1990. *The Domestication of Europe: Structure and Contingency in Neolithic Societies*. Oxford: Blackwell.

Hodder, I. 2011. Human-Thing Entanglement: Towards an Integrated Archaeological Perspective. *Journal of the Royal Anthropological Institute* 17:154–77.

Hodder, I. 2012. *Entangled: An Archaeology of the Relationships between Humans and Things*. Oxford: Wiley-Blackwell.

Hodder, I. 2016. *Studies in Human-Thing Entanglement*. Online publication available at http://www.ian-hodder.com/books/studies-human-thing-entanglement, accessed 9 February 2017.

Holbraad, M. 2007. The Power of Powder: Multiplicity and Motion in the Divinatory Cosmology of Cuban Ifá. In *Thinking Through Things: Theorising Artefacts Ethnographically*, edited by A. Henare, M. Holbraad and S. Wastell. London: Routledge, 42–56.

Holbraad, M. 2010. The Whole Beyond Holism: Gambling, Divination and Ethnography in Cuba. In *Experiments in Holism: Theory and Practice in Contemporary Anthropology*, edited by N. Bubandt and T. Otto. Oxford: Wiley-Blackwell, 67–86.

Holbraad, M. 2012a. Things as Concepts: Anthropology and Pragmatology. In *Savage Objects*, edited by G. Pereira. Guimaraes: INCM, 17–30.

Holbraad, M. 2012b. Truth Beyond Doubt: Ifá Oracles in Havana. *Hau: Journal of Ethnographic Theory* 2:81–110.

Holliman, S. E. 1997. The Third Gender in Native California: Two-Spirit Undertakers Amongst the Chumash and Their Neighbours. In *Women in Prehistory: North America and Mesoamerica*, edited by C. Claassen and R. A. Joyce. Philadelphia: University of Pennsylvania Press, 173–88.

Holliman, S. E. 2000. Archaeology of the 'Aqi: Gender and Sexuality in Prehistoric Chumash Society. In *Archaeologies of Sexuality*, edited by R. A. Schmidt and B. Voss. London: Routledge, 179–96.

Hoskins, J. 2006. Agency, Objects and Biography. In *Sage Handbook of Material Culture*, edited by C. Tilley, W. Keane, S. Küchler, M. Rowlands and P. Spyer. London: Sage, 74–85.

Howey, M. C. L. 2011. Colonial Encounters, European Kettles, and the Magic of Mimesis in the Early Sixteenth and Late Seventeenth Century Indigenous Northeast and Great Lakes. *International Journal of Historical Archaeology* 15:329–57.

Ingold, T. 2000. *The Perception of the Environment: Essays in Livelihood, Dwelling and Skill*. London: Routledge.

Ingold, T. 2007a. Materials against Materiality. *Archaeological Dialogues* 14:1–16.

Ingold, T. 2007b. *Lines*. London: Routledge.

Ingold, T. 2011. *Being Alive: Essays in Movement, Knowledge and Description*. London: Routledge.

Ingold, T. 2012. Toward an Ecology of Materials. *Annual Review of Anthropology* 41: 427–42.

Ingold, T. 2013. *Making: Anthropology, Archaeology, Art and Architecture*. London: Routledge.

Ingold, T. 2015. *The Life of Lines*. London: Routledge.

Itan, Y., A. Powell, M. A. Beaumont, J. Burger and M. G. Thomas. 2009. The Origins of Lactose Persistence in Europe. *PLoS Computational Biology* 5:1–13.

Jacobs, S.-E., and J. Cromwell. 1992. Visions and Revisions of Reality: Reflections on Sex, Sexuality, Gender, and Gender Variance. *Journal of Homosexuality* 23:43–69.

Jensen, C. B. 2016. New Ontologies? Reflections on Some Recent 'Turns' in STS, Anthropology and Philosophy. Unpublished paper presented at Osaka University, 24 July 2016, available electronically from https://www.academia.edu/25710614/New_Ontologies_Reflections_on_Some_Recent_Turns_in_STS_Anthropology_and_Philosophy, accessed 9 February 2017.

Johannsen, N. N. 2015. Practising Archaeology with Composite Cosmologies: On Import and Alternation in Theory. *Current Swedish Archaeology* 23:47–59.

Johnson, M. 1996. *An Archaeology of Capitalism*. Oxford: Blackwell.

Johnson, M. 1999. *Archaeological Theory: An Introduction*. Oxford: Blackwell.

Johnson, M. 2010. *Archaeological Theory: An Introduction*. Second ed. Oxford: Wiley-Blackwell.

Johnson, M. 2011. A Visit to Down House: Some Interpretive Comments on Evolutionary Archaeology. In *Evolutionary and Interpretive Archaeologies: A Dialogue*, edited by E. E. Cochrane and A. Gardner. Walnut Creek, CA: Left Coast Press, 307–24.

Johnson, M. 2012. Phenomenological Approaches in Landscape Archaeology. *Annual Review of Anthropology* 41:269–84.

Jones, A. M. 2002. *Archaeological Theory and Scientific Practice*. Cambridge: Cambridge University Press.

Jones, A. M. 2005. Lives in Fragments? Personhood in the European Neolithic. *Journal of Social Archaeology* 5:193–224.

Jones, A. M. 2007. *Memory and Material Culture*. Cambridge: Cambridge University Press.

Jones, A. M. 2012. *Prehistoric Materialities: Becoming Material in Prehistoric Britain and Ireland*. Oxford: Oxford University Press.

Jones, A. M., and B. Alberti (with contributions from C. Fowler and G. Lucas). 2013. Archaeology after Interpretation. In *Archaeology After Interpretation: Returning Materials to Archaeological Theory*, edited by B. Alberti, A. M. Jones and J. Pollard. Walnut Creek, CA: Left Coast Press, 15–42.

Jones, A. M., and E. Sibbesson. 2013. Archaeological Complexity: Materials, Multiplicity, and the Transitions to Agriculture in Britain. In *Archaeology after Interpretation: Returning Materials to Archaeological Theory*, edited by B. Alberti, A. M. Jones and J. Pollard. Walnut Creek, CA: Left Coast Press, 151–72.

Jones, S. 1997. *The Archaeology of Ethnicity: Constructing Identities in the Past and Present*. London: Routledge.

Joyce, R. A. 1998. Performing the Body in Prehispanic Central America. *Res: Anthropology and Aesthetics* 33:147–65.

Joyce, R. A. 2000. Girling the Girl and Boying the Boy: The Production of Adulthood in Ancient Mesoamerica. *World Archaeology* 31:473–83.

Joyce, R. A. 2001. *Gender and Power in Prehispanic Mesoamerica*. Austin: University of Texas Press.

Joyce, R. A. 2008. *Ancient Bodies, Ancient Lives: Sex, Gender, and Archaeology*. London: Thames and Hudson.

Joyce, R. A. 2015. Things in Motion: Itineraries of Ulua Marble Vases. In *Things in Motion: Object Itineraries in Anthropological Practice*, edited by R. A. Joyce and S. D. Gillespie. Santa Fe, NM: School of Advanced Research Press, 21–38.

Joyce, R. A., and S. D. Gillespie, eds. 2015a. *Things in Motion: Object Itineraries in Anthropological Practice*. Santa Fe, NM: School of Advanced Research Press.

Joyce, R. A., and S. D. Gillespie. 2015b. Making Things out of Objects that Move. In *Things in Motion: Object Itineraries in Anthropological Practice*, edited by R. A. Joyce and S. D. Gillespie. Santa Fe, NM: School of Advanced Research Press, 3–19.

Joyce, R. A., and J. Lopiparo. 2005. Postscript: Doing Agency in Archaeology. *Journal of Archaeological Method and Theory* 12:365–74.

Keane, W. 1997. *Signs of Recognition: Powers and Hazards of Representation in an Indonesian Society*. Berkeley: University of California Press.

Keane, W. 2005. Signs Are Not the Garb of Meaning: On the Social Analysis of Material Things. In *Materiality*, edited by D. Miller. London: Duke University Press, 182–205.

Keane, W. 2006. Subjects and Objects. In *Handbook of Material Culture*, edited by C. Tilley, W. Keane, S. Küchler, M. Rowlands and P. Spyer. London: Sage, 197–202.

Klejn, L. S. 2013. *Soviet Archaeology: Trends, Schools, and History*. Oxford: Oxford University Press.

Kluckhohn, C. 1949. *Mirror for Man: The Relation of Anthropology to Modern Life*. New York, NY: Whittlesey House.

Knappett, C. 2005. *Thinking Through Material Culture: An Interdisciplinary Perspective*. Philadelphia: University of Pennsylvania Press.

Knappett, C. 2011. *An Archaeology of Interaction: Network Perspectives on Material Culture and Society*. Oxford: Oxford University Press.

Knappett, C. 2014. Materiality in Archaeological Theory. In *Encyclopedia of Global Archaeology*, edited by C. Smith. New York: Springer, 4700–8.

Kopytoff, K. 1986. The Cultural Biography of Things: Commoditization as Process. In *The Social Life of Things: Commodities in Cultural Perspective*, edited by A. Appadurai. Cambridge: Cambridge University Press, 64–91.

Kuhn, T. 1962. *The Structure of Scientific Revolutions*. Chicago, IL: Chicago University Press.

La Salle, M. 2010. Community Collaboration and Other Good Intentions. *Archaeologies: Journal of the World Archaeology Congress* 6:401–22.

Laland, K. N., J. Odling-Smee, and S. Myles. 2010. How Culture Shaped the Human Genome: Bringing Genetics and the Human Sciences Together. *Nature Reviews Genetics* 11:137–48.

Last, J. 1995. The Nature of History. In *Interpreting Archaeology: Finding Meaning in the Past*, edited by I. Hodder, M. Shanks, A. Alexandri, V. Buchli, J. Carman, J. Last and G. Lucas. London: Routledge, 141–57.

Latour, B. 1987. *Science in Action: How to Follow Scientists and Engineers through Society*. Cambridge, MA: Harvard University Press.

Latour, B. 1993. *We Have Never Been Modern*. Translated by C. Porter. Cambridge, MA: Harvard University Press.

Latour, B. 1999. *Pandora's Hope: Essays on the Reality of Science Studies*. Cambridge, MA: Harvard University Press.

Latour, B. 2005. *Reassembling the Social: An Introduction to Actor Network Theory*. Oxford: Oxford University Press.

Latour, B. 2009. Perspectivism: 'Type' or 'Bomb'? *Anthropology Today* 25:1–2.

Latour, B. 2013. *An Enquiry into Modes of Existence: An Anthropology of the Moderns*. Cambridge, MA: Harvard University Press.

Lele, V. P. 2006. Material Habits, Identity, Semeiotic. *Journal of Social Archaeology* 6: 48–70.

Leone, M. P. 1984. Interpreting Ideology in Historical Archaeology: Using the Rules of Perspective in the William Paca Garden in Annapolis, Maryland. In *Ideology, Power and Prehistory*, edited by D. Miller and C. Tilley. Cambridge: Cambridge University Press, 25–36.

Leroi-Gourhan, A. 1993. *Gesture and Speech*. Cambridge, MA: MIT Press.

Lévi-Strauss, C. 1964. *Totemism*. London: Merlin Press.

Lewontin, R. 2000. *The Triple Helix: Gene, Organism and Environment*. Cambridge, MA: Harvard University Press.

Liebmann, M. 2008. Introduction: The Intersection of Archaeology and Postcolonial Studies. In *Archaeology and the Postcolonial Critique*, edited by M. Liebmann and U. Z. Rizvi. Walnut Creek, CA: AltaMira, 1–20.

Liebmann, M., and U. Z. Rizvi, eds. 2008. *Archaeology and the Postcolonial Critique*. Walnut Creek, CA: AltaMira.

Lightfoot, K. G., A. Martinez, and A. Schiff. 1998. Daily Practice and Material Culture in Pluralistic Social Settings: An Archaeological Study of Culture Change and Persistence from Fort Ross, California. *American Antiquity* 63:199–222.

Lindstrøm, T. C. 2015. Agency 'in Itself'. A Discussion of Animate, Animal and Human Agency. *Archaeological Dialogues* 22:207–38.

LiPuma, E. 1998. Modernity and Forms of Personhood in Melanesia. In *Bodies and Persons: Comparative Perspectives from Africa and Melanesia*, edited by M. Lambek and A. Strathern. Cambridge: Cambridge University Press, 53–79.

Loren, D. D. 2001. Social Skins: Orthodoxies and Practices of Dressing in the Early Colonial Lower Mississippi Valley. *Journal of Social Archaeology* 1:172–89.

Loren. D. D. 2003. Refashioning a Body Politic in Colonial Louisiana. *Cambridge Archaeology Journal* 13:231–7.

Loren, D. D. 2007. Corporeal Concerns: Eighteenth-Century Casa Paintings and Colonial Bodies in Spanish Texas. *Historical Archaeology* 41:23–36.

Lorimer, H. 2006. Herding Memories of Humans and Animals. *Environment and Planning D: Society and Space* 24:497–518.

Lorimer, J. 2010. Elephants as Companion Species: The Lively Biogeographies of Asian Elephant Conservation in Sri Lanka. *Transactions of the Institute of British Geographers* 35:491–506.

Lowenthal, D. 1985. *The Past is a Foreign Country.* Cambridge: Cambridge University Press.

Lucas, G. 2012. *Understanding the Archaeological Record.* Cambridge: Cambridge University Press.

Lucas, G. 2015. The Mobility of Theory. *Current Swedish Archaeology* 23:13–32.

Lydon, J., and U. Z. Rizvi, eds. 2010. *Handbook of Postcolonial Archaeology.* Walnut Creek, CA: Left Coast Press.

Lyman, R. L., and M. J. O'Brien 1998. The Goals of Evolutionary Archaeology: History and Explanation. *Current Anthropology* 39:615–52.

McCafferty, G. G., and S. D. McCafferty. 2003. Questioning a Queen? A Gender-Informed Evaluation of Mote Alban's Tomb 7. In *Ancient Queens: Archaeological Explorations*, edited by S. Nelson. Walnut Grove, CA: Altamira Press, 41–58.

McCafferty, S. D., and G. G. McCafferty. 1994. Engendering Tomb 7 at Monte Albán, Oaxaca: Respinning an Old Yarn. *Current Anthropology* 35:143–66.

McFadyen, L. 2008. Building and Architecture as Landscape Practice. In *Handbook of Landscape Archaeology*, edited by B. David and J. Thomas. Walnut Creek: Left Coast Press, 307–14.

McFadyen, L. 2013. Designing with Living: A Contextual Archaeology of Dependent Architecture. In *Archaeology after Interpretation: Returning Materials to Archaeological Theory*, edited by B. Alberti, A. M. Jones and J. Pollard. Walnut Creek, CA: Left Coast Press, 135–50.

McNay, L. 2000. *Gender and Agency: Reconfiguring the Subject in Feminist and Social Theory.* Cambridge: Polity.

Malafouris, L. 2013. *How Things Shape the Mind: A Theory of Material Engagement.* London: The MIT Press.

Marshall, Y., and B. Alberti 2014. A Matter of Difference: Karen Barad, Ontology and Archaeological Bodies. *Cambridge Archaeological Journal* 24:19–36.

Mauss, M. 1973 [1935]. Techniques of the Body. *Economy and Society* 2:70–88.

Mauss, M. 1990. *The Gift: The Form and Reason for Exchange in Archaic Societies.* London: Routledge.

Meillassoux, Q. 2008. *After Finitude: Essays on the Necessity of Contingency.* London: Continuum.

Menard, L. 2001. *The Metaphysical Club: A Story of Ideas in America.* New York: Farrar, Straus and Giroux.

Mercer, R., and F. Healy. 2008. *Hambledon Hill, Dorset, England: Excavation and Survey of a Neolithic Monument Complex and its Surrounding Landscape.* Swindon, UK: English Heritage.

Merleau-Ponty, M. 1962. *Phenomenology of Perception.* London: Routledge.

Meskell, L. 2004. *Object Worlds in Ancient Egypt: Material Biographies Past and Present.* London: Berg.

Meskell, L. 2005. Introduction: Object Orientations. In *Archaeologies of Materiality*, edited by L. Meskell. Oxford: Blackwell, 1–17.

Meskell, L., and R. W. Preucel, eds. 2006. *A Companion to Social Archaeology*. Oxford: Blackwell.

Miller, D. 1994. *Modernity, an Ethnographic Approach: Dualism and Mass Consumption in Trinidad*. London: Berg.

Miller, D. 1995. Consumption and Commodities. *Annual Review of Anthropology* 24:141–61.

Miller, D. 2005. Materiality: An Introduction. In *Materiality*, edited by D. Miller. Durham, NC: Duke University Press, 1–50.

Miller, D. 2006. Objectification. In *Handbook of Material Culture*, edited by C. Tilley, W. Keane, S. Küchler, M. Rowlands and P. Spyer. London: Sage, 60–73.

Miller, D. 2008. *The Comfort of Things*. Cambridge: Polity.

Miller, D. 2010. *Stuff*. London: Polity.

Miller, D., and C. Tilley, eds. 1984. *Ideology, Power and Prehistory*. Cambridge: Cambridge University Press.

Mrozowski, S. A. 2006. *The Archaeology of Class in Urban America*. Cambridge: Cambridge University Press.

Nanda, S. 1999. *Neither Man nor Woman: The Hijras of India*. 2nd ed. Belmont, CA: Wadsworth.

Neustupný, E. 1998. Structures and Events: The Theoretical Basis of Spatial Archaeology. In *Space in Prehistoric Bohemia*, edited by E. Neustupný. Prague, Czech Republic: Institute of Archaeology, Academy of Sciences of the Czech Republic, 9–44.

Nilsson Stutz, L. 2003. *Embodied Rituals and Ritualized Bodies: Tracing Ritual Practices in Late Mesolithic Burials*. Stockholm, Sweden: Almqvist & Wiksell Intl.

Normark, J. 2009. The Making of a Home: Assembling Houses at Nohcacab, Mexico. *World Archaeology* 41:430–44.

Normark, J. 2012. The Road of Life: Body-Politic in the Maya Area. In *To Tender Gender: The Pasts and Futures of Gender Research in Archaeology*, edited by I.-M. Back Denielsson and S. Thedéen. Stockholm, Sweden: Stockholm University, 117–36.

Normark, J. 2014. An Object-Oriented Gender Study of Queen Chop the Earth at Yo'okop, Mexico. In *Med Hjärta Och Hjärna: En Vänbok Till Elisabeth Arwill-Nordbladh*, edited by H. Alexandersson, A. Andreeff and A. Bünz. Gothenburg, Sweden: University of Gothenburg, 355–66.

Olsen, B. 2003. Material Culture after Text: Remembering Things. *Norwegian Archaeological Review* 36:87–104.

Olsen, B. 2007. Keeping Things at Arm's Length: A Genealogy of Symmetry. *World Archaeology* 39:579–88.

Olsen, B. 2010. *In Defense of Things: Archaeology and the Ontology of Objects*. Plymouth, UK: Altamira Press.

Olsen, B. 2012. After Interpretation: Remembering Archaeology. *Current Swedish Archaeology* 20:11–34.

Olsen, B., M. Shanks, T. Webmoor, and C. L. Witmore. 2012. *Archaeology: The Discipline of Things*. Berkeley: University of California Press.

Olsen, B., and C. Witmore. 2015. Archaeology, Symmetry and the Ontology of Things. A Response to Critics. *Archaeological Dialogues* 22:187–97.

Ortner, S. B. 1984. Theory in Anthropology since the Sixties. *Comparative Studies in Society and History* 26:126–66.

Overton, N., and Y. Hamilakis. 2013. A Manifesto for a Social Zooarchaeology: Swans and Other Beings in the Mesolithic. *Archaeological Dialogues* 20:111–36.

Paleček, M., and M. Risjord. 2012. Relativism and the Ontological Turn within Anthropology. *Philosophy of the Social Sciences* 43:3–23.

Parker Pearson, M., and Ramilisonina. 1998. Stonehenge for the Ancestors: The Stones Pass on the Message. *Antiquity* 72:308–26.

Parmentier, R. J. 1994. *Signs in Society: Studies in Semiotic Anthropology.* Bloomington: Indiana University Press.

Pauketat, T. R., ed. 2001a. *The Archaeology of Traditions: Agency and History Before and After Columbus.* Gainesville: University Press of Florida.

Pauketat, T. R. 2001b. Practice and History in Archaeology: An Emerging Paradigm. *Anthropological Theory* 1:73–98.

Pauketat, T. R. 2008. Founders' Cults and the Archaeology of *Wa-kan-da*. In *Memory Work: Archaeologies of Material Practices*, edited by B. J. Mills and W. H. Walker. Santa Fe, NM: School of Advanced Research, 61–79.

Pauketat, T. R. 2013a. Bundles of/in/as Time. In *Big Histories, Human Lives*, edited by J. Robb and T. R. Pauketat. Santa Fe, NM: School for Advanced Research, 35–56.

Pauketat, T. R. 2013b. *An Archaeology of the Cosmos: Rethinking Agency and Religion in Ancient America.* London: Routledge.

Peers, L. 1999. 'Many Tender Ties': The Shifting Contexts and Meaning of the S BLACK bag. *World Archaeology* 31:288–302.

Peirce, C. S. P. 1958–65. *Collected Papers of Charles Sanders Peirce, Volumes 1–8*, edited by C. Hartshorne and P. Weiss. Cambridge, MA: Harvard University Press.

Peirce, C. S. P. 1998 [1893]. Immortality in the Light of Synechism. In *The Essential Peirce: Selected Philosophical Writings, Volume 2 (1893–1913)*, edited by Peirce Edition Project. Bloomington: Indiana University Press, 1–3.

Peirce, C. S. P. 1998 [1894]. What is a Sign? In *The Essential Peirce: Selected Philosophical Writings, Volume 2 (1893–1913)*, edited by Peirce Edition Project. Bloomington: Indiana University Press, 4–10.

Peirce, C. S. P. 1998 [1895]. Of Reasoning in General. In *The Essential Peirce: Selected Philosophical Writings, Volume 2 (1893–1913)*, edited by Peirce Edition Project. Bloomington: Indiana University Press, 11–26.

Peirce, C. S. P. 1998 [1903a]. The Categories Defended. In *The Essential Peirce: Selected Philosophical Writings, Volume 2 (1893–1913)*, edited by Peirce Edition Project. Bloomington: Indiana University Press, 160–78.

Peirce, C. S. P. 1998 [1903b]. The Nature of Meaning. In *The Essential Peirce: Selected Philosophical Writings, Volume 2 (1893–1913)*, edited by Peirce Edition Project. Bloomington: Indiana University Press, 208–25.

Peirce Edition Project, eds. 1998. *The Essential Peirce: Selected Philosophical Writings, Volume 2 (1893–1913).* Bloomington: Indiana University Press.

Perry, E. M., and R. A. Joyce 2001. Providing a Past for 'Bodies That Matter': Judith Butler's Impact on the Archaeology of Gender. *International Journal of Sexuality and Gender* 6:63–76.

Piggott, S. 1954. *The Neolithic Cultures of the British Isles.* Cambridge: Cambridge University Press.

Pinney, C. 2005. Things Happen: Or, From Which Moment Does That Object Come? In *Materiality*, edited by D. Miller. Durham, NC: Duke University Press, 256–72.

Preucel, R. W. 2006. *Archaeological Semiotics.* Malden, MA: Blackwell.

Preucel, R. W. 2012. Archaeology and the Limitations of Actor Network Theory. Unpublished paper presented at Harvard University, Cambridge, Massachusetts, 10 October 2012. Available electronically from https://www.academia.edu/10272554/Archaeology_and_the_Limitations_of_Actor_Network_Theory, accessed 9 February 2017.

Preucel, R. W., and A. A. Bauer. 2001. Archaeological Pragmatics. *Norwegian Archaeological Review* 34:85–96.

Preucel, R. W., and C. N. Cipolla. 2008. Indigenous and Postcolonial Archaeologies. In *Archaeology and the Postcolonial Critique*, edited by M. Liebmann and U. Z. Rizvi. Lanham, MD: AltaMira, 129–40.

Preucel, R. W., and S. A. Mrozowski. 2010. The New Pragmatism. In *Contemporary Archaeology in Theory*, edited by R. W. Preucel and S. A. Mrozowski. Oxford: Wiley-Blackwell, 3–49.

Renfrew, C., ed. 1973. *The Explanation of Cultural Change: Models in Prehistory*. London: Duckworth.

Rizvi, U. Z. 2015. Decolonizing Archaeology: On the Global Heritage of Epistemic Laziness. In *Two Days after Forever: A Reader of the Choreography of Time*, edited by O. Kholeif. Santa Monica, CA: RAM Publications, 154–63.

Robb, J. 2009. People of Stone: Stelae, Personhood, and Society in Prehistoric Europe. *Journal of Archaeological Method and Theory* 16:162–83.

Robb, J. 2010. Beyond Agency. *World Archaeology* 42:493–520.

Robb, J. 2013. Material Culture, Landscapes of Action, and Emergent Causation: A New Model for the Origins of the European Neolithic. *Current Anthropology* 54:657–83.

Robb, J., and O. J. T. Harris. 2013. *The Body in History: Europe from the Palaeolithic to the Future*. Cambridge: Cambridge University Press.

Robb, J., and T. R. Pauketat. 2013. From Moments to Millennia: Theorising Scale and Change in Human History. In *Big Histories, Human Lives: Tackling the Problem of Scale in Archaeology*, edited by J. E. Robb and T. R. Pauketat. Santa Fe, NM: SAR Press, 3–33.

Russell, N. 2011. *Social Zooarchaeology: Humans and Animals in Prehistory*. Cambridge: Cambridge University Press.

Russell, N., and K. J. McGowan. 2003. Dance of the Cranes: Crane Symbolism at Çatalhöyük and Beyond. *Antiquity* 77:445–55.

Sahlins, M. 1985. *Islands of History*. Chicago, IL: University of Chicago Press.

Sahlins, M. 2014. On the Ontological Scheme of Beyond Nature and Culture. *Hau: Journal of Ethnographic Theory* 4:281–90.

Said, E. 1978. *Orientalism*. New York, NY: Vintage.

Saussure, F. 1986. *Course in General Linguistics*. Chicago, IL: Open Court.

Schiffer, M. B. 1983. Toward the Identification of Formation Processes. *American Antiquity* 48:675–706.

Schmidt, R. A., and B. Voss, eds. 2000. *Archaeologies of Sexuality*. London: Routledge.

Service, E. R. 1962. *Primitive Social Organisation: An Evolutionary Perspective*. New York: Random House.

Shanks, M. 2007. Symmetrical Archaeology. *World Archaeology* 39:589–96.

Shanks, M. 2012. *The Archaeological Imagination*. London: Routledge.

Shanks, M., and C. Tilley. 1982. Ideology, Symbolic Power and Ritual Communication: A Reinterpretation of Neolithic Mortuary Practices. In *Symbolic and Structural Archaeology*, edited by I. Hodder. Cambridge: Cambridge University Press, 129–54.

Shanks, M., and C. Tilley. 1987a. *Reconstructing Archaeology: Theory and Practice*. London: Routledge.

Shanks, M., and C. Tilley. 1987b. *Social Theory and Archaeology*. Cambridge: Polity.

Shennan, S. J. 1975. The Social Organisation at Brač. *Antiquity* 39:279–88.

Shennan, S. J. 2002. *Genes, Memes and Human History*. London: Duckworth.

Shennan, S. J. 2008. Evolution in Archaeology. *Annual Review of Anthropology* 37:75–91.

Shennan, S. J. 2012. Darwinian Cultural Evolution. In *Archaeological Theory Today*, edited by I. Hodder. Cambridge: Polity, 15–36.

Silliman, S. W. 2001. Agency, Practical Politics and the Archaeology of Culture Contact. *Journal of Social Archaeology* 1:190–209.

Silliman, S. W. 2005. Culture Contact or Colonialism? Challenges in the Archaeology of Native North America. *American Antiquity* 70:55–74.

Silliman, S. W. 2009. Change and Continuity, Practice and Memory: Native American Persistence in Colonial New England. *American Antiquity* 74:211–30.

Silliman. S. W. 2015. A Requiem for Hybridity? The Problem with Frankensteins, Purées, and Mules. *Journal of Social Archaeology* 15:277–98.

Skeates, R. 2010. *An Archaeology of the Senses: Prehistoric Malta*. Oxford: Oxford University Press.

Smith, A. T. 2001. The Limitations of Doxa: Agency and Subjectivity from an Archaeological Point of View. *Journal of Social Archaeology* 1:155–71.

Smuts, B. 2001. Encounters with Animal Minds. *Journal of Consciousness Studies* 8:293–309.

Sofaer, J. 2006. *The Body as Material Culture: A Theoretical Osteoarchaeology*. Cambridge: Cambridge University Press.

Sofaer Derevenski, J. 1997. Age and Gender at the Site of Tiszapolgár-Basatanya, Hungary. *Antiquity* 71:875–89.

Sørensen, M. L. S. 2000. *Gender Archaeology*. London: Routledge.

Sørensen, T. F. 2013. We Have Never Been Latourian: Archaeological Ethics and the Posthuman Condition. *Norwegian Archaeological Review* 46:1–18.

Sørensen, T. F. 2015. More Than a Feeling: Toward and Archaeology of Atmosphere. *Emotion, Space and Society* 15:64–73.

Sørensen, T. F. 2016. Hammers and Nails. A Response to Lindstrøm and to Olsen and Witmore. *Archaeological Dialogues* 23:115–27.

Spector, J. 1991. What This Awl Means: Toward a Feminist Archaeology. *In Engendering Archaeology: Women and Prehistory*, edited by J. Gero and M. Conkey. Oxford: Blackwell, 388–406.

Spector, J. 1993. *What This Awl Means: Feminist Archaeology at a Wahpeton Dakota Village*. St Paul: Minnesota Historical Society Press.

Spivak, G. C. 1988. Can the Subaltern Speak? In *Marxism and the Interpretation of Culture*, edited by C. Nelson and L. Grossberg. Urbana: University of Illinois Press, 271–313.

Spriggs, M. 2008. Ethnographic Parallels and the Denial of History. *World Archaeology* 40:538–52.

Strathern, M. 1988. *The Gender of the Gift: Problems with Women and Problems with Society in Melanesia*. Cambridge: Cambridge University Press.

Strathern, M. 1992. *After Nature: English Kinship in the Late 20th Century*. Cambridge: Cambridge University Press.

Strathern, M. 2004. *Partial Connections*. Oxford: Altamira Press.

Strathern, M. 2013. *Learning to See in Melanesia: Masterclass Series 2*. Manchester, UK: HAU Society for Ethnographic Theory.

Tarlow, S. 1999. *Bereavement and Commemoration: An Archaeology of Mortality*. Oxford: Blackwell.

Tarlow, S. 2000. Landscapes of Memory: The Nineteenth-century Garden Cemetery. *European Journal of Archaeology* 3:217–39.

Tarlow, S. 2012. The Archaeology of Emotion and Affect. *Annual Review of Anthropology* 41:169–85.

Thomas, J. 1993. The Politics of Vision and the Archaeologies of Landscape. In *Landscape: Perspectives and Politics*, edited by B. Bender. London: Berg, 19–48.

Thomas, J. 1996. *Time, Culture and Identity: An Interpretive Archaeology*. London: Routledge.

Thomas, J. 2004. *Archaeology and Modernity*. London: Routledge.

Thomas, J. 2006. Phenomenology and Material Culture. In *The Handbook of Material Culture*, edited by C. Tilley, W. Keane, S. Küchler, M. Rowlands and P. Spyer. London: Sage, 43–59.

Thomas, J. 2007. The Trouble with Material Culture. *Journal of Iberian Archaeology* 9/10: 11–23.

Thomas, J. 2015a. The Future of Archaeological Theory. *Antiquity* 89:1287–96.

Thomas, J. 2015b. Why 'the Death of Archaeological Theory'? In *Debating Archaeological Empiricism: The Ambiguity of the Material Evidence*, edited by C. Hillerdal and J. Siapkas. London: Routledge, 11–31.

Thrift, N. 2008. *Non-Representational Theory: Space, Politics, Affect*. London: Routledge.

Tilley, C. 1994. *A Phenomenology of Landscape: Paths, Places and Monuments*. Oxford: Berg.

Tilley, C. 1996. *An Ethnography of the Neolithic: Early Prehistoric Societies in Southern Scandinavia*. Cambridge: Cambridge University Press.

Tilley, C. 2004. *The Materiality of Stone: Explorations in Landscape Phenomenology*. Oxford: Berg.

Tilley, C. 2012. Walking the Past in the Present. In *Landscapes Beyond Land: Routes, Aesthetics, Narratives*, edited by A. Árnason, N. Ellison, J. Vergunst and A. Whitehouse. Oxford: Berghahn, 15–32.

Tilley, C., W. Keane, S. Küchler, M. Rowlands, and P. Spyer, eds. 2006. *Handbook of Material Culture*. London: Sage.

Todd, Z. 2016. An Indigenous Feminist's Take on the Ontological Turn: 'Ontology' is Just Another Word for Colonialism. *Journal of Historical Sociology* 29:4–22.

Treherne, P. 1995. The Warrior's Beauty: The Masculine Body and Self-Identity in Bronze Age Europe. *Journal of European Archaeology* 3:105–44.

Trigger, B. 1984. Alternative Archaeologies: Nationalist, Colonialist, Imperialist. *Man (NS)* 19:355–70.

Trigger, B. 2006. *A History of Archaeological Thought: Second Edition*. Cambridge: Cambridge University Press.

Tringham, R. 1991. Households with Faces: The Challenge of Gender in Prehistoric Architectural Remains. In *Engendering Archaeology*, edited by J. Gero and M. Conkey. Oxford: Blackwell, 93–131.

Trudelle Schwarz, M. 1997. *Molded in the Image of the Changing Woman: Navajo Views on the Human Body and Personhood*. Tucson: University of Arizona Press.

Van der Veen, M. 2014. The Materiality of Plants: Plant-People Entanglements. *World Archaeology* 46:799–812.

van Dommelen, P. 2002. Ambiguous Matters: Colonialism and Local Identities in Punic Sardinia. In *The Archaeology of Colonialism*, edited by C. L. Lyons and J. K. Papadopoulos. Los Angeles, CA: Getty Research Institute, 121–47.

Viveiros de Castro, E. 1998. Cosmological Deixis and Amerindian Perspectivism. *Journal of the Royal Anthropological Institute* 4:469–88.

Viveiros de Castro, E. 2004. The Transformation of Objects into Subjects in Amerindian Ontologies. *Common Knowledge* 10:463–84.

Viveiros de Castro, E. 2010. Intensive Filiation and Demonic Alliance. In *Deleuzian Intersections: Science, Technology, Anthropology*, edited by C. B. Jensen and K. Rödje. Oxford: Berghahn, 219–54.

Viveiros de Castro, E. 2015. Who is Afraid of the Ontological Wolf? Some Comments on an Ongoing Anthropological Debate. *Cambridge Anthropology* 33:2–17.

Voss, B. 2008a. Gender, Race and Labor in the Archaeology of the Spanish Colonial Americas. *Current Anthropology* 49:861–93.

Voss, B. 2008b. Sexuality Studies in Archaeology. *Annual Review of Anthropology* 37:317–36.

Wallace, S. 2011. *Contradictions of Archaeological Theory: Engaging Critical Realism and Archaeological Theory*. London: Routledge.

Watkins, J. 2000. *Indigenous Archaeology: American Indian Values and Scientific Practice*. Walnut Creek, CA: Altamira Press.

Watts, C. M. 2008. On Mediation and Material Agency in the Peircian Semeiotic. In *Material Agency: Toward a Non-Anthropocentric Approach*, edited by C. Knappett and L. Malafouris. New York: Springer, 187–207.

Webmoor, T. 2007. What About 'One More Turn after the Social' in Archaeological Reasoning? Taking Things Seriously. *World Archaeology* 39:563–78.

Webmoor, T., and C. L. Witmore 2008. Things Are Us! A Commentary on Human/Things Relations under the Banner of a 'Social Archaeology'. *Norwegian Archaeological Review* 41:1–18.

Weismantel, M. 2015. Seeing like an Archaeologist: Viveiros de Castro at Chavín de Huantar. *Journal of Social Archaeology* 15:139–59.

Whelan, M. 1991. Gender and Historical Archaeology: Eastern Dakota Patterns in the 19th Century. *Historical Archaeology* 25:17–32.

White, L. A. 1959. *The Evolution of Culture*. New York: McGraw-Hill.

Whitridge, P. 2004. Whales, Harpoons, and Other Actors: Actor-Network-Theory and Hunter-Gatherer Archaeology. In *Hunters and Gatherers in Theory and Archaeology*, edited by G. M. Crothers. Carbondale: Center for Archaeological Investigations, Southern Illinois University, 445–74.

Whittle, A. 2003. *The Archaeology of People: Dimensions of Neolithic Life*. London: Routledge.

Whittle, A., F. Healy, and A. Bayliss 2011. *Gathering Time: Dating the Early Neolithic Enclosures of Southern Britain and Ireland*. Oxford: Oxbow Books.

Wilkinson, D. 2013. The Emperor's New Body: Personhood, Ontology and the Inka Sovereign. *Cambridge Archaeological Journal* 23:417–32.

Williams, H. 2003. Keeping the Dead at Arm's Length: Memory, Weaponry, and Early Medieval Mortuary Technologies. *Journal of Social Archaeology* 5:253–75.

Witmore, C. L. 2006. Vision, Media, Noise and the Percolation of Time: Symmetrical Approaches to the Mediation of the Material World. *Journal of Material Culture* 11: 267–92.

Witmore, C. L. 2007. Symmetrical Archaeology: Excerpts of a Manifesto. *World Archaeology* 39:546–62.

Witmore, C. L. 2012. The Realities of the Past. In *Modern Materials: Proceedings from the Contemporary and Historical Archaeology in Theory Conference*, edited by B. Fortenberry and L. McAtackney. Oxford: British Archaeological Reports, 25–36.

Witmore, C. L. 2014. Archaeology and the New Materialisms. *Journal of Contemporary Archaeology* 1:203–46.

Wolf, E. R. 1982. *Europe and the People without History*. Berkeley: University of California Press.

Wolfe, C., ed. 2003. *Zoontologies: The Question of the Animal*. Minneapolis: University of Minnesota Press.

Wylie, A. 2002. *Thinking from Things: Essays in the Philosophy of Archaeology*. Berkley, CA: University of California Press.

Yarrow, T. 2003. Artefactual Persons: The Relational Capacities of Persons and Things in the Practice of Excavation. *Norwegian Archaeological Review* 36:65–73.

Yarrow, T. 2008. In Context: Meaning, Materiality and Agency in the Process of Archaeological Recording. In *Material Agency*, edited by C. Knappett and L. Malafouris. New York: Springer, 121–37.

Zedeño, M. N. 2009. Animating by Association: Index Objects and Relational Taxonomies. *Cambridge Archaeological Journal* 19:407–17.

Zubrow, E. 2015. Paradigm Lost: The Rise and Fall and Eventual Recovery of Paradigms in Archaeology. In *Paradigm Found: Archaeological Theory – Present, Past and Future. Essays in Honour of Evžen Neustupný*, edited by K. Kristiansen, L. Šmejda and J. Turek. Oxford: Oxbow, 167–76.

INDEX